KU-505-092

GROUNDED THEORY

A Practical Guide

MELANIE BIRKS
& JANE MILLS

Los Angeles | London | New Delhi
Singapore | Washington DC

© Melanie Birks and Jane Mills 2011

First published 2011

Apart from any fair dealing for the purposes of research or
private study, or criticism or review, as permitted under the
Copyright, Designs and Patents Act, 1988, this publication may
be reproduced, stored or transmitted in any form, or by any
means, only with the prior permission in writing of the publishers,
or in the case of reprographic reproduction, in accordance
with the terms of licences issued by the Copyright Licensing
Agency. Enquiries concerning reproduction outside those terms
should be sent to the publishers.

SAGE Publications Ltd
1 Oliver's Yard
55 City Road
London EC1Y 1SP

SAGE Publications Inc.
2455 Teller Road
Thousand Oaks, California 91320

SAGE Publications India Pvt Ltd
B 1/I 1 Mohan Cooperative Industrial Area
Mathura Road
New Delhi 110 044

SAGE Publications Asia-Pacific Pte Ltd
33 Pekin Street #02-01
Far East Square
Singapore 048763

Library of Congress Control Number available

British Library Cataloguing in Publication data

A catalogue record for this book is available from the British Library

ISBN 978-1-84860-992-1
ISBN 978-1-84860-993-8 (pbk)

Typeset by C&M Digitals (P) Ltd, Chennai, India
Printed by CPI Antony Rowe, Chippenham, Wiltshire
Printed on paper from sustainable resources

Contents

List of activities

List of boxes

List of figures

List of tables

About the authors

Melanie Birks completed her PhD titled *Becoming professional by degree: A grounded theory study of nurses in Malaysian Borneo* at Monash University in 2007. Melanie submitted her thesis by full publication, including a number of articles about grounded theory methods. Currently she is employed as a Senior Lecturer at Monash University where she has worked for the past 13 years. Melanie has a passion for both nursing and teaching. Her role in the School of Nursing and Midwifery involves programme coordination and teaching at both undergraduate and post graduate level, most significantly in the first year of the pre-service course and post-registration degree programmes. She has extensive experience in international education, having taught in Hong Kong, Singapore, Papua New Guinea and Malaysia. Her doctoral thesis employed grounded theory methodology to explore changes experienced by registered nurses in Malaysian Borneo as a result of undertaking study at tertiary level. Currently, Melanie continues to undertake research in areas of education and health. Her interest in research is reflected in her publication history, which includes journal articles and book chapters. Most recently, she has coauthored a research text for undergraduate students in the health disciplines, *Using research in healthcare practice* (2010) with Dr Jane Mills. Visit Melanie Birks' website at www.med.monash.edu.au/nursing/staff/birks.html.

Jane Mills completed her PhD titled *Rural nurses' experiences of mentoring: A constructivist grounded theory* at Monash University in 2006. Jane also submitted her thesis by full publication, including articles about grounded theory methods. Currently she is employed as a Senior Lecturer/Deputy Head of School in the School of Nursing, Midwifery and Nutrition at James Cook University, Cairns Campus, Australia. Jane has authored over 50 peer-reviewed journal articles in addition to *Community as partner: Theory and practice in nursing Australia/New Zealand edition* (2008) and *Using research in healthcare practice* (2010) with Dr Melanie Birks. To date, the large majority of Jane Mills' research has been undertaken in the areas of rural and remote nursing, primary health care and general practice nursing. Jane has been the recipient of a number of competitive and contract research grants, including an Australian National Health and Medical Research Council Postdoctoral Primary Health Care Fellowship. Currently she supervises a cohort of postgraduate students, many of whom are using grounded theory. Visit Jane's website at www.jcu.edu.au/nursing/staff/JCUPRD_052454.html.

Acknowledgements

Through our own experiences of graduate study, we realize the challenges of undertaking higher degree research. In our academic careers we have witnessed graduate students struggle with understanding philosophical and methodological concepts and have ourselves experienced frustration and confusion when attempting to negotiate the intellectual hurdles encountered when producing research worthy of the awarding of a doctoral degree. In writing this text, we hope to demystify some of the complexities associated with grounded theory. A balance is necessary between engaging in the internal intellectual dialogue that is required and meeting the practical requirements of undertaking research at graduate level. We hope this book assists the reader in achieving this balance.

We wish to thank our eternally patient families for their support while we worked on producing this text. We also wish to acknowledge our research mentors Professor Karen Francis and Professor Ysanne Chapman. Indeed, Ysanne encouraged us to write this book. Our thanks also go to all those who shared their experience of grounded theory in the 'Windows into grounded theory' that feature throughout this text. In particular, we acknowledge the time given to us by Dr Barry Gibson and Professor Tony Bryant in the developmental stages of this book. Finally, we are grateful for the professional guidance of our publisher, Dr Patrick Brindle, and editorial assistance of Mr David Hodge at SAGE Publications.

1   Essentials of grounded theory

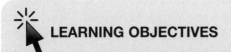
LEARNING OBJECTIVES

This chapter will help you to:

1   Summarize the historical background of grounded theory

2   Discuss methodological influences on grounded theory as an approach to research

3   Outline key positions taken in the literature about grounded theory

4   Identify a personal philosophical position

5   Define essential grounded theory methods

Introduction

Grounded theory is one of the most popular research designs in the world. Not only are there thousands of publications that report on studies using grounded theory methods, but there is also a collection of seminal texts that researchers can use to guide their study and ensure the rigour of their work. So why then, you may ask, is there a need for another book on grounded theory? For beginning researchers, including graduate students, the magnitude of information that exists about grounded theory methods and findings has made engaging in a grounded theory study a complicated endeavour. Trying to understand the general principles of grounded theory in context of the debate and discussion that is so much a part of this research tradition can be incredibly difficult. Where to start? What to read? Who to 'follow' and why? This book aims to provide you with a place to begin as you explore the wider grounded theory literature. Reading this text will assist you to become an informed reader of grounded theory articles and seminal texts, allowing you to make wise investments of your time. As you will come to understand, grounded theorists take various philosophical and methodological positions that influence the implementation of a set of essential grounded theory methods. Each chapter in this text addresses these differences and highlights the implications they may have when undertaking a study.

The grounded theory generations

Recently there has been an influx of new books about grounded theory, many of which have documented the beginnings of the method and the original work of Anselm Strauss and Barney Glaser (Covan, 2007; Stern, 2009). In 1960, Anselm Strauss joined the University of California, San Francisco (UCSF) School of Nursing. The UCSF School of Nursing has a proud intellectual history: Edith Bryan, the first American nurse to earn a doctoral degree, was its founding leader in 1918 (UCSF, 2007). In appointing the then 44-year-old Strauss to a professorial position, the school's leaders were strategically investing in his intellectual capital with the aim of establishing a doctoral studies programme. Shortly after his appointment, the Department of Social and Behavioral Science was created within the school and Strauss appointed its inaugural Director.

In 1961, at the age of 33 years, Barney Glaser had completed his PhD at Columbia University in New York under the guidance of Paul Lazerfeld and Robert Merton (Covan, 2007). At this time, Strauss was successful with a grant application for a four-year funded study to examine the experience of dying, and recruited Glaser to the research team. It was during this study that the grounded theory methods we know today began to coalesce. In 1967, after completion of *Awareness of dying*, Glaser and Strauss published *The discovery of grounded theory*. Together they made their scholarly motivation for this publication quite clear, stating that:

> We would all agree that in social research generating theory goes hand in hand with verifying it; but many sociologists have been diverted from this truism in their zeal to test either existing theories or a theory that they have barely started to generate. (p. 2)

The notion of generating new theory from data, as opposed to testing existing theory, resonated with other social scientists and grounded theory as a research design became increasingly popular. For the next 10 years, Strauss and Glaser taught together at UCSF, with many of their students now forming a coterie who would carry on their legacy. While Strauss continued teaching at UCSF until 1987, and later as an Emeritus Professor, Glaser left the academy to write, publish, consult and teach around the world.

Increasingly there is a trend in the literature to categorize Glaser and Strauss as the first generation of grounded theorists. At UCSF they created a challenging and supportive teaching environment that was a crucible for many of those who have

Table 1.1 Seminal grounded theory texts

Year	Author	Title
1967	Glaser and Strauss	*The discovery of grounded theory*
1978	Glaser	*Theoretical sensitivity*
1987	Strauss	*Qualitative analysis for social scientists*
1990	Strauss and Corbin	*Basics of qualitative research: Grounded theory procedures and techniques*
1992	Glaser	*Basics of grounded theory analysis*
1994	Strauss and Corbin	'Grounded theory methodology: An overview' in *Handbook of qualitative research* (1st Edition)
1995	Charmaz	'Grounded theory' in *Rethinking methods in psychology*
1998	Strauss and Corbin	*Basics of qualitative research: Grounded theory procedures and techniques* (2nd Edition)
2000	Charmaz	'Grounded theory: Objectivist and constructivist methods' in *Handbook of qualitative research* (2nd Edition)
2005	Clarke	*Situational analysis: Grounded theory after the postmodern turn*
2006	Charmaz	*Constructing grounded theory: A practical guide through qualitative analysis*

become known as second-generation grounded theorists (Morse et al., 2009). It is the second generation of grounded theorists who have written about their interpretations of Glaser and Strauss's grounded theory methods and who have in many cases used the original work as a launching pad for their own iterations (Bowers & Schatzman, 2009; Charmaz, 2006; Clarke, 2005).

Table 1.1 is ordered chronologically and lists those works considered by us to be seminal grounded theory texts because they are characterized by their originality of thought and subsequent influence. Making a decision about what to classify in this way is an arbitrary process; however, the citation rate of each of these works provides an indication of scholarly opinion. It is not suggested that a novice grounded theorist read the books in this list from top to bottom, even though supervisors sometimes recommend this.

Over the years, much has been made of a supposed split between Strauss and Glaser following the publication of Strauss and Corbin's text *Basics of qualitative research: Grounded theory procedures and techniques* in 1990. Glaser's rebuttal (1992) sparked a debate among grounded theory scholars (Boychuk-Duchscher & Morgan, 2004; Heath & Cowley, 2004) about the relative merits of each scholar's work that continues today. It is worth noting, however, that in spite of the intellectual discussion that surrounds variations in the use of grounded theory methods, Glaser and Strauss's personal and professional relationship endured until Strauss' death in 1996.

You will frequently see reference to Glaser and Strauss's different perspectives on grounded theory in the literature. Often a researcher will demonstrate (a sometimes almost fanatical) adherence to either a traditional Glaserian or an evolved Straussian version of grounded theory. This text aims to provide a balanced view of grounded theory methods without adopting a dichotomous position. Few things are ever black and white, especially when it comes to research with an overtly interpretive component, and there is much to be learned from all antecedent grounded theorists.

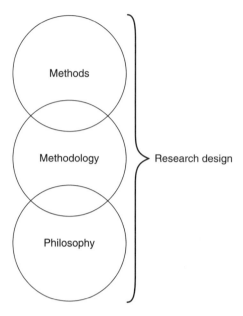

Figure 1.1   Components of a research design

Philosophy, methodology and methods

One of the key aims of a doctoral research programme, and to a certain extent other graduate programmes, is to instil in students knowledge of various philosophies and in turn the methodologies and methods that are linked to these schools of thought. It is important to understand the difference between a methodology and a set of methods. Stemming from a congruent philosophy, a methodology is a set of principles and ideas that inform the design of a research study. Methods, on the other hand, are practical procedures used to generate and analyse data. There is a fluid interplay that occurs between methodology and method in the process of undertaking a research study, represented very simply in the crossover between each of these domains in Figure 1.1. The methodological framework with its underpinning philosophy influences how the researcher works with the participants, in other words the position they take in the study. Depending on their philosophical beliefs and adopted methodology, researchers take either a position of distance or acknowledged inclusion in both the field and in the final product of the study (see Chapter 4). As well, and crucially for grounded theory, the methodology subscribed to influences the analysis of the data as it focuses the researcher's attention on different dynamics and alerts them to possible analytic configurations in the process of conceptual and theoretical abstraction.

   In this chapter, our purpose is to discuss philosophical and methodological influences on grounded theory. For a broader and more comprehensive explanation of the various paradigmatic positions that can be assumed by a researcher we recommend you seek out other texts that address these issues in detail (for example, Guba and Lincoln's chapter 'Paradigmatic controversies, contradictions, and emergent confluences' in the *Handbook of Qualitative Research 3rd Edition*, edited by Denzin and Lincoln (2005) or similar works).

One of the major criticisms of the first generation of grounded theorists, and in this we include Juliet Corbin who co-wrote some of the seminal texts with Strauss, is that they did not write about grounded theory as a methodological/methods package; rather, they wrote only about the various strategies and techniques (methods) that could be used. Fortunately this has been rectified to an extent in the latest edition of Corbin and Strauss's (2008) book, which includes a chapter, absent from the earlier editions, explaining pragmatism and symbolic interactionism as the philosophies that methodologically underpin Strauss's iteration of grounded theory methods. Glaser has never really entered the conversation about grounded theory methodology, rather his writing has focused on grounded theory method and what constitutes a grounded theory itself. Conversely to Strauss and Corbin, he has dismissed the applicability of any specific philosophical or disciplinary position, including symbolic interactionism, in his belief that adopting such a perspective reduces that broader potential of grounded theory (Glaser, 2005). Because of the language that Glaser uses when writing about emergence in the process of concurrent data collection and analysis, as well as in the later stages of analysis when the core category is also said to emerge, he is generally cited as a critical realist researching within the post-positivist paradigm (Annells, 1996).

Methodological gaps in seminal texts written by first-generation grounded theorists have meant that students of grounded theory needed to figure out what was (to borrow a famous grounded theory mantra) 'going on' ontologically and epistemologically in order to plan and execute a rigorous study that would pass examination. Because of this, many second-generation grounded theorists developed methodological frameworks for grounded theory methods that are clearly underpinned by various philosophies. Rather than argue for one genre of grounded theory in this book, you will note that we move across a range of these now established methodological positions in order to demonstrate their influence on grounded theory methods. We have also made an assumption, in concert with others (Bryant & Charmaz, 2007), that there is a set of methods essential to grounded theory research design that must be used in order for the final product to be considered as such.

Throughout this book, we encourage you to identify your own underlying assumptions about the world, to decide how you are positioned philosophically and in turn methodologically. To help you to achieve this we will provide you with some strategies later in this chapter. Once you have accomplished this task, you will be in a much better position to draw the best from a variety of thinkers about how grounded theory methods can be used in individual research designs. This is what many of the second-generation grounded theorists themselves have done, with the result that grounded theory research design has moved into new methodological spaces (Charmaz, 2000; Clarke, 2005).

Methodological influences on grounded theory

Grounded theory is most often derived from data sources of a qualitative (interpretive) nature. Qualitative research studies originate from early world explorers who document their experiences of encountering the tribes of foreign lands while collecting cultural artefacts, all in the name of colonization.

Denzin and Lincoln (2005) identify eight moments of qualitative research originating at different points of history and influenced by the social milieu of the time. The eight moments of qualitative research are not moments that have ever passed, rather they continue today and shape the variety of methodological positions that researchers take in their designs. Methodologically, grounded theory has been influenced by researchers situated in the second, third, fourth and fifth of these eight moments of qualitative research. The dates attached to the following explanations of these relevant moments are provided to indicate their period of dominance.

The second moment (from the end of the Second World War to 1970) is known as the 'golden age of rigorous qualitative analysis' (Denzin & Lincoln, 2005: 16) during which time Glaser and Strauss developed grounded theory methods. Philosophically in the second moment post-positivism is the dominant school of thought, resulting in researchers working within an ontological and epistemological frame where there is an assumed reality worth discovering as a detached objective observer.

The third moment of qualitative research dawned soon after the publication of *Discovery of grounded theory*, as a response to cultural ruptures in American society (2005). This phase is called blurred genres (1970–86) and is characterized by qualitative researchers questioning their place in research texts. Constructivist thinking became very influential in this moment, and of importance to grounded theory, as Charmaz began to think about a grounded theory using this methodological lens.

It was not until the fourth moment of qualitative research (2005), dubbed the crisis of representation (1986–95), that Charmaz began to publish about constructivist grounded theory (Charmaz, 1995). Charmaz's work is clearly influenced by the third and fourth moments in its focus on the place of the author in the text, their relationship with participants, and the importance of writing in constructing a final text that remains grounded in the data (Charmaz, 2000; 2006).

The fifth moment of qualitative research overlaps and extends the fourth and is termed the triple crisis as it adds legitimation and praxis to representation. Legitimation questioned measures for deciding on the merit of qualitative research outcomes, while the crisis of praxis provoked questions about the ability of textual analyses of society to effect change (Denzin & Lincoln, 2005). Postmodernist thought permeated much of this debate and influenced the next key movement in grounded theory, Clarke's work on situational analysis (2005).

In Box 1.1, Merilyn Annells discusses situating her own study within the fifth moment of qualitative research and the influence this had on establishing her philosophical position. Note how Annells supports researchers taking a broad and evolving view of grounded theory and the advice she gives for ensuring success in adopting a non-traditional position.

 BOX 1.1 WINDOW INTO GROUNDED THEORY

Merilyn Annells on philosophical positioning

Although I did a small study in 1991 that I thought was grounded theory (GT) research, my first real GT study commenced in 1994 as part of my PhD research. The 1991 study included GT research processes but was descriptive, exploratory qualitative research achieving conceptual ordering but not a full explanatory scheme as per GT.

With my PhD research, fortunately a supervisor knew that in 1994 we were in the 'fifth moment' of qualitative research, which, according to Norman Denzin and Yvonne Lincoln, was being defined and shaped by dual crises of representation and legitimation. Therefore, I was encouraged to consider in which paradigm of qualitative research my philosophical position about inquiry positioned me – so I studied the writings of Egon Guba and Yvonne Lincoln to discover that I was embedded in the constructivist paradigm.

However, this led me to a dilemma. How could I do GT research that would be ontologically, epistemologically and methodologically constructivist? GT literature in that era did not satisfactorily answer the question. Disciples of Glaserian or Straussian modes of GT were polarized about 'rightness' of the modes, but mostly silent about philosophical perspectives. So I 'took the bull by the horns' and did my own extensive analysis of writings by GT's major identities Barney Glaser, Anselm Strauss and Juliet Corbin. My opinion became that Glaserian GT was post-positivist and controversially that Straussian GT was leaning toward constructivism although still showing signs of post-positivism with symbolic interaction foundations. This led me to applying the Straussian mode but in an ostensibly constructivist way, and I had to write a solid defense of this choice.

What helped was meeting with Juliet Corbin in the US in 1995 to discuss my analysis of data for the study, and in 1996, prior to his death, having correspondence about my philosophical analyses of GT with Anselm Strauss. Several articles were published in the mid-1990s presenting my philosophical analyses of GT modes – this led to critical comment by others. Nevertheless, having eminent examiners of the thesis added credibility to the research and the philosophical analyses. These examiners were the qualitative research methodologist, Margarete Sandelowski, and the pioneer grounded theorist nurse researcher who worked with Glaser and Strauss in the 1960s, Jeanne Quint Benoliel.

What has remained constant is my conviction that GT can be conducted within any qualitative paradigmatic position if ensuring commensurable process and

(Continued)

> *(Continued)*
>
> claims of outcome. This needs to be thoroughly justified when planning and reporting the study. Additionally, I believe that GT is evolving and it is not only OK but also beneficial to have multiple modes of GT from which to choose. PhD candidates who I have supervised have justifiably and successfully used quite different approaches to GT. These days there is plenty of literature about the philosophical underpinnings of GT so a student does not have to try and work it out but if there is something about GT that needs some new thought and opinion, don't hesitate to delve into it. Viva la GT!

Annell's perspective reinforces our assertion earlier in this chapter that dividing grounded theory into either traditional or Glaserian grounded theory and evolved or Straussian grounded theory is not very helpful. Doing so fails to account for the subtleties and differences in grounded theory research design that have developed in the third, fourth and fifth moments of qualitative research. Methodologically, there are no right or wrong approaches to using grounded theory methods; however, there are differences that need to be taken into account. It is the methodological differences in how essential grounded theory methods are used that we will explore and explain in the chapters that follow.

Discerning a personal philosophical position

You may already be very clear about how you see yourself philosophically and in turn methodologically. For some, this hard thinking work is part of their scholarly history and training, but others may have yet to attempt this task in an orderly way. The importance of discerning a personal philosophical position before you begin to conceptualize a research study is highlighted in the following quote:

> All research is interpretive; it is guided by the researcher's set of beliefs and feelings about the world and how it should be understood and studied. Some beliefs may be taken for granted, invisible, only assumed, whereas others are highly problematic and controversial. (Denzin & Lincoln, 2005: 22)

Articulating their beliefs and feelings about the world and reflecting on these equips a researcher to make decisions of a methodological nature, which in turn affects how the essential grounded theory methods are used. As to whether a researcher's beliefs and feelings are highly problematic and controversial, the question must be asked: for whom might this be the case? Chapter 4 discusses positioning the researcher at length; however, if there is some early work that needs to be done to think through a philosophical position, now is the time to 'clear a space for the writing voice, hacking away at the others with [a] machete' (Lamott, 1994), and begin to write.

Activity 1.1

Identifying your underlying assumptions about the world

Make sure that you will be uninterrupted and comfortable (get a cup of coffee and perhaps a chocolate biscuit). Prepare to time yourself to write for six minutes without stopping.

Think about the following questions:

1 How do we define our self?
2 What is the nature of reality?
3 What can be the relationship between researcher and participant?
4 How do we know the world, or gain knowledge of it?

Now write for six minutes, without stopping, about the questions listed. Do not worry about style, spelling or punctuation – just get your thoughts down on paper. Don't stop to critique your work – just concentrate on writing.

Put this piece of writing away for a couple of days and then come back to it. Print it out, get a highlighter pen and go through it. Find the gems in the dross, focus on these and write some more. Look for the gaps, reflect on what else you need to read and consider. Write some more. Never throw anything away; instead, file it carefully for another day.

Essential grounded theory methods

As will be discussed in the following chapters, many research studies purporting to be grounded theories are often a qualitative descriptive analysis (Glaser, 2007) of a particular phenomena. *The Sage handbook of grounded theory* (Bryant & Charmaz, 2007) has brought the question of what are the salient characteristics of grounded theory research design to the forefront of contemporary discussions about grounded theory. We consider the following to constitute a set of essential grounded theory methods: initial coding and categorization of data; concurrent data generation or collection and analysis; writing memos; theoretical sampling; constant comparative analysis using inductive and abductive logic; theoretical sensitivity; intermediate coding; selecting a core category; theoretical saturation; and theoretical integration. The remainder of this chapter provides a brief introduction to each of these methods to create a sense of how they are used in undertaking a grounded theory study. The following chapters will examine each of these methods in relation to producing an integrated grounded theory while discussing the various debates and ideas present in the literature.

Initial coding and categorization of data

Initial or open coding is the first step of data analysis. It is a way of identifying important words, or groups of words, in the data and then labelling them accordingly.

In vivo codes are when the important words or groups of words (usually verbatim quotes from participants) are themselves used as the label, while categories are groups of related codes (Holloway, 2008). Categories are referred to as theoretically saturated when new data analysis returns codes that only fit in existing categories, and these categories are sufficiently explained in terms of their properties and the dimensions.

There are various terms used to describe coding in grounded theory, which can become confusing. In the original text, Glaser and Strauss (1967) paid little attention to describing the process of coding, assuming that the reader would know what this entailed. Since then, the process of coding in grounded theory studies has had phases of being quite elaborate (Strauss & Corbin, 1990) to in more recent times becoming much more straightforward (Charmaz, 2006).

Concurrent data generation or collection and analysis

Fundamental to a grounded theory research design is the process of concurrent data generation or collection and analysis. To achieve this, the researcher generates or collects some data with an initially purposive sample. The data from these initial encounters is coded before more data is collected or generated. It is this concept that differentiates grounded theory from other types of research design that required the researcher either initially to collect and subsequently analyse the data, or to construct a theoretical proposition and then collect data to test their hypothesis (Glaser & Strauss, 1967).

Writing memos

Memos have been wonderfully described as 'intellectual capital in the bank' (Clarke, 2005: 85). More prosaically, memos are written records of a researcher's thinking during the process of undertaking a grounded theory study. As such, they vary in subject, intensity, coherence, theoretical content and usefulness to the finished product. However harshly you may critique your efforts at memo writing, never throw a memo away as you cannot anticipate when it might suddenly become vitally important. Memo writing is an ongoing activity for grounded theorists as memos are generated from the very early stages of planning a study until completion. Your memos will in time transform into your grounded theory findings. Writing consistently and copiously will help build your intellectual assets.

Theoretical sampling

Researchers use theoretical sampling to focus and feed their constant comparative analysis of the data. During this iterative process, it will become apparent that more information is needed to saturate categories under development. This often occurs when you want to find out more about the properties of a category, conditions that a particular category may exist under, the dimensions of a category or the relationship between categories (Strauss & Corbin, 1998). To sample theoretically, the researcher makes a strategic decision about what or who will provide the most information-rich source of data to meet their analytical needs. Writing memos is an important technique to use in this process, as it allows the researcher to map out possible sources to sample theoretically, while at the same time creating an important audit trail of the decision-making process for later use.

Constant comparative analysis

Part of the process of concurrent data collection and analysis is the constant comparison of incident to incident, incident to codes, codes to codes, codes to categories, and categories to categories. This is termed constant comparative analysis and is a process that continues until a grounded theory is fully integrated.

Grounded theory methods are referred to as inductive in that they are a process of building theory up from the data itself. Induction of theory is achieved through successive comparative analyses. The logic of abduction is also much more apparent in the recent literature about grounded theory methods (Charmaz, 2006; Reichertz, 2007; Richardson & Adams St Pierre, 2005). Abductive reasoning occurs at all stages of analysis, but particularly so during the constant comparative analysis of categories to categories leading to theoretical integration. When using abductive reasoning, the researcher 'has decided ... no longer to adhere to the conventional view of things ... Abduction is therefore a cerebral process, an intellectual act, a mental leap, that brings together things which one had never associated with one another: A cognitive logic of discovery' (Reichertz, 2007: 220)

Theoretical sensitivity

Theoretical sensitivity is first cited in Glaser and Strauss's seminal text (1967) as a two-part concept. Firstly, a researcher's level of theoretical sensitivity is deeply personal; it reflects their level of insight into both themselves and the area that they are researching. Secondly, a researcher's level of theoretical sensitivity reflects their intellectual history, the type of theory that they have read, absorbed and now use in their everyday thought. Researchers are a sum of all they have experienced. The concept of theoretical sensitivity acknowledges this fact and accounts for it in the research process. As a grounded theorist becomes immersed in the data, their level of theoretical sensitivity to analytical possibilities will increase.

Intermediate coding

Intermediate coding is the second major stage of data analysis following on from initial coding. In saying this, the researcher moves between initial and intermediate coding during the process of concurrent data generation or collection and analysis, and the constant comparison of data. The researcher employs intermediate coding in two ways: firstly, to develop fully individual categories by connecting sub-categories, and fully developing the range of properties and their dimensions; and, secondly, to link categories together. Initial coding is often said to fracture the data, whereas intermediate coding reconnects the data in ways that are conceptually much more abstract than would be produced by a thematic analysis. Axial coding is the most advanced form of intermediate coding and has been a feature of the work of Strauss (1987) and Strauss and Corbin over time (1990).

Identifying a core category

Developing categories through the process of intermediate coding will increase the level of conceptual analysis apparent in the developing grounded theory. At this time, the researcher may choose to select a core category that encapsulates and explains the grounded theory as a whole. Further theoretical sampling and selective coding focus on actualizing the core category in a highly abstract conceptual manner. This is achieved through full theoretical saturation of both the core category and its subsidiary categories, sub-categories and their properties.

Advanced coding and theoretical integration

Advanced coding is critical to theoretical integration. Theoretical integration is the most difficult of the essential grounded theory methods to accomplish well. A grounded theory generally provides a comprehensive explanation of a process or scheme apparent in relation to particular phenomena. It is comprehensive because it includes variation rather than assuming there is a one-size-fits-all answer to a research question. Advanced coding procedures include the use of the storyline technique (Strauss & Corbin, 1990) as a mechanism of both integrating and presenting grounded theory. Glaser (2005) employs theoretical coding during the advanced coding stage. Theoretical codes can be drawn from existing theories to assist in theoretical integration while adding explanatory power to the final product of a grounded theory study by situating it in relation to a theoretical body of knowledge.

Generating theory

The final product of a grounded theory study is an integrated and comprehensive grounded theory that explains a process or scheme associated with a phenomenon. This theory is generated by the researcher (Glaser & Strauss, 1967) using the methods we have just provided an overview of. Figure 1.2 illustrates how the essential methods fit together during the process of grounded theory research.

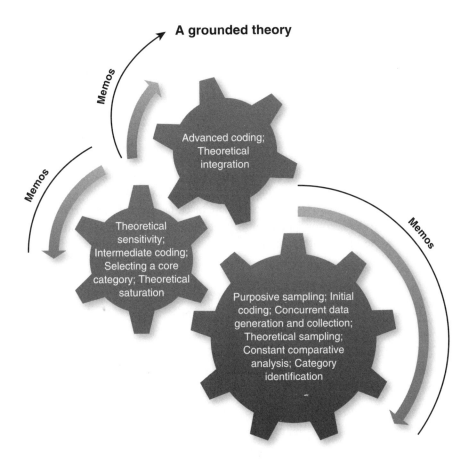

Figure 1.2 Essential grounded theory methods

We have purposefully grouped essential grounded theory methods into three cogs that can drive a machine (you) to generate grounded theory. The largest cog includes purposive sampling, initial coding, concurrent data generation and collection and analysis, theoretical sampling, constant comparative analysis and category identification. This cog constitutes the most straightforward and easiest to accomplish of the methods. Together, large cog methods form the powerhouse of grounded theory research design, enabling you both to generate and refine data. The two smaller cogs include concepts and techniques that are no less important. Rather, small-cog methods take your study to a level of sophistication that will lift your analysis beyond qualitative description. The lower of the small cogs includes theoretical sensitivity, intermediate coding, identifying a core category and theoretical saturation. Engaging in these methods will further refine your analysis while increasing the comprehensiveness of the final product. The upper small cog includes complex methods of advanced coding and theoretical integration. This is where a grounded theory either comes together, or not, as the case may be. Writing memos lubricates each of the cogs as they rotate around each other during the research process. Without high-quality memos, the machine will very quickly grind to a halt. If one of the small cogs become jammed, or has absent components, then a grounded theory will never be produced. It is as simple as that.

Conclusion

This chapter has provided you with an introduction to grounded theory research. In the chapters that follow, you will have the opportunity to explore in detail the critical elements of grounded theory introduced so far. By now, you will have written your first memo, and perhaps eaten several chocolate biscuits! Both of these are extremely important tasks to be accomplished before you begin to plan your grounded theory study, which is the subject of Chapter 2.

 CRITICAL THINKING QUESTIONS

1 How important do you think the prevailing research culture was in shaping Glaser and Strauss's original work on grounded theory?

2 Consider second-generation grounded theorists. What do you think were the most important influences on their work?

3 Essential grounded theory methods are multi-faceted. Identify the purposes of each of these.

4 Reflect on the different methodological influences apparent in grounded theory research. What type of language would you expect each of the seminal authors to use in relation to both participants and their findings?

 WORKING GROUNDED THEORY

Review the 'Working grounded theory' example presented in Appendix A. Note:

• The preconceptions this researcher held about grounded theory prior to commencing the study.

• The relationship this researcher had with the seminal works on grounded theory.

• The personal philosophical position of the researcher and how this was expressed.

2 Planning a grounded theory study

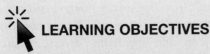

LEARNING OBJECTIVES

This chapter will help you to:

1 Discuss the unique characteristics of grounded theory research

2 Describe instances where investigation using grounded theory is indicated

3 Outline the stages of planning a grounded theory study

4 Identify elements of an effective written proposal to conduct grounded theory research

5 Discuss the use of grounded theory methods in diverse research designs

Introduction

The first chapter of this text provided an important introduction to the philosophical and methodological foundations of grounded theory. Understanding the history, principles and methods of this approach to research ensures that you are well positioned to grasp the fundamental concepts that underpin data generation, collection and analysis in order to render quality grounded theory. In this chapter we will explore issues relating to planning in grounded theory research. A structured framework for planning your study is proposed, along with guidelines to assist you in using essential grounded theory methods in diverse research designs.

The grounded theory difference

The methodology for use in any research design is determined by the aims of the particular study. Many qualitative research methodologies seek to describe and explore phenomena. The essential grounded theory methods described in the previous chapter, and elaborated on throughout this text, go beyond simple description and exploration. Grounded theory differs from other approaches to research in that it serves to explain the phenomenon being studied. The strategies used in data collection and analysis result in the generation of theory that explicates a phenomenon from the perspective and in the context of those who experience it. Theory as the product of the investigative processes is the hallmark of grounded theory research. This theory is directly abstracted from, or grounded in, data generated and collected by the researcher.

Not all studies purporting to be grounded theory actually result in a theory that demonstrates explanatory power. Some may claim to generate theory, yet the process of abstraction is inadequately demonstrated, leading to doubts about how effectively this theory is grounded in the data. Grounded theory methods are inherently effective in their own right and we will describe later in this chapter how they can also be employed to assist in achieving specific aims within diverse research designs. Simply employing selected grounded theory methods, however, will not generate grounded theory. Rather, a selective approach is more likely to result in descriptive, exploratory research that has been referred to as qualitative data analysis (QDA) by Glaser (2004) and the generic inductive qualitative model (GIQM) by Hood (2007). Both these authors contend that a failure to make the distinction between the value and purpose of exploratory descriptive research and grounded theory serves to devalue and erode the latter. Figure 2.1 indicates where many researchers who erroneously claim to have produced a grounded theory usually diverge from the distinguishing features of this approach. Often it is those elements of grounded theory research design that make possible abstraction and theoretical integration at the higher level (represented by the shaded cogs in Figure 2.1) that are absent in such studies.

When is grounded theory appropriate?

How do you know whether grounded theory is appropriate for your intended study? Often researchers are attracted to the relatively straightforward methods that characterize grounded theory and do not thoroughly consider whether it is the best approach for achieving their research aims. Because of the unique nature of grounded theory methods, we can identify the type of instances where its use is appropriate. Grounded theory is indicated when:

- Little is known about the area of study.

- The generation of theory with explanatory power is a desired outcome.

- An inherent process is imbedded in the research situation that is likely to be explicated by grounded theory methods.

Grounded theory results in the generation of new knowledge in the form of theory; therefore areas where little is known about a particular topic are most deserving of

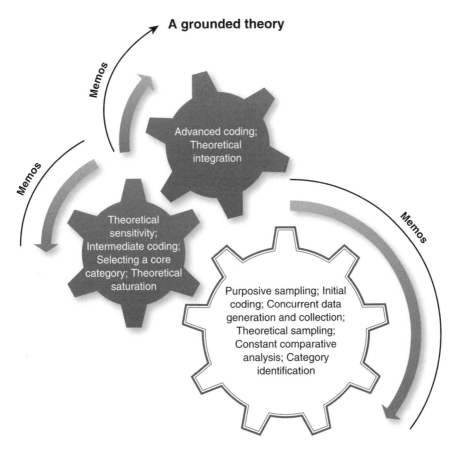

Figure 2.1 Grounded theory versus descriptive, exploratory research

research effort. Not much can be gained from energy expended to investigate issues that have already been explored extensively. Conversely, it should also be noted that while research designs with an interpretive component are usually not intended for generalization, there are often specific questions in unique situations that cannot be addressed by findings from studies conducted in similar yet disparate settings. All researchers should be able to demonstrate that their proposed study will generate knowledge that is relevant and significant. In employing grounded theory, you should also be satisfied that it is new and unique. Skeat and Perry (2008), for example, identified the potential for grounded theory to contribute to theory about the discipline of speech and language therapy. Similarly, Nilsson (2006) discussed the potential of grounded theory to redress the limited amount of human and organizational focused knowledge in the area of logistics.

As identified previously, grounded theory is the preferred choice when the intent is to generate theory that explains a phenomenon of interest to the researcher. When planning a study, therefore, you should be clear that the aim is to move your analytical processes beyond simple description through exploration. Innumerable descriptive, exploratory studies have been undertaken on a vast array of topics that have contributed significant knowledge to their discipline areas. If your purpose is to describe and explore rather than explain, you are encouraged to look to other approaches for research more suited to your specific aims.

The concept of 'process' is often described as a characteristic feature of grounded theory. Some debate exists as to the significance of process in grounded theory and how this concept can be defined. While Glaser (1978) discusses the specific concept of the basic social process at length, he notes that process is a possible, although not necessarily essential, element of grounded theory. Charmaz (2006), however, believes that process is central to grounded theory and advocates the use of 'gerunds' (the noun form of a verb) to emphasize action in the employ of essential grounded theory methods. Emphasizing process during analysis forces you to identify relationships evident in your study arena (Charmaz, 2006). The value of adopting process as central to grounded theory is enhanced when we broaden our conception of what we mean by the term itself. Corbin and Strauss (2008) define process as an 'ongoing action/interaction/emotion taken in response to situations, or problems' (p. 96). Process, therefore, need not be limited to conceptions of time, phases or stages, but can be seen as occurring in all aspects of the natural, dynamic nature of life.

 Activity 2.1

Use of grounded theory in published research

Access a database of literature from a discipline different from your own. Undertake a search of articles using the key term 'grounded theory'. You will need to limit your search further (for example, to recent years and full text articles) to make your results manageable. Retrieve a small selection of articles of interest to you (perhaps 10–12). Identify using Figure 2.1 which essential grounded theory methods were employed by the authors.
   Do the authors of these articles:

- Discuss existing knowledge in the area of study?
- Indicate that the generation of theory with explanatory power is the intended outcome of their research?
- Identify an inherent process in the research situation that has been explicated by their use of grounded theory methods?

Planning a grounded theory study

The popularity of grounded theory among novice researchers is often linked to its more tangible application in research design than is often the case in other approaches to research, particularly those that employ qualitative data. The intention of this chapter is not to present a universal overview of the planning process for a research project; you are encouraged to consult the various generic research texts for that purpose. Rather, the following discussion will focus on those aspects of planning that require specific attention in a grounded theory study. The stages of planning are summarized for convenience in Box 2.1.

 ### BOX 2.1 STAGES OF PLANNING

1 Acknowledge assumptions
2 Clarify the research question and aims
3 Review the literature
4 Develop a research design
5 Identify ethical and legal issues
6 Determine required resources
7 Develop timeline

Acknowledge assumptions

Researchers will often choose an area of research because of their passion for the topic or a personal interest that stems from experience. Clearly such interest is borne from the existence of some degree of knowledge about the intended area of study. Much discussion has been had in the literature about Glaser's (1992) directive that the researcher must maintain an open mind when entering into an area of study and to what extent this can, or indeed should, be done in reality. As we will discuss in Chapter 4, the ability to generate theory is dependent on the researcher being theoretically sensitive to the concepts evident in the data. A balance is therefore required between maintaining an open mind and being able to identify concepts of theoretical significance throughout the process of data collection and analysis. As a researcher, you must be able to avoid imposing your preconceptions on the developing theory while ensuring, as Strubing (2007) advises, that the knowledge and experience you possess is used effectively in the application of essential grounded theory methods.

Acknowledging your existing assumptions, experience and knowledge of the area of research is an effective mechanism for establishing where you stand in relation to your proposed study. By articulating your thoughts, feelings and ideas before you begin, you ensure that your study is transparent from the outset. How you choose to record your assumptions about your study is a matter of preference; however, we recommend the use of memoing as discussed in the following chapter. Drafting memos from the outset of your study establishes an audit trail of your research and gets you into the habit of logging your project from an early stage.

What issues constitute 'assumptions' about your research that you may need to identify? There are a number of factors that can be better understood once confronted through acknowledgement. These include:

- Your philosophical position (how you see the world) and how it relates to both the topic area of your study and your application of grounded theory methods and principles (as you will have done through completing the activity in the previous chapter).

- What you already know about the topic of your research, from both formal study and personal/professional experience.

- What you expect you will find from your research; while it is important not to influence the outcome, often it is only through acknowledging your predictions that such preconception can be avoided.

- Any apprehension, concerns or fears you have in relation to your study and how your strengths and limitations may impact on the process.

Undertaking any type of research study, particularly for a graduate student, is a process of learning. Setting your compass points at the beginning of your project is the most effective means of making sure that you do not lose your bearings along the way. Acknowledging your assumptions as part of the planning process for your study ensures that you yourself are grounded throughout all stages of your research adventure.

Clarify the research question and aims

In most studies, the research question directs how the study proceeds. In grounded theory, it is the research process that generates the question. A key characteristic of traditional grounded theory research is that the researcher enters the field of study without the narrow research questions or hypotheses common in other research designs. Glaser has consistently referred to the concept of 'emergence' in relation to grounded theory outcomes (see for example Glaser, 1978; 1992; 2004). When we speak of grounded theory as emergent, we are referring to the process, rather than the products, of research. Grounded theory does not spontaneously arise; rather, it is generated, developed and integrated by the researcher through the application of the essential grounded theory methods.

Originally, Glaser and Strauss (1967) proposed that even the research problem itself must 'emerge'. Strauss and Corbin's assertion in their 1990 text that the research question be narrow and function to establish boundaries to the research was a key element in the 'emergence versus forcing' debate that underpinned Glaser's (1992) subsequent rebuttal. Glaser's (1998) stance is based on his belief that for a problem to be of relevance, it must come from those for whom it has significance (or, we would suggest, be generated with them). Strauss and Corbin's

(1990; 1998; and subsequently Corbin & Strauss, 2008) position is typically much more pragmatic and relevant to the contemporary, professional research situation. Current requirements for the conduct of research, some of which echo the dominance of the scientific method, do of course impose a need for the researcher to demonstrate a focused research topic. Whether this topic is expressed as a question, problem statement or hypothesis will be determined by the research design adopted by the researcher.

In undertaking a grounded theory study, you will no doubt be required to produce some type of formal proposal (discussed later in this chapter) that will include a statement of your intended research. In identifying the research question and specific aims for your research study, it is possible to find some middle ground between Glaser's (1992) suggestion that the research functions from a position of 'abstract wonderment' (p. 22) and Strauss and Corbin's more defined approach. Where possible, state your research questions broadly and in terms that reflect a problem-centred perspective of those experiencing or living the phenomenon to be studied. Avoid locking yourself into a specific topic of study as this will hinder your application of grounded theory methods and draw strong criticism from experienced grounded theorists who review your work. The research question will become refined early in the research process (Glaser, 1992). Until that occurs, ensure that your identified area of study is sufficiently broad to allow for the flexible and dynamic nature of the research methods to be employed. Examples of how a research question may be expressed are presented in Box 2.2.

 BOX 2.2 EXAMPLES OF RESEARCH QUESTIONS

1 How do asylum seekers experience freedom in their adopted country following internment?
2 What influences managers in financial institutions to seek professional advancement?
3 How do women in the Sudan develop financial independence?

 Activity 2.2

Identifying research questions

Review your local newspaper. Identify potential topics for research. State these as research questions suitable for investigation using grounded theory.

Review the literature

Use of the literature in grounded theory is perhaps one of the most contentious and misunderstood aspects of this approach to research. The literature has significance at all stages of a grounded theory study but for convenience we can discuss the literature as being used: to enhance theoretical sensitivity; as data during analysis; and as a source of theoretical codes.

It is the use of the literature in the initial stages of a grounded theory study that has stimulated the most debate. As is the case with many approaches to qualitative research, a formal review of the literature is delayed in grounded theory to prevent the researcher imposing existing theories or knowledge on the study processes and outcomes. Glaser and Strauss (1967) acknowledge, however, that no researcher enters the field as a blank slate. Strauss and Corbin (1990) reiterate this position, but the failure of these authors to direct the researcher away from the topical literature in the early stages of a study resulted in Glaser (1992) voraciously reaffirming the importance of avoiding reading in the substantive area completely. In saying this, Glaser does, however, encourage the grounded theorist to engage with the literature from the very beginning of a study, but outside the topic area to avoid contaminating and constraining the analysis of data with extant codes and concepts.

In reality there is very little difference between the positions of these authors. None deny that a researcher will enter into a study with a broad range of knowledge about their proposed area of study (with much of this having no doubt been drawn from the literature) and neither promotes a thorough review of the literature before undertaking a grounded theory study. We suggest, however, that there are many ways in which a limited and purposive preliminary review can assist a researcher in the early stages, not the least of which is the early enhancement of theoretical sensitivity.

Reviewing the literature on the topic of a proposed study provides an indication of the extent of current knowledge and work undertaken in the field. Urquhart (2007) argues that this is an effective means of orientating the grounded theorist to the field of study, without necessarily prejudicing them towards existing theoretical concepts. Often a review of the literature is required in formal proposals for approval or funding of research to justify the need for the study. Where possible, contain the depth and breadth of your exploration of the literature to the minimum necessary to meet such requirements. Undertaking the exercise of articulating your assumptions, as described above, can be effective in identifying your existing knowledge and perceptions about the area of study and can serve to limit the impact that an unavoidable excursion into the literature can have on your research. Glaser's (1998) perspective on how literature can and should be used in the early stages of research is summarized in Box 2.3. Further to these comments he does advise that, where procedural dictates require a literature review before the commencement of a study, the researcher should take the opportunity to treat the literature as data (a concept we discuss in Chapter 5).

BOX 2.3 GLASER ON THE USE OF THE LITERATURE

Reading the literature is a problem for many people doing grounded theory. The traditional approach is to study the literature in a substantive area before one starts the research. Grounded theory's very strong dicta are (a) **do not do a literature review in the substantive area and related areas where the research is to be done**, and (b) when the grounded theory is nearly completed during sorting and writing up, then the literature search in the substantive area can be accomplished and woven into the theory as more data for constant comparison.

To state the point bluntly, these dicta have the purposes of keeping the grounded theory researcher as free and as open as possible to discovery and to the emergence of concepts, problems and interpretations from the data. The likely results of a pre-research literature review are inimical to generating grounded theory. They are:

First, the researcher can be grabbed by received concepts that do not fit or are relevant.

Second, the researcher may develop a preconceived, 'professional' problem of no relevance to the substantive area, the research of which yields nothing but derailment from what is actually going on.

Third, the researcher will become imbued with speculative, non-scientifically related interpretations and connections that find their way into the grounded theory, which are not relevant or do not work. Grounded theory provides its own emergent interpretations as part of it. There is no need for speculation.

Fourth, the researcher will likely become 'awed out' by other authors, especially the pundits in the field, which detracts from one's own self-valuation as a creator of theory.

Fifth, the researcher becomes rhetoricalized, thus sounding all the time like the literature and not sounding as the emergent theory would have it. Thus the researcher's theoretical sensitivity is eroded to rhetorical jargon.

Sixth and lastly, which literature is relevant is unknown until the main concern of the substantive participants emerges with its continual resolving. The relevant literature may be actually far afield from the preconceived literature and not known until much later. It in turn will shed light on the traditional litera-ture as will the grounded theory. Thus time is saved from studying the wrong literature. It is focused on an exacting contribution to the relevant literature.

However, the researcher should be constantly reading voraciously in other substantive areas during their research. Choose areas that (a) will not precon-ceptually contaminate the emerging theory, and (b) will keep theoretical sensitivity, learning of theoretical codes and knowledge of the usage of social theory.

Source: Glaser, B. G. (1998). *Doing grounded theory: issues and discussions*. Mill Valley, CA: Sociology Press, pp. 67–8. Used with permission.

The greatest advantage that the literature affords a researcher in the early stages of a study is that it provides examples of how other researchers have employed grounded theory methods. There is an abundance of literature from various disciplines on the use of grounded theory methods in whole or in part. These works provide an opportunity for you to learn from the experiences of others and can inform your study from a methodological rather than substantive position.

In many research methodologies, theoretical frameworks may be drawn from the literature to direct a study and facilitate interpretation of findings. As grounded theory seeks to generate theory that is grounded in the data and not influenced by preconceived ideas about the area of study, there is usually no theoretical framework employed to guide the research. While the imposition of an external framework as the basis of your study is inconsistent with the basic principles of grounded theory, Corbin and Strauss (2008) do suggest that theoretical frameworks have some practical value, mostly in respect of interpreting the findings. In Chapter 7, we will discuss the use of theoretical frameworks in the process of theoretical coding as your grounded theory takes shape.

Develop a research design

A research design is the blueprint for your study; it identifies your philosophical and methodological position and the methods that you will employ to achieve your research goals. In order to develop an appropriate plan to guide your research it is important that you fully understand the essential grounded theory methods outlined in the previous chapter, and elaborated on throughout this text, before embarking on your study.

In Chapter 1, we presented an overview of the methodological influences on the use of grounded theory methods. The original work by Glaser and Strauss (1967) outlined grounded theory methods in a general way compared with the more procedural approach suggested by Strauss and Corbin in their 1990 text and later editions. Grounded theorists such as Charmaz (2006) and Clarke (2005) developed new approaches to the use of grounded theory methods influenced by their diverse philosophical and methodological positions. As discussed in the previous chapter, it is not necessary to subscribe to one version of grounded theory throughout your study. Your own philosophical position will determine whether you align yourself with one particular author or another, or perhaps draw from each of them to varying degrees in your application of essential grounded theory methods.

When designing your grounded theory research study, you may find yourself frustrated by the need to consider the evolving nature of this approach. Alternatively you may relish the flexible and unrestricted potential that it affords you. This is particularly the case when a broad area of study is identified but the specific issue eludes you. Herein lies a particular strength of grounded theory methods. Exploit them where practical to allow the research problem to become delineated as you engage with the data.

You will, however, need to consider some practicalities of the research design. The fluid, dynamic nature of grounded theory is not an excuse for sitting back and seeing where the trail serendipitously leads you. Theoretical sampling will determine how data will be generated, from what sources and in what locations, as the study progresses. Overall *you* will determine how essential grounded theory methods will be used in your study and to what extent. In the planning stages of your study, however, consideration of these issues can avoid problems arising at later stages that can impact on the progress and quality of your research.

One of the most important things that you will do in the planning stage of your study is to specify the unit of analysis. In Box 2.4, Barry Gibson discusses how specifying the unit of study and maintaining a focus on this often overlooked factor was critical in his own research.

 BOX 2.4 WINDOW INTO GROUNDED THEORY

Barry Gibson on specifying the unit of study

In the second chapter of *Discovery* on 'Generating Theory' there is a little section called 'Specifying a Concept' that has a nugget of information that virtually everyone who begins to do grounded theory for the first time seems to miss. The section simply talks about specifying the unit of analysis. The process is described as 'painstaking' and is crucial to generating a decent theory. Yet most people begin their grounded theories with little thought concerning their unit of analysis, assuming that the unit of their grounded theory is the individual or people who have problems. In *Discovery* the units of traditional sociological analysis are described as 'taxi-dance halls', 'ghettoes' and 'high schools' amongst other things. Clearly individuals will be operating in such settings but the focus of analysis is not on the individuals but rather the situation which is problematical.

I remember tackling this issue in my PhD. I was studying dental practices that were specially set up to treat HIV positive patients. In the first practice I looked at it was clear the dentist did not want to be treating such patients and his strategy was one of avoidance. These patients were clearly dangerous and carried the threat of contagion to this dentist. As a consequence he would not use local anaesthetic, which caused immense suffering to his patients. He also wore what one patient described as 'the lawnmower man suit' (goggles, visor, green scrubs, two pairs of gloves and mask). The suit was alarming to his patients. Looking at this clinic it became essential to find other units to compare it to. I needed to find places where dentists did not think treating such patients was contagious and therefore dangerous.

In order to find the other units I had to specify the properties of the clinic that were relevant to the emerging theory. One property was the number of dentists in

(Continued)

(Continued)

the clinic. This clinic had only one dentist working in isolation. Traditionally solo dentist units are conservative so I needed other units where there were teams of dentists working together. Another property of the clinic was its location. The first clinic was in a location where there was a very small population of people who were HIV positive. HIV was still 'exotic' and unusual in contrast to other places. A third property was longevity. The first clinic was only recently established.

I ended up attending two other practices, one where there were two dentists and another where there were four dentists. These other practices were located in very different areas. In one, the population attending the clinic was derived from a wider environment where the principal means of transmission of HIV was through heterosexual drug use. The other clinic was serving a vocal and active homosexual community. Both of the additional clinics had been established for long periods of time in contrast to the first clinic. In the end it became clear that the definition of danger varied in each location and that this definition contrasted with that of risk and I had an emerging 'cutting point' theory. There was a 'cutting point' where dentists would clearly decide to treat and decide to treat in a partic- ular way. All of the properties of the first clinic mitigated against the dentist being able to treat his population with appropriate sensitivity. He was scared and felt he was operating in dangerous conditions. In contrast the other dentists saw themselves as in control. There was a risk of contagion but it was tiny. Being able to take control and define the situation as a situation of risk enabled them to treat their respective populations with sensitivity and appropriately. Because they were working in units where responsibility was shared they could support each other. The first dentist was isolated and scared and this showed in the way he treated his patients in an atmosphere of fear. Likewise he had only just started to treat them whereas the other clinics had a history of expertise going back over ten to twenty years.

It was a tricky process exposing the different layers of the cutting point and it took a very long time to build the analysis. In the end the common thing in each setting was the way the cutting point between risk and danger varied. Specifying the unit of analysis and paying attention to it throughout your study is crucial to developing a solid grounded theory. That one page in *Discovery* was worth so much to me at the time. It remains an essential element of how I understand grounded theory.

Identify ethical and legal issues

Grounded theory methods, while providing broad scope for the researcher in terms of explicating, exploring and explaining phenomena, can nevertheless be problematic. The requirement to identify potential ethical and legal issues at the outset of a research study can be difficult as it is not possible to know at this stage the nature of the data that will be collected, who it will be collected from or how many sources of data will be sought. Your local institutional review boards (IRBs or ethics committees) will assess any potentially problematic issues and it is therefore important that you consider and address these in you application for ethics clearance. Be prepared to defend your broad research focus and provide examples of data sources and strategies for collection and generation (for example, sample or initial interview questions). Demonstrate an understanding of contemporary legal and ethical issues. What privacy legislation may impact on your intention to access certain documents? What measures will you put in place to prevent, minimize or respond to distress in an interview situation when you do not know where the questions will lead? These questions must be considered in addition to the ethical and legal issues that may impact on any research that involves humans, regardless of the methodology.

Grounded theory research is flexible and ever changing; be sure to allow for the possibility of ethical amendments in your original application for study approval (Duffy, Ferguson, & Watson, 2004). With the use of grounded theory comes enormous potential for the conduct of rich research, but also the need for responsible conduct in respect of ethical and legal considerations.

Determine required resources

A realistic determination of resources required to undertake grounded theory research is necessary to ensure that your study stays on track. Grounded theory encourages the use of data of various types from various sources. Through theoretical sampling techniques, you will identify the most appropriate data sources as your research progresses. A number of resources will be required to assist you as you undertake collection and analysis of this data. Engaging with grounded theory as a dynamic research process, however, will limit your ability to identify specifically which resources you will require during the planning stage of your study. While you may not be able to account for every likely contingency, you will be able to establish at least the minimal requirements for your study. Most likely the biggest resource requirements (over and above your time) will have financial implications. Do you need to purchase equipment such as computer hardware, data management software and/or digital voice recorders? Will you need to undertake training programmes or attend conferences/seminars? Where do you intend to commence data collection? Are you likely to be led to places that will require you to travel extended distances? Do you intend to offer participants reimbursement or compensation for their time? Will you need to employ a professional transcriber?

Thinking broadly about potential resource requirements and planning accordingly can prevent unnecessary frustration and delays as you become engrossed in your research. Before commencing your study, consider potential sources of funding and assistance that may reduce the financial burden and identify individuals who may offer support and direction when you need it most.

Develop timeline

Establishing a timeline for your grounded theory study is an important strategy for keeping you focused on your research, ensuring that you achieve your goals as effectively and efficiently as possible. You will no doubt find that undertaking research, particularly at graduate level, is a journey from which you will grow both personally and professionally. You will follow many paths as you become immersed in your study, some of which may prove more fruitful than others. It is important to remember that your research is also a project, one that requires application and direction in order to secure its completion. Once again time is a flexible concept at the mercy of the fluid nature of the grounded theory research process and for this reason time-dependent planning increases in importance.

Establish timelines prior to commencement of your study to determine intended completion dates for key components of your project. External factors that may influence your study must be taken into account. Identify submission dates for IRB applications. Ensure that holiday periods or other scheduled events do not prevent access to potential participants or other data sources. Most of all it is important to build in flexibility and contingency. IRBs may require additional information and time for consideration of your ethics application; gatekeepers may delay access to data sources; participants may not be available; an unanticipated need to return to the field may be indicated even in the later stages of your study. It is unlikely that you will be prepared for every change in direction or hurdle that will arise. Planning for what is known or likely is your best defence against loss of your valuable time when the unexpected does occur.

 Activity 2.3

Research design in grounded theory

Refer to the articles that you collected in Activity 2.1 earlier in this chapter. How do the authors discuss their use of grounded theory methods? Is there a detailed description of their research design or do they simply state that grounded theory has been employed? Have the authors described how they addressed any potential ethical or legal issues? Do any of the papers present a discussion of the author's experience of conducting the research using grounded theory methods?

Writing a formal proposal

Almost every research study requires submission of a written proposal of some description. The most common examples can be found in applications for enrolment into higher degree courses or to secure ethics approval from the relevant institutional committee. In addition, applications for research grants and scholarships also require submission of a detailed proposal to the funding body.

Attention to detail in the preparation of your written proposal to conduct research will minimize the possibility that resubmission will be required or that the application will be rejected or declined outright. Most forms of written research proposals will contain a discussion of many of the items contained in Box 2.1. The specific purpose of your proposal will determine the extent to which each of these components will take precedence. All proposals will require that you demonstrate the relevance and significance of your proposed study in addition to an ability to conduct research at this level. Applications for ethics clearance will require greater emphasis on measures to protect participants while submissions for funding will focus more heavily on resource requirements and your ability to complete the research within the identified timeframe.

Reviewing bodies are becoming more familiar with research that includes a qualitative component, yet there remains a dominance of quantitative methodologies in the scholarly arena that influences how non-positivist approaches such as grounded theory are perceived in the academic environment and beyond (Hesse-Biber, 2007). Grounded theory is particularly prone to scrutiny by those most familiar with more structured research methodologies. Reviewing bodies are often more comfortable with research designs that state categorically the number of persons, records, locations, etc., that will be accessed and for what purpose. In your written proposal be sure to describe grounded theory as a research design that evolves and demonstrate the rationale for this approach. Acknowledge the implications of employing such a fluid research design and describe measures that you will put in place to prevent and manage any potential, unforeseen adverse outcomes. Be conscious of the fact that you may need to return to the approving body at a later stage with any necessary amendments and build such flexibility into your proposal.

Grounded theory methods in diverse research designs

It is common for studies conducted within another methodological framework to employ grounded theory methods because of their value in the analytical process. Grounded theory methods are in and of themselves effective tools that can be employed in a variety of ways. The hybrid utilization of the essential grounded theory methods is legitimate and encouraged; however, as we discussed earlier in this chapter, there are problems associated with studies that claim to be grounded theory but cannot legitimately be described as such. It is important, therefore, to ensure that your use of grounded theory methods is adequately and accurately described to preserve the credibility of your work.

There are many examples of published research that have employed grounded theory methods within other research designs. Often the researcher is using a grounded theory approach but does not aim to generate theory. A varied application of grounded theory methods and principles is used in these studies where the ultimate outcome is description and exploration of phenomena. Vågan (2009) used grounded theory methods in his study of how medical students in Norway perceived their identity when learning communication skills. Bahora, Sterk and Elifson (2009) also employed grounded theory techniques in their investigation of recreational ecstasy use in the United States. In both of these studies, the authors described their research method as 'modified grounded theory', with findings presented as themes that provided insight into the phenomena being explored.

Grounded theory methods are of particular value in mixed methods studies that employ broad and diverse research strategies drawn from both qualitative and quantitative domains. In mixed methods studies, grounded theory methods are often used to ensure rigorous management of the qualitative component of the research. Cagle and Wells (2008) demonstrated the use of grounded theory methods for this purpose in their design of a mixed methods study exploring the cancer care giving experience of Mexican–American women.

Researchers undertaking studies using a single overarching methodological framework, such as phenomenology, case study, historical research, ethnography and action research, may choose to employ grounded theory methods to varying degrees in their research design. Annells (2006) promotes the application of grounded theory with other established methodologies providing the study is structured to accommodate the different strengths, weaknesses and purposes of each. The extent to which specific grounded theory methods can be relied upon will be determined by how well they fit with the researcher's methodological goals and philosophical position.

When using grounded theory strategies and techniques in diverse research designs, the rules are quite simple:

- Identify the overarching methodological framework(s) of your study.

- Be guided in your choice and application of grounded theory methods by the aims of your study; avoid selecting their use on the basis of personal preference alone.

- Ensure that you possess adequate knowledge of the principles that underlie each of the methods you intend to use.

- Plan your use of each of the selected methods in the context of your study as a whole.

- Cleary describe the modification and use of grounded theory methods in any reports or publication of your research.

Conclusion

The application of grounded theory principles and methods is a flexible, fluid, evolving process. The dynamic nature of the grounded theory research process presents the researcher with enormous advantages over more rigid approaches to investigating phenomena. There remains, however, the potential for a researcher to lose their way if there is inadequate attention to planning during the early stages of a study. Whether your intention is to generate theory, or exploit the value of grounded theory methods in more diverse research designs, producing a detailed plan will ensure that you remain focused and identify areas of weakness before they become problematic. In the following chapter, we will discuss issues relating to quality in grounded theory research and provide you with practical guidelines for ensuring that the attention to detail initiated during the planning stage continues as your study is implemented.

 CRITICAL THINKING QUESTIONS

1 Consider your own profession. Are there general or specific areas of knowledge that would benefit from the generation of theory through research?

2 The concept of process can potentially be defined quite broadly. Think about your everyday activities. Identify obvious and more obscure examples of process in your daily routine. How does examining events in this way change your perspective on them?

3 Locate examples of application proformas for the conduct of research (for example, ethics applications, funding requests, course enrolment documentation). You will find examples of these on the internet or can possibly obtain them from your affiliate organization. Review the components of each and consider how effectively they may accommodate an application for grounded theory research.

 WORKING GROUNDED THEORY

Review the 'Working grounded theory' example presented in Appendix A. Note:

- The characteristics of this study that made it appropriate to investigation by grounded theory.

- The stages of planning a grounded theory study discussed in this chapter that are evident in this example.

- Strategies used by the researcher to address issues related to the development of a written proposal to conduct the study.

3 Quality processes in grounded theory research

LEARNING OBJECTIVES

This chapter will help you to:

- Define the term 'quality' in relation to research generally and grounded theory specifically

- Identify factors that influence quality in studies using grounded theory methods

- Describe personal, methodological and procedural strategies that can be employed to ensure quality in grounded theory research

- Discuss the significance of memoing as an essential grounded theory method

Introduction

A natural phenomenon among graduate students is a tendency to question their ability to undertake research at higher degree level. Working with graduate research students we often hear concerns expressed about their ability to do research 'properly'. Conducting research can be daunting for the novice and it is expected that a conscientious student will have questions and concerns, particularly in the early stages of a project. How can you be sure that your application of essential grounded theory methods is appropriate? Will your study stand up to close scrutiny from others? How do you ensure that your efforts will produce 'good research'? In Chapter 9 we examine evaluation of grounded theory for the purpose of judging the *products* of grounded theory research. When we refer to the products of grounded theory we mean those produced by your own efforts and those produced by others. In this chapter we will discuss strategies and techniques that you can employ in the *process* of conducting your research to ensure quality in both your study experience and the outcomes generated from this undertaking.

What is 'quality' in research?

What do we mean when we talk about quality in relation to research? The concept of quality receives a good deal of attention in the literature, including considerable debate surrounding how quality can and should be evaluated with respect to research undertaken within various paradigmatic frameworks. In Chapter 9, we will explore these arguments and examine the current dialogue in relation to quality in research. At this stage it is important to emphasize the need for attention to quality processes in the conduct of a grounded theory study. Regardless of the philosophical and methodological approach used to guide a study, the credibility of the research outcomes is dependent on the researcher employing measures to ensure quality throughout the entire process. In other words, you must be able to demonstrate *rigour* in the conduct of your research.

In the context of research, the concept of quality is synonymous with rigour. Often perceptions of rigour involve images of severe or difficult situations. The weather may be described as rigorous, as may military training or academic assessment. In such circumstances there is a high degree of control and limited room for error. Conceptualizing rigour in this way is appropriate when considering quality as it applies to the conduct of your research. This is not to suggest that you should stifle the creativity that is essential to the generation of a quality grounded theory. Rather, you must be sufficiently in control of the processes that you employ in order to accommodate or explain all factors that can impact on, and thereby potentially erode, the value of your research outcomes.

As discussed in Chapter 2, the growing popularity of grounded theory methods over recent decades can be tied to its greater attention to procedural detail, particularly following publication of the more prescriptive guidelines devised by Strauss and Corbin in 1990 (and subsequently 1998, and Corbin & Strauss, 2008). Other researchers may employ a grounded theory design in their study because they see it as offering a smorgasbord from which they can pick and choose what methods to use and how to use them. In conducting your research, regardless of how flexible, ethereal or intangible you consider your philosophical position, research topic or methodological interpretation to be, you must be rigorous in conducting your study if you wish to produce a credible outcome.

Factors influencing quality in grounded theory research

A number of factors influence quality in the conduct of grounded theory research. For convenience, we categorize these determinants as *researcher expertise*, *methodological congruence* and *procedural precision* (Figure 3.1).

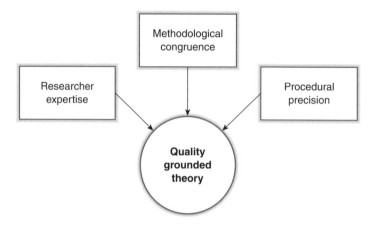

Figure 3.1   Factors influencing quality in the conduct of grounded theory research

Researcher expertise

The fact that you are reading this text suggests that you do not have extensive experience in undertaking research, or perhaps are an experienced researcher who is a newcomer to grounded theory. The complexities of grounded theory terminology and some of the original works on the topic can leave a novice researcher a little overwhelmed when commencing a study (and often throughout the later stages). We concur with Stern (2007) who reassures us that even she did not truly understand grounded theory until she had been through the process of producing one herself. This phenomenon is common to many aspects of personal and professional life. In scholarship, if we view a doctoral degree as a 'research apprenticeship', we recognize this as a process of knowledge acquisition and skill development. In many cases, therefore, a researcher may have limited research experience when commencing a grounded theory study. Nevertheless, most will possess experiential knowledge that will make an important contribution as they undertake their research. Even the neophyte researcher is likely to possess a number of generic skills that will contribute to their research endeavours. Skills in scholarly writing, accessing resources and the ability to manage a project are examples of such abilities.

You may draw comfort from the preceding discussion and our assurances that your generic skills will stand you in good stead as you undertake your grounded theory study. You will nonetheless need to acquire considerable knowledge about grounded theory methods from the beginning phases of conceptualization of your research through to theory generation. This can be achieved through a variety of means and should be consistent with your resources and preferred scholarly style. As discussed in Chapter 1, there are a number of grounded theory texts that will aid in knowledge development. While you need not read all from cover to cover, there is enormous variation in the style and content of these books and you should seek them out in order to establish what they are able to offer you in terms of understanding grounded theory methods and processes from your own methodological perspective.

In most instances, it is the philosophical position of the author(s) of these texts that will determine their approach to grounded theory. The stage at which a given text was written determines the author's focus and reflects major developments in grounded theory at that time. Grounded theory is, and will continue to be, a work in progress and you should be sure to access all editions of a title – do not assume that later editions are essentially the same as earlier ones. Whether or not you choose to align yourself with a given author or approach to grounded theory, be sure to read widely and with purpose. Keep an open mind and be willing to learn from the various grounded theorists who have contributed to the literature. You will be doing yourself a disservice to avoid scholarly contributions from authors who you feel do not subscribe to your adopted position on grounded theory. You may also find that colleagues and supervisors may attempt to steer you in one direction or another. Be sure to listen to all such advice, but do not feel obliged to take a direction that shuts you off from alternative views.

In addition to extensive reading of the available literature, you should explore other options to develop your knowledge, skills and understanding of research methods. Opportunities to participate in workshops that specialize in grounded theory should be seized; however, these are often limited. You should nevertheless seek out conferences, workshops and seminars that address research issues generally as these provide an opportunity to discuss your research activities with other researchers who have varying levels of experience and expertise. There are a number of resources available on the internet, including articles, mailing lists and forums, that will promote your engagement with the research community and provide you with a wealth of resources.

 Activity 3.1

Search for internet resources

Conduct an internet search for resources to assist in developing your expertise in grounded theory research. Don't limit your search to documents – there are a number of resources on video sharing sites that you may find valuable.

Identify and sign up to online research communities to engage in discussion with researchers from a broad range of disciplines with varying levels of expertise.

Corbin and Strauss (2008) identify a number of conditions that foster quality in research, the majority of which relate directly to personal and professional researcher characteristics. Self-awareness, clarity of purpose, commitment to hard work and internal motivation to do research are examples of these characteristics. Note that these are largely a manifestation of individual attitude. Your attitude will determine how successful you are in achieving the personal and professional goals that are tied to your research. We often hear potential researchers lament that they have yet to find a topic that they feel intensely passionate about. We reiterate our advice from the previous chapter that your research study should be managed as a *project*. You need to have an appreciation of the importance of your study, you need to feel an affinity for the topic area and you must be committed to achieving quality outcomes. These characteristics are more important than a romanticized attachment to an idea of research.

Methodological congruence

Throughout this text we emphasize the importance of acknowledging your personal philosophy in relation to your study area. How you see the world will influence how you approach your study and the techniques that you use in achieving your research goals. As discussed in Chapter 1, methodological congruence occurs when there is accordance between:

- Your personal philosophical position.

- The stated aims of your research.

- The methodological approach you employ to achieve these aims.

Quality is most evident in those studies that demonstrate congruence in their research design (Nelson, 2008). Failure to demonstrate methodological congruence will, therefore, bring into question the quality of your research. Weed (2009), in examining research design in 12 studies purporting to use grounded theory in sports and exercise psychology, found that the majority of articles examined failed to achieve such congruence. While the identification of these flaws is intended as a constructive critique, it calls into question the quality of the studies and the subsequent value of the findings.

Methodological congruence is the foundation of a credible research study. Invest time prior to the commencement of your research establishing methodological congruence. You need to be able to engender trust (in both yourself and the outcomes of your study) among those most likely to benefit from your research efforts. Do not make promises that you do not keep in conducting your research. Do not describe your study as grounded theory when it does not achieve this status. Do be honest about the limitations of your research. Do acknowledge and rectify philosophical and methodological inconsistencies as they arise. Your research design will no doubt continue to evolve; such is the nature of grounded theory. The construction of a sturdy anchor will ensure that you do not drift too far off course as your study progresses.

Procedural precision

In the previous chapter we discussed the importance of planning your grounded theory study. Within this context we also identified the process of undertaking grounded theory research as an emergent one; that is, it is not possible at the outset of your study to identify exactly where you will be led by your data and concurrent analytical developments. This is not to suggest that you are at the mercy of forces beyond your control in the implementation of your study, but it is here that your expertise as a researcher will be tested (Lincoln & Guba, 1985). Careful attention to the rigorous application of grounded theory methods is critical if you wish to develop theory that will be judged as a quality product (Glaser, 2004).

Burns (1989), when writing about qualitative research generally, discusses a similar concept of 'procedural rigour' (p. 49). In this work she focuses almost exclusively on processes related to the generation and collection of data. This perspective is limited for our purposes in that it does not address the fact that grounded theory involves complex processes that precede and surpass the gathering of data.

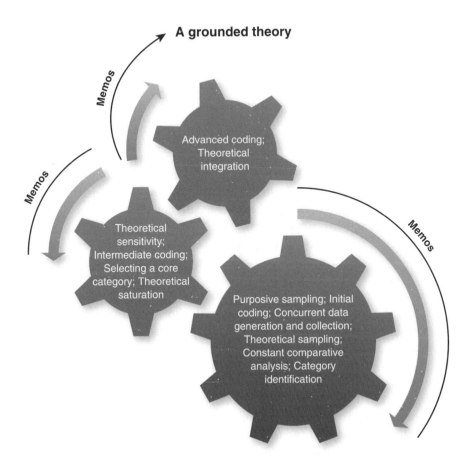

Figure 3.2 Essential grounded theory methods

In the following chapters, the use of essential grounded theory methods (presented in Figure 3.2) is described in practical terms with the intent of developing your skills in their use and your appreciation of the importance of meticulous application. The use of memos, as a critical element in the promotion of quality in grounded theory research, is given special attention later in this chapter. In the meantime we will examine some general concepts that permeate the entire grounded theory research process. In order to ensure procedural precision, you must pay due attention to:

- Maintaining an audit trail.

- Managing data and resources.

- Demonstrating procedural logic.

Maintenance of an audit trail is essential in any research project. The decisions that you make in relation to your research should be recorded as you carry out your research activities. Failure to produce a record of your decision-making trail can result in backtracking and confusion at later stages, particularly in lengthy projects (Corbin & Strauss, 2008). Maintaining a record of research activities, changes in research direction and a rationale for choices made can protect you from loss of confidence and prevent you from 'second guessing' decisions made. Securing confidence in your own actions is a prerequisite for securing the confidence of those who may judge the products of your research. How you record events and decisions throughout your study is a personal choice. You may retain a log book, diary or electronic file for this purpose. Incorporating this process into memos, as discussed later in this chapter, is a practical approach and one that we recommend.

Cutcliffe and McKenna (2004) have argued that audit trails do nothing to establish credibility of research findings in studies using qualitative data, particularly when the researcher is an 'expert'. We, on the other hand, contend that a requirement for transparent accountability, whether in professional or scholarly activities, is incontrovertible. One cannot argue that experience negates the need for demonstrating procedural precision in research work. Certainly, research with an interpretive component may result in the generation of concepts through more ethereal means. This does not mean that the tangible processes that foster and engender such intuitive renderings cannot be articulated. Conversely, Burns (1989) argues that audit trails in qualitative research should be so detailed as to result in other authors being able to replicate your processes and reach the same conclusions. As discussed in the following chapters, however, each grounded theory researcher will have an individual perspective on a piece of research and a unique relationship with data, including that which was gathered by someone else. The outcome of a second researcher's experience with the data is therefore unlikely to mirror that of the first.

When planning your study you should make decisions about how you intend to manage the data that you collect. Qualitative data, for example, is often obtained from a relatively small number of sources, yet the amount of data generated from even a single interview can be extensive. You need to establish mechanisms to record, store, retrieve, analyse and review data and other resources that you will generate and collect while undertaking your research. Various software programs are available that will help you to organize and manage your data. These range from simple word processing and spreadsheet applications (for an example of how one such program can be used to manage qualitative data, see Meyer & Avery, 2009), through common quantitative data analysis systems, to powerful qualitative data management programs that can store digital voice recordings, interview transcripts, images and memos. Bong (2002) argues that use of the latter ensures that analyses are more rigorous, while simultaneously making the process more creative and enjoyable. Whatever system you decide to use, remember that these are tools to assist you in the conduct of your research. It is not what approach you use, but rather how you use it that will determine how effective your data management procedures will be.

Regardless of how you choose to manage your data, your system should be logical and secure, and your files should be backed up frequently. An awful lot of analytical products can be produced in a single day of intense activity, products that can be wiped away in seconds as a result of a virus or system failure. The way you store your data, the duration for which you retain it, and whether it may be used for secondary analysis in a future study (as discussed in Chapter 5) will be governed by prescriptive policies of institutional bodies (such as review boards and ethics committees) and you should therefore be familiar with these.

Grounded theory methods are inherently logical, which is often a factor that many researchers find attractive. Throughout this chapter we have emphasized the relationship between rigorous use of these methods and a quality end product. Correct application of essential grounded theory methods will safeguard this procedural logic, thereby preventing credibility gaps in your research. You will no doubt experience analytical breakthroughs while working with your data. The generation of abstract theory from concrete data is dependent on conceptual leaps, many of which may occur at unexpected times, such as when you are asleep (Burns, 1989). Our own experience is that analytical breakthroughs are most likely to occur when pen and computer keyboard are inaccessible, such as in the shower or while driving! In spite of the disregard your subconscious self may have for due process, you must be careful to preserve procedural logic by returning to your original data to ensure that conceptual leaps can be supported by your analysis, thus avoiding bringing into question the grounding of your theory.

Keeping track of the processes used in your research and establishing structured mechanisms for managing your data, as discussed above, are investments in your credibility. In so doing you are positioning yourself well to respond to questions relating to how you came to the end point of your analysis, such as may be required, for example, when presenting an oral defence of your dissertation or when publishing your theory. While publication constraints in scholarly journals may limit your ability to articulate fully the measures that you employed to preserve quality, you should nevertheless endeavour to make reference to these, where possible, in the discussion of your methods. Remember, procedures to ensure quality must not only be done, but also be *seen* to be done.

Memoing – The cornerstone of quality

Memos in grounded theory research are records of thoughts, feeling, insights and ideas in relation to a research project. As will be discussed later in this chapter, memoing is not optional, as it is fundamental to the development of grounded theory (Lempert, 2007). While we will make reference to the use of memos throughout the research process in subsequent chapters, we introduce memoing here as it is the most significant factor in ensuring quality in grounded theory. The intent of this discussion is to address common questions that novice researchers often pose in relation to memoing as an essential method in grounded theory research.

Why do I need to memo?

In Chapter 1 we introduced the concept of memoing as the critical lubricant of a grounded theory 'machine' (as indicated in Figure 3.2). Stern (2007) regards memos as the mortar that holds together the building blocks (data) that comprise a grounded theory. These metaphors together reinforce the importance of memos to both processes and outcomes in grounded theory research. A useful mnemonic for understanding the broad functions of memoing is 'MEMO' – Mapping research activities; Extracting meaning from the data; Maintaining momentum; and Opening communication (Birks, Chapman, & Francis, 2008).

Regardless of how you engage with memoing in your research, you should, at the very least, use memos to map your activities in support of maintaining the audit trail for your research, the importance of which was discussed earlier in this chapter. Planned activities, unforeseen circumstances and changes in direction can all be considered and recorded in the safe confines of a memo, along with your rationale for decisions made and responses to various contingencies. Even if you choose to log activities in a formal, more structured manner elsewhere, you should still use memoing to explore the meaning and consequences of events that occur along the way.

In working with data, the researcher extracts meaning using a process of interpretation. Memoing enables you to articulate, explore and question these interpretations as you engage with the data (Birks et al., 2008). Your theoretical sensitivity is raised, better equipping you to answer Glaser's (1978: 57) classic question 'what is actually happening in the data?' Memoing gives you the opportunity to interrogate the data with the aim of developing abstract concepts necessary for the construction of theory. Any deficiencies or gaps in your analytical thinking can be detected at an early stage when you are able to see these thoughts in black and white (Corbin & Strauss, 2008). Most importantly, memoing is an uninhibited activity in which you are free to explore your ideas, instincts and intuition in relation to your research. You are able to take risks without fear of being committed to your evolving thought processes (Clarke, 2005). Recording your ideas in memo form does not lock you into them; rather, it frees you up to challenge your developing analysis.

Memos provide a series of snapshots that chronicle your study experience and the internal dialogue that is essential when conducting any research, particularly that with an interpretive component. Memos are working documents that you will rely on to record and revisit earlier thinking and reorient yourself to your research when analytical processes become complex (Charmaz, 2006; Corbin & Strauss, 2008; Goulding, 2002). Momentum is therefore maintained, as you are able to converse with yourself both in real time and retrospectively through the use of memos.

Memos also provide a mechanism for communicating with other stakeholders in a research study. Research rarely occurs in isolation. Teams often undertake funded research and graduate students work closely with a supervisor or supervisory panel. While memoing is usually a personal process, communication with others in team research is facilitated by the use of memos. Memos (or extracts where there is a desire to keep private any reflections of a more personal nature) can be circulated to other members as appropriate to share ideas and inspire thinking within a research team. Melendez (2008), for example, in his study of black football players attending a predominantly white college, used memos to disseminate patterns evident in the data to his supervisor and other members of a research group. Embryonic ideas can be explored and new insights gained through the contribution of all those involved in a study. Memoing facilitates and encourages this process.

From the preceding discussion you will see that memos serve both concrete and abstract purposes. They assist you in maintaining an audit trail in the form of a contemporaneous record of events, while also facilitating communication with others who may have an interest in your research processes. Most significantly, memoing is the single most effective mechanism for raising your data to a conceptual level. Through the use of memos, your concrete data is abstracted and momentum is maintained as you progress through your analysis. Ultimately, as will be discussed in the following chapters, your memos will serve as catalysts in data generation and analysis, form the foundation of your final theory, and provide substance for the written presentation of your research.

When do I memo?

Some authors refer to memoing as a process that occurs from data collection to theory construction (Bryant & Charmaz, 2007; Wiener, 2007) or as being unique to analysis (Corbin & Strauss, 2008). We contend that your use of memos should commence from the time your study is first conceptualized. In so doing you have the opportunity to benefit from memoing during the planning of your research, while also establishing the habit of memo writing at an early stage. The process will then be well established when you reach the critical data collection and analysis phases of your research.

Charmaz (2006) recognizes the power that writing gives the researcher and specifically acknowledges the value of memoing as a technique for initiating and maintaining productivity. Harnessing this power from the outset of your study will ensure that you maximize the effectiveness and efficiency of your research actions.

As your study progresses you will continue to memo at every stage. You may choose to set aside a specific time of the day or week to memo routine activities and maintain a procedural audit trail, or may establish a habit of memoing after every data collection event and coding session. For the most part, however, memoing cannot be scheduled. The timing of memo writing is as unpredictable as the nature and timing of the thoughts that spur this process. Memoing should therefore be given priority over every other activity. In working with your data you will often find an idea is sparked. When this occurs, you should stop what you are doing in order to write a memo, adhering to what Glaser (1978) calls his 'prime rule' (p. 83). In time, you will find the process becomes natural and spontaneous. Your memo writing will continue throughout your study, and perhaps even after completion, as a form of 'debriefing'.

What do I memo?

In the early stages of a research study you may be wondering what it is that you could write about in your memos. There are a number of things that can be written about in respect of your research. If you are having trouble grasping the concept of memoing, view your memos as a type of research log, diary or journal. Initially you may find it a little daunting writing about your study and the processes of your research. The memos written early in your project will probably be stilted and fragmented (Lempert, 2007). You may find it particularly difficult to put down in words your feelings about your research. As your comfort grows with the process, you will find the depth and richness of content will increase and the ability to reflect on your experiences will prove valuable to you personally, while simultaneously enhancing the quality of your study.

Some of the things that you may choose to write about in your memos include:

- Your feelings and assumptions about your research.

- Your philosophical position in relation to your research.

- Musings on books and papers that you have read.

- Potential issues, problems and concerns in relation to your study design.

- Reflections on the research process, including factors that influence quality in your study, such as those discussed above.

- Procedural and analytical decision making.

- Codes, categories and your developing theory.

In addition to what you write in your memos, illustrations and diagrams can be included that clarify your thinking about relationships in the data and enhance conceptualization (these will be discussed further in later chapters). You may also wish to include raw data, such as quotations from participants or observations extracted from fieldnotes. These inclusions prove particularly important when memoing about coding and category development as they reinforce and clarify your analytical decision making. You must be sure, however, to reference such extractions to ensure that later reading does not render unclear the distinction between your own conceptualizations and original data (Glaser, 1978). As your study progresses, you will find that you write memos about earlier memos as your level of abstraction is raised, confirming Lempert's (2007) assertion that memos are therefore themselves data, and should be treated as such.

How do I memo?

A number of authors provide various suggestions and guidelines for memo writing (see for example Charmaz, 2006; Corbin & Strauss, 2008; Glaser, 1978; Richards, 2005), and all agree that flexibility and freedom are essential to the process. From these authors we can derive two rules of memoing: that you *must* do it (for reasons that we have clearly established) and that you should find an approach that works for you. How you memo is inconsequential, that you do so is critical (Corbin & Strauss, 2008). Having said that, we can proffer some advice to assist you in establishing an approach to memoing that will be most appropriate for you.

The first consideration when writing memos is that you should not be constrained by the normal conventions of writing and documentation. When writing memos, the emphasis is on spontaneity and natural flow. Charmaz (2006) describes a process of freewriting, where you are encouraged to write whatever comes into your mind without limitation. Doing so encourages you to trust the process and builds your skills in expressing your thoughts. Remember that your memos are your personal documents. They can be reproduced in a modified form at a later time should you wish to share your insights with your research colleagues, as discussed earlier.

Memos may initially consist of only one or two lines and you may or may not add to them later. As Glaser (1978) suggests, your memos should remain open for as long as necessary. Closing off a memo can result in prematurely closing an analytical pathway (Lempert, 2007). Consider all memos as 'active' until your final theory is constructed. In this regard we suggest that you view your memos as dynamic documents. Making subsequent additions to your memos is preferable to amendment in order to prevent deleting insights; an action that you might later regret. Rather, aim to build on or revoke earlier thinking through additional comments, as this has the added advantage of chronicling your changing thought processes.

Some authors have suggested systems for the categorization of memos that aim to distinguish them on the basis of content and purpose (see for example Birks et al., 2008; Charmaz, 2006; Strauss & Corbin, 1990; 1998). While working this way may be valuable as you develop your skills in memoing, you will no doubt find that overlap will occur, particularly in later stages of analysis, leading you to merge or eliminate classifications. Do not be afraid to experiment with your own system, however; the flexible nature of memoing makes it difficult for you to make terminal errors as you work at finding an approach that suits you best.

With this in mind, there are some practical strategies that you should put in place early in your study to avoid confusion and problems occurring at a later stage. You should develop a system of labelling and filing your memos to facilitate easy access to them at a later date. Use short descriptive titles that reflect the content of each memo. Date each memo and each subsequent addition or amendment that reflects your developing thinking. These measures ensure that you are able to cross-reference efficiently within and between memos and data sources (Corbin & Strauss, 2008). You may be surprised how often you will refer to other memos, particularly as your analysis becomes more complex and advanced. Box 3.1 presents an example of a memo that illustrates many of the above points.

 BOX 3.1 EXAMPLE OF A MEMO

MEMO 6/10 (Additions made 13/10 & 18/10) – NEW KNOWLEDGE, NEW THINKING

This memo results from the writing of the memo for 'Thinking differently' of 4/10 and revised today.

Participants have indicated that it is knowledge that leads to thinking differently, specifically thinking critically. As indicated in the 'Thinking differently' memo, reading, reflection and knowledge are all linked to thinking differently. As reading is a method of gaining knowledge, and reflection is itself a way of thinking differently, essentially this reduces down to the relationship between knowledge and thinking. Is this a process? What is actually occurring? The following diagram is modified from that in the 'Thinking differently' memo to simplify what I am trying to establish:

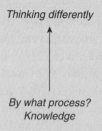

Thinking differently

By what process?
Knowledge

I have always said that tertiary education changes how you think. Why? Because it makes you look at both sides of an argument, it forces you to demonstrate your process of analysis. Is this related to the knowledge (subject matter) itself? The participants speak specifically of 'knowledge', not 'learning' in the context of thinking differently. Do they mean the same thing to them, or are they identifying actual subjects? When the participants speak of knowledge in relation to changed thinking, are they speaking of specific knowledge gained such as learning about the change management process and learning about critical thinking frameworks?

Or are they talking about the process of learning itself? Researching, writing assignments, learning how to develop a critical argument, do they see developing these processes as acquiring knowledge? Is there a difference? I think there is. We are talking about developing cognitive processes, skills if you like. Knowledge I feel is something more concrete.

I did refer to these cognitive skills at one point as 'collateral learning'. I already have a code for this which contains examples of learning that was achieved outside of the subject content, e.g. computer skills, organizational skills, time management. Are those skills different from what I am referring to here? I think so. This to me is a higher order of cognitive functioning. They are, in fact, learning to 'think differently' by going through the process of learning such as they have through completing their course.

Why does this matter? Does it matter? Does it matter what caused the change in thinking? Yes, I think it does. This may well be an element of the process, however that may manifest itself. New knowledge, new life – does 'thinking differently' link the new knowledge with the new life? If so, is it the actual knowledge or the process by which it is acquired that leads to 'thinking differently' for these participants? In other words, is it specific knowledge or is it a result of the journey? Is it both? I suspect that it is and will look for more clues in the data. I know this will either fade away or coalesce as analysis progresses, and may likely be something that needs clarifying in the focus groups. I also assume that this is discussed in the educational literature and if it gains significance I'll no doubt turn to that during theoretical coding.

I guess in summary I am asking:

- How significant is knowledge in 'thinking differently'?

- When participants speak of knowledge, what form does it take – specific subject matter (outcome), developing higher order cognitive skills (process)?

- What significance (if any) does this have in the big picture?

Additional comments 13/10

Reviewing the 'Gaining knowledge' and 'We learned a lot' codes has helped to clarify the above to some extent, or at least to move it past some of the confusion. The memos for those codes and also that entitled 'learning and knowledge' should be read in conjunction with this.

I believe that I have clarified the distinction between 'Gaining knowledge' and 'We learned a lot'. 'We learned a lot' refers to a process. 'Gaining knowledge' is an outcome of this. 'Collateral learning' is also an outcome, in fact almost all codes are touched by 'We learned a lot' and 'Gaining knowledge'. I isolate 'Collateral learning' because it is what distinguishes 'We learned a lot' from 'Gaining knowledge', a task that initially seemed impossible (see memos for these codes).

(Continued)

(Continued)

I see the process at this point as:

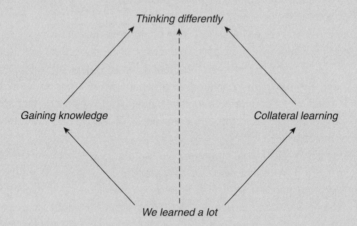

This diagram takes into account the participants' statements that it is the knowledge that makes them think differently, and my assumption that collateral learning is a significant factor in this process. I have said above that I don't see collateral learning as being those higher order cognitive processes that explain 'Thinking differently'. While the data in the 'Collateral learning' code has yet to be reviewed, I feel that it is in fact part of the process that contributes to 'Thinking differently'. I have tentatively linked 'We learned a lot' and 'Thinking differently' directly in this diagram because I think that there is something beyond what is contained in the other codes that is changing the way participants think. I may be wrong.

This diagram is of course only a small piece of the puzzle but one that may help in clarifying the process.

In answer to the above questions:

- How significant is knowledge in 'Thinking differently'? – Unknown how significant, but that it is significant remains clear.

- When participants speak of knowledge, what form does it take – specific subject matter (outcome), developing higher order cognitive skills (process)? The focus group interviews will clarify this, but I believe that it is both the process (learning) and outcome (knowledge) that contribute to thinking differently. I now see the higher order cognitive skills as actually being what 'Thinking differently' is.

- What significance (if any) does this have in the big picture? – Perhaps only a small part of the process. As is discussed in the memo 'learning and knowledge'

> (12–13/10) thinking differently is one outcome of all of those codes that cluster around the concept of 'new knowledge'. All of the other outcomes that lead to 'new life' flow on from these.
>
> *Additional comments 18/10*
>
> The memo 'constructing knowledge' produced yesterday and revised today further extends this discussion.

How you choose to create and store memos is a personal choice. Most researchers these days produce memos electronically. While handwriting of memos is a less practical option, you may find yourself doing so if inspiration hits when you are away from your computer. Digital recording of memos is also an option, although eventual transcription may be required to enable you to work with the contents in a meaningful way. You can, for example, use different font styles, sizes and colours or may highlight sections of your memos either on a computer or by hand. For this reason you may also wish to print and file memos, particularly those produced during more advanced analysis, should you prefer to work with hard copies as suggested by Glaser (1978), for the purpose of sorting as discussed in Chapter 7.

 Activity 3.2

Write a memo

Using the guidelines outlined above, write a memo about what you have read in this chapter. How do you feel about the prospect of writing memos as you work through your research? Do you have any reservations? Give consideration to how the process will best work for you. What skills do you have, or will need to develop (for example, familiarity with software programs) in order to memo effectively and efficiently?

Conclusion

Quality is important in many aspects of our personal and professional lives. In regard to research, quality is critical if the outcomes of a study are to be respected. In grounded theory research, quality is dependent upon attention to a number of factors that can influence the potential value of the resultant theory. Researcher expertise, methodological congruence and procedural precision are required if both the researcher and study outcomes are to be deemed credible. This chapter has explored strategies that should be implemented to ensure that high-standard grounded theory is produced. Rigorous application of essential grounded theory methods, as described in the following chapters and aided by the diligent use of memoing, is fundamental to ensuring quality in the processes and products of research. Your perception of quality, and your attitude to it in your own research, will determine how successful you are in producing grounded theory. Apathy and imprecision in the conduct of your research will inevitably be reflected in the end product.

 CRITICAL THINKING QUESTIONS

1 Consider your own definition of the word 'quality'. How often do you see reference to quality in everyday life? In what contexts is quality most likely to be an important consideration? How does your conceptualization of quality impact on your feelings in relation to your own research?

2 What characteristics do you possess that can affect the quality of your research? Think about both strengths and weaknesses that you have that may impact on how you conduct your grounded theory study. What resources or strategies could you employ to enable you to capitalize on the strengths and overcome your weaknesses?

3 Identify experienced grounded theory researchers that you have access to who have demonstrated quality in the conduct of research. Consider what you may ask them, given the opportunity, about their perception of quality and rigour in their own work.

 WORKING GROUNDED THEORY

Review the 'Working grounded theory' example presented in Appendix A. Note:

- The attitude of this researcher towards issues of quality from the outset of her study.

- Personal, methodological and procedural strategies that she relied upon to promote quality in the process and outcomes of her grounded theory research.

- The significance that memoing held for this researcher as an essential grounded theory method.

4 Positioning the researcher in a grounded theory study

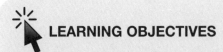

LEARNING OBJECTIVES

This chapter will help you to:

- Discuss the significance of positioning the researcher in a grounded theory study

- Identify strategies that can be used to support the researcher's adopted position

- Discuss the concepts of reflexivity and reciprocity in relation to grounded theory research

- Define the term 'theoretical sensitivity'

- Describe strategies and techniques that can be used to raise a researcher's theoretical sensitivity

Introduction

This chapter will discuss the position of the researcher in the context of various grounded theory traditions. Two main strategies to support the researcher's adopted position will be explained: these are developing reflexive practice and establishing relationships between the researcher and participants. Theoretical sensitivity will be defined and discussed in relation to a priori knowledge of the researcher and their familiarity with the literature related to the broad area of enquiry. In all approaches to grounded theory research, theoretical sensitivity is an important concept and one that is often difficult to grasp even by experienced researchers. Techniques to enhance and raise the researcher's theoretical sensitivity

LIVERPOOL JOHN MOORES UNIVERSITY
LEARNING SERVICES

will be described and explored in relation to the various methodological approaches to the use of essential grounded theory methods.

Positioning yourself as a grounded theorist

In Chapter 1, we asked you to undertake an activity to help you identify some of your underlying assumptions about the world. In answering the four questions posed, you will have generated a memo that tells something of your philosophical position, which in turns informs your methodological preference. Questions asked were:

1   How do we define our self?

2   What is the nature of reality?

3   What can be the relationship between researcher and participant?

4   How do we know the world, or gain knowledge of it?

Some people get very uncomfortable thinking about what they consider to be 'fluffy' questions such as these. However, the answers to each will guide how you position yourself as a grounded theorist and, in turn, how you work with participants, the approach you take to data generation/collection and analysis, and the way you formulate your final grounded theory.

When considering the question of how we define our self, think about the various roles that you engage in on a daily basis. You might consider yourself an expert in your chosen professional field, but a novice researcher. In addition, you may have other 'selves' where you are a member of a religious congregation, a minority cultural group, play a team sport, parent of young or older children, be a spouse, a daughter, a son. All of us have multiple selves that we live out, and all of these roles impact on how we think about the world. When we begin a research study we do not only think about this work as a novice researcher – rather we draw upon the totality of our life experience in deciding how to proceed. The multiple selves that we live out, or the 'many hats' that we wear, influence the methodological approach we choose and in turn how we use essential grounded theory methods. For example, if you come to grounded theory as an experienced architect who relies upon exact, reliable measurements to carry out your work, your methodological preference may well be for a post-positivist approach to grounded theory. This is because your experience tells you there is a fundamental truth about the concept of measurement that you use in your everyday life, therefore surely this same principle applies to discovering 'a' fundamental process that individuals draw upon to manage their lives. A world governed by fundamental truth is for you a possibility, so therefore it influences how you approach your grounded theory study.

Activity 4.1

Identifying your multiple 'selves'

Review the memo that you initially wrote answering the four questions listed in the previous section. At that point in time, how did you define your self? Did you consider the multiple roles that you undertake in your everyday life? Thinking about your initial response to the question, how insightful were you about the complexity of your life and what that might mean for your research study? Write another memo about your response to that same question now.

The question of 'truth' or the nature of reality lies at the heart of a discussion about methodological preference. As Guba and Lincoln (2004) argue, 'whether or not the world has a 'real' existence outside of human experience of that world is an open question' (p. 202). The methodological schools of thought that shape the use of essential grounded theory methods are clearly divided on the question of reality. As our previous example illustrates, a post-positivist approach to grounded theory posits that there is an objective reality that exists outside of human perception but that it is only ever imperfectly perceived. Constructivists and postmodernists, on the other hand, assume what is called a relativist position, where reality is understood as 'relative to a specific conceptual scheme, theoretical framework, paradigm, form of life, society or culture … there is a non-reducible plurality of such conceptual schemes' (Bernstein, 1983: 8).

The literature about symbolic interactionism presents mixed views on the nature of reality. Early interpretations of Blumer's seminal work *Symbolic interactionism: perspective and method* (1969) view his discussion of an 'obdurate reality' as indicative of a post-positivistic position (Annells, 1996; Charon, 2001). Blumer argues that the empirical world offers points of resistance and so is obdurate in nature. Charmaz (2000) proposes a reinterpretation of Blumer's obdurate reality to 'change our conception of it from a real world to be discovered … to a world *made real* in the minds and through the words and actions of its members' (p. 523). This reformulation provides for symbolic interactionists to assume a relativist position where reality is constantly reformulating as a fluid construction of individuals and, in turn, their social reference groups.

Interrogating your own philosophical position requires thinking through what you believe to be true about the nature of reality. Once you have made a decision about where you are ontologically, you need to examine your beliefs about how researchers can legitimately gain knowledge about the world. Ontology (the study of the nature of reality) and epistemology (the nature of justifiable knowledge) are intrinsically linked. Your philosophical beliefs about reality guide your thoughts about how legitimate knowledge can be acquired. The question of what constitutes legitimate knowledge is one that qualitative researchers are frustrated by in the current climate of evidence-based practice where research findings are ranked according to their degree of objectivity and generalizability (Mantzoukas, 2007). Denzin (2009) has declared that in this moment the majority of qualitative research methodologies are 'under fire', the outcome of which is reduced competitive grant funding for researchers positioned outside of a positivist/post-positivist school of thought. We will revisit this argument in Chapter 10.

So, you may be asking, what does this mean for the use of essential grounded theory methods? The short answer to this is that your methodological position dictates if you consider yourself an objective instrument of data collection *from* participants, or a subjective active participant in data generation *with* participants. Figuring out where you are methodologically will 'overtly reshape the interactive relationship between researcher and participants in the research process' (Mills, Bonner, & Francis, 2006: 9). Ultimately, though, it is about the relationship between the researcher and the data, how it is collected or generated, what it consists of and how it is analysed. In order to be methodologically congruent in your research design (as discussed in Chapter 3) you need to be conscious of your philosophical position.

Reflexivity and grounded theory

A key strategy to promote quality in the use of essential grounded theory methods is the maintenance of an audit trail, the importance of which was discussed in detail in Chapter 3. Memos are recommended as a useful way to maintain your audit trail of the procedural aspects of undertaking a grounded theory study. Such an audit trail of memos however, also provides a mechanism for tracing your interactions with both participants and the data. Reflective writing about the research process, captured in the form of memos, will provide you with a tool to monitor both your methodological congruence and how you move across your history when undertaking a grounded theory study. The act of writing and then analysing this writing in light of your philosophical/methodological position will necessitate your making 'meaningful linkages between the personal and emotional on the one hand, and the stringent intellectual operations to come on the other' (Lofland & Lofland, 1995: 15). Critically analysing your reflective writing therefore is a reflexive act. We define reflexivity as an active process of systematically developing insight into your work as a researcher to guide your future actions. Regardless of your methodological position, there is an imperative for grounded theorists to be reflexive researchers.

In saying this, the question of what constitutes reflexivity, the value of reflexive practices in ensuring the quality of research processes and the contribution that reflexivity can make to the generation and analysis of data are the topics of a new debate in both the grounded theory literature and the broader qualitative enquiry literature. As discussed in Chapter 3, Cutcliffe and McKenna (2004) argue against reflexive techniques such as memo and journal writing, positing that they are poor-quality assurance measures for expert researchers. This argument continues elsewhere with specific reference to the concept of reflexivity, which Cutcliffe (2003) rejects as useless based on the assumption that it is impossible for individuals to attain a complete knowledge of self. Because of the complexity of self, engaging in reflexive processes could only ever partially realize the broad scope of knowledge that actually underpins our thinking and actions as much of this is unconsciously realized, such as tacit knowledge and 'knowledge produced during empathic exchange' (Cutcliffe, 2003: 144).

Glaser (2001) also rejects reflexivity as an appropriate strategy to include in a grounded theory research design, warning that it will lead to 'reflexivity paralysis' (p. 47) in relation to analysis. Later readings of Glaser's position suggest that in making this statement he is not rejecting the development of a researcher's self-insight, rather he is rejecting a researcher's desire to locate their work in a particular theoretical construct (McGhee, Marland, & Atkinson, 2007). Neill (2006) provides an interesting treatise on a post-positivistic approach to reflexivity in grounded theory, concluding that the effect of the researcher is automatically accounted for in the data with the exception of sampling, where it is necessary to account for the decisions made to ensure transparency.

Even though the term 'reflexivity' is not apparent in the early seminal grounded theory texts, Strauss (1987), as a symbolic interactionist, clearly identified that researchers' biographies exert influence on the use of essential grounded theory methods and the need for this to be accounted for during the research process. Strauss and Corbin (1998) later advocate that researchers keep a written record of their metaphorical journey, usually in the form a reflective journal, with the aim of learning from their experiences.

More recently, grounded theorists have explicitly addressed the concept of reflexivity in their work. In particular, Clarke (2005) analyses the lack of reflexivity apparent in a post-positivistic approach to grounded theory, concluding that 'instead of hiding behind method ... we [need to] become more visible and accountable for, in, and through our research' (p. 13). In concert with Clarke's post modernist view of reflexivity, Charmaz (2006) acknowledges an obligation for constructivist grounded theorists to incorporate reflexivity as a strategy in their research design.

So practically, how do you 'do' reflexivity? We included the word 'systematically' in our definition of reflexivity as a reference to assuring the quality of your work as a grounded theorist. Memos can provide a written record of reflexivity, if, as you write about your actions and feelings, the influences on your thinking, you incorporate an analysis of impact and outcome. Writing a memo that is reflexive in intent is not a one-off event; rather, taking a systematic approach to reflexive memo writing means attending to this task regularly and working out a way to build upon and learn from your previous efforts (see the example provided in Chapter 3).

Peshkin (1988) investigated his own subjectivity by recording how he felt during particular moments of the fieldwork phase of one of his research studies on community school relationships in different contexts. Using 5″ × 8″ cards, Peshkin wrote about specific situations that aroused his feelings, be they positive or negative, happy or sad, and importantly when he felt motivated to move beyond the role of a researcher into being a participant advocate. Even though Peshkin did not use the word 'reflexivity' to describe this aspect of his work as a researcher, his action of analysing the written records of his subjectivity to identify what he called 'subjective I's' (p. 18) resulted in developing insight into how his underlying assumptions about the world influenced both data analysis and presentation of the findings. As he says, 'I have looked for myself where, knowingly or not, I think we all are – and unavoidably belong: in the subjective underbrush of our own research experience' (1988: 20).

The work of Peshkin has more recently been developed by phenomenologist Bradbury-Jones (2007) where the concept of reflexivity is tied to the identification of subjective 'I's' in the analysis of journal writing. As discussed in Chapter 3, the writing of memos can capture a textual documentary of your lived experience as a grounded theorist, as can journal writing. Consciously creating a record of *how you feel* during this process will allow you reflexively to analyse much more than just an audit trail of decisions made in relation to operational or analytical processes.

The idea of analysing your subjective self in relation to grounded theory process resonates with the work of Charmaz (1991) who defines self as 'the organized set of internalized attachments, commitments, attributes, images and identifications with which a person creates a concept of self' (p. 72). Shibutani (1962), an early symbolic interactionist, had already developed the notion of multiple perspectives of self, the inclusion of which further develops this definition, saying that individuals have a variety of perspectives they use as frames of reference depending on which societal group they find themselves with at the time. As such, a perspective is one of many organized views that make up our worlds and includes what is taken for granted about the characteristics of objects, of events and of human nature (Shibutani, 1962). The idea that our 'self' is somehow made up of multiple perspectives resonates with Charmaz's (2006) much more recent statement that we are 'part of our constructed theory and this theory reflects the *vantage points* inherent in our varied experience, whether or not we are aware of them' (p. 149, emphasis added).

 Activity 4.2

Identifying the subjective 'I'

This is an activity for those of you who have had some experience or involvement with grounded theory research. Choose a memo that is about your thoughts and feelings in relation to the research process. Set aside any previous analysis of the memo and re-examine it afresh. Can you identify any moments where you spoke from one of your multiple 'selves'? Can you name this persona? What might that mean for your overall analysis of the data?

Incorporating a reflexive agenda that seeks to find subjective 'I's', multiple perspectives of self or the vantage points of influence on your grounded theory research design may at first glance seem to fall within the remit of those who have positioned themselves methodologically as constructivists, symbolic interactionists or post modernists (see Chapter 1). We would challenge, however, that this is also important work for those who consider themselves to be post-positivists, as the idea of maintaining objective separation without a mechanism for monitoring behaviour, feelings and thought is impossible. After all, it is only through the analysis of your subjectivity through the judicious process of reflexivity that you can guide your own actions in a more insightful way. This is consistent with the post-positivist approach to reflexivity in qualitative research that is referred to as 'bracketing', a process that aims to sustain objectivity (Dowling, 2006).

While we empathize with those moments of analysis where the elements of a theory do appear to 'emerge' from the data as a result of constant comparative analysis, a moment that Cutcliffe (2003) describes as the magic of qualitative research, our firm belief is that critically analysing these flashes of brilliance/emergence in light of your own history, context and culture remains extremely important. Even if you believe that the data has a life of its own that you are uncovering through the use of essential grounded theory methods (Glaser, 2001), you need to be accountable for your actions and decisions as the researcher facilitating this process – writing reflexive memos is the most truthful and methodologically congruent way to meet this need.

Relationships between researcher and participants in grounded theory

Historically, first-generation grounded theorists paid scant attention to their relationships with participants, instead viewing participants' words and actions as a source of data, data that they needed to obtain in an objective manner (Glaser, 1978; Glaser & Strauss, 1967; Strauss & Corbin, 1990). Collins (1998) describes this as a 'smash and grab' approach (para 1.1), whereby participants are relieved of whatever useful data they may have.

Over time, Strauss and Corbin (1994) demonstrate a shift in how they view their interaction with participants, stating 'the interplay between researcher and the actors studied – if the research is intensive – is likely to result in some degree of reciprocal shaping' (p. 280). In their later text they clarify their definition of interplay as the 'researcher … actively reacting to and working with data' (1998: 58). This, and the last edition of their text (Corbin & Strauss, 2008), acknowledges the co-construction of meaning between researcher and participant as implicit in the generation of data from an unstructured interview (see Chapter 5).

Positioning yourself methodologically as anything other than a post-positivist grounded theorist requires a transformation of the traditional participant/researcher relationship, and for the researcher to prioritize and analyse the interaction that occurs between the two. Epistemologically constructivists, post modernists and the great majority of symbolic interactionists believe it is impossible to separate researcher from participant in the generation of data; however, this is what taking a post-positivist position requires. Glaser (1998) emphasizes the importance of not taping interviews, as recording, transcribing and analysing the interaction between researcher and participant work against a post-positivistic positioning of relying on fieldnotes as data. Writing a one-sided account of the interview in this format effectively separates the researcher and participant as the constant comparison of abstract categories perceived by the researcher during the interview is pursued at the cost of participants' voices. It is this cost that many of the second-generation grounded theorists are not willing to bear (Charmaz, 2006; Clarke, 2005; Morse et al., 2009), arguing that the study of data in the form of recordings and transcripts exposes more about the 'nuances of ... language and meanings' (Charmaz, 2006: 34) than fieldnotes will ever be able to reveal. Each methodological position places a different value on the contribution that various forms of data can make to a grounded theory, although essential grounded theory methods for analysing data remain the same – no matter what constitutes the data.

Regardless of the position taken by the grounded theorist, during the process of narrative interaction, researcher and participant give and take from each other. The complexity of the area of interest being explored becomes apparent and the conversation in turn gains density as meaning is clarified. Interviews therefore become the 'site for the construction of knowledge, [where] clearly the researcher and informant produce this knowledge together' (Hand, 2003: 17). In the construction of such knowledge, information generated needs to reveal depth, feeling and reflexive thought. This approach is representative of contemporary beliefs about grounded theory interviewing as a method of data generation. Interviews are not neutral, context-free tools; rather, they provide a site for interplay between two people that leads to data that is negotiated and contextual (Mills et al., 2006). As we will discuss in later chapters, the final product of a grounded theory study is an abstract construction of the researcher's making, with both researcher and participants generating data that informs this theory.

Counteracting imbalances of power: Establishing reciprocity

Engaging in a grounded theory study means researchers commit to a relationship of reciprocity with the participants that ideally includes a reflexive consideration of existing power differentials. Strategies used to achieve this will vary between different methodological positions taken and the degree of separation or objectivity aimed for. In *Discovery*, Glaser and Strauss (1967) identified establishing rapport with people to be studied as a time-consuming task and one that is not always essential as data can often be obtained by the researcher 'without the people he talks with, overhears or observes recognizing his purpose … he may obtain his data clandestinely in order to get it quickly, without explanations, or to be allowed to obtain it at all' (p. 75). Since the 1960s, relationships between researchers and participants in a grounded theory study have been influenced by codes of ethical conduct that disallow covert behaviour such as this. Recognizing the need to establish a relationship with participants that is mutually beneficial is closely aligned to the ethical principle of beneficence, which guides researchers to do no harm (Nagy, Mills, Waters, & Birks, 2010).

Strategies that can assist moving the researcher and participant to a more equal position of power within the relationship are the researcher assuming a more reflexive stance and proactively planning for the time they and the participants spend together. Box 4.1 contains questions that provoke thinking about power differentials that might exist in the research relationship.

 ## BOX 4.1 **POWER DIFFERENTIALS**

1 How is this [person] like me?
2 How [are they] not like me?
3 How are these similarities and differences being played out in our interaction?
4 How is that interaction affecting the course of the research?
5 How is it illuminating or obscuring the research problem? (Seibold, cited in Reinharz, 1992)

You may find the questions in Box 4.1 useful when working with current or potential grounded theory participants, although asking these types of questions may not be as straightforward as you think. Your responses might reveal insights of which you may not be proud. If you are feeling uncomfortable, be reassured that it is this type of honesty in your writing that leads to greater self-insight. Even though we would all like to consider ourselves open minded and accepting of the colourful tapestry of life, sometimes it is hard to adopt a non-judgemental stance and to resist the urge to assign values to either participants' responses or participants themselves (Holloway & Fulbrook, 2001). When undertaking research with an interpretive element, our history can subconsciously come back to haunt us and influence our work. Proactive planning prior to entering the field can help to mitigate the likelihood of this resulting in negative experiences for participants and self.

Once you enter the field there are several additional strategies that help move the researcher and participants to a more equal sharing of power. These are: scheduling interviews at a time and location of the participant's choice; using a relatively flexible and unstructured approach to questioning so that participants assume more power over the direction of the conversation; sharing the researcher's understanding of the key issues arising; and assuming an open stance towards the participant – sharing personal details and answering questions asked both during the interview and afterwards (Mills et al., 2006; O'Connor, 2001). The famous notion of 'no intimacy without reciprocity' (Oakley, 1981: 61) is borne out by the last point, with the researcher needing to invest their own personality in the research process in order to establish a less hierarchical relationship. Mishler (1991) also provides guidance on minimizing power imbalances between participant and researcher, urging the yielding of control over the flow and content of the interview; a focus on the benefits to participants, who gain greater insight into their own worlds through the research process; the creating of spaces for participants' voices in the interpretation of data and the eventual findings; and ensuring that researchers act as advocates for participants.

In order to tap greater depths in mutual meaning making during grounded theory interviews, the researcher needs to engage with participants, through a willingness to understand a participant's response in the context of the interview as a whole (Collins, 1998). This understanding develops through the open interchange between participant and researcher, which Mishler (1991) describes as a 'circular process through which [the] meaning [of a question] and that of its answer are created in the discourse between interviewer and respondent as they try to make continuing sense of what they are saying to each other' (p. 53).

Theoretical sensitivity

Theoretical sensitivity is a difficult concept to grasp because of its intangible nature. What is theoretical sensitivity? How do you get it? What do you do with it? What is the difference between theoretical sensitivity and the ultimate crime of forcing the data (Glaser, 1992)? There is often a tendency for scholars just to 'skate over' the concept of theoretical sensitivity when these questions are posed, as many struggle to understand or express its meaning and value in grounded theory research. As we will explain, however, theoretical sensitivity is instrumental to the development of grounded theory and not fully embracing it in your study will result in a shallow product.

Theoretical sensitivity was identified in *Discovery* as an important attribute of a sociologist who wanted to engage in grounded theory research and was contingent on 'his personal and temperamental bent … and ability to have theoretical insight into his area of research, combined with an ability to make something of his insights' (Glaser & Strauss, 1967: 46). Strauss and Corbin (1990) devote a chapter to theoretical sensitivity in their first text, recognizing its importance for theory development through the researcher's insight into what is meaningful and significant in the data. In their later work (Strauss & Corbin, 1998), they referred to the concept simply as 'sensitivity', discussing it in contrast to objectivity (Corbin & Strauss, 2008), possibly as a strategy to diffuse Glaser's (1992) criticism of their original discussion of theoretical sensitivity. In this text, our purpose is to transcend the debate, reduce the confusion and increase your comfort levels in relation to theoretical sensitivity and its essential contribution in your own research.

Defining and developing theoretical sensitivity

We define theoretical sensitivity as the ability to recognize and extract from the data elements that have relevance for your emerging theory. Theoretical sensitivity has three important characteristics:

1   It reflects the sum of your personal, professional and experiential history.

2   It can be enhanced by various techniques, tools and strategies.

3   It increases as your research progresses.

Grounded theory is one of the most commonly used approaches to research in graduate studies. These researchers are excited, passionate and committed to a minimum of three years to undertake their study. One of the downsides, though, is that novice grounded theorists do not know what they do not know and are unconscious of the importance of what they do know when they start out! In understanding theoretical sensitivity, it is important to assess what it is that you know because of your history. First and foremost, consider the characteristics of your multiple selves discussed above, and how these position you in respect of your research.

Professionally, you are probably a person in the know in your particular field, which you have now chosen to research. Undoubtedly you will have discipline-relevant theoretical knowledge from prior learning. In the process of applying for admission to a graduate programme, you will have been required to undertake a partial review of the relevant literature. The combination of a priori experiential and theoretical knowledge can take these and many other forms, but whichever way you look at it, you will have form. By identifying your baseline position before you begin, you can work at consciously developing your theoretical sensitivity during the research process. As Glaser and Strauss (1967) say, 'the researcher does not approach reality as a *tablu rasa* [blank slate]. He must have a perspective that will help him see relevant data and abstract significant categories from his scrutiny of the data' (p. 3). The danger from Glaser's (1992) perspective, as discussed in Chapter 2, is the potential for the researcher consciously or unconsciously to apply existing theoretical schemes to their own data.

Kelle (2007) provides a thoughtful analysis of theoretical sensitivity in relation to category building where he identifies the conflict between theoretical sensitivity and forcing the data as a conundrum for both teachers and students of grounded theory research methods. In Box 4.2, Vicki Drury (Drury, Francis, & Chapman, 2008a; 2008b) writes about her own experience of potentially forcing data analysis by wanting to apply her own theoretical conceptualizations in a grounded theory study of mature-aged rural nursing students' experiences of undergraduate education.

BOX 4.2 WINDOW INTO GROUNDED THEORY

Vicki Drury on theoretical sensitivity and forcing data analysis

My experience has taught me the importance of being aware of one's own conceptual assumptions prior to embarking on analysis in grounded theory. When we begin a research study, we often think we have some idea of what to expect in terms of the data. This may be because you, the researcher, empathise with the participants or it may be that you set out to discover the answer to a question and you want that answer! In my own study, I identified that mature students spoke of attributes of resilience, which resonated with me, as I had been a mature student. Of course, I had not set out to force my preconceived ideas and theory onto the data and I think that is the lesson here – you become so enmeshed in the data and in your analysis that you can lose sight of the larger picture. Your theoretical sensitivity becomes theoretical fixation. If I had identified my baseline assumptions prior to beginning the analysis process, this situation would not have occurred. The problem that arose from forcing the data was that I became trapped – I was unable to connect the other categories to the core category of resilience that I had forced. I looked at the analysis from all perspectives but still focused on the core category of resilience so no matter what I did I was unable to progress. Finally, a colleague suggested that I write a storyline, which I did. I found even writing the storyline and not imposing the forced category on to it was difficult. Reflecting on the storyline, I became aware that not only was the forced category not the core category, it in fact was not even a category! This meant that I now had to look at the data through a different lens. When you have spent a lot of time scrutinising the data and have made conclusions it can be incredibly difficult to do this. I found I was blocked and simply could not seem to move forward.

Eventually I sat down with my supervisor and a colleague in an attempt to find the core category. They made notes and asked me questions, moving through all the data I had collected. As we did this, we found that all the data was leading back to one point. When it was suggested that perhaps this could be the core category, and we began diagramming relationships, it became evident that it was indeed the core category.

The data that I had previously coded was not wasted. This data connected to the core category in a way that had not occurred when I inadvertently tried to force the data. Identification of the core category and diagramming the relationship of other categories resulted in the development of a model. Following weeks of deliberation and stagnation, all these developments occurred in a single day.

Strategies to promote theoretical sensitivity are discussed in the seminal texts published by Strauss and Corbin (1990; 1998) and remain in the latest edition led by Corbin (Corbin & Strauss, 2008), even though they are extremely contentious in the ongoing debate about what constitutes essential grounded theory methods. One technique for raising sensitivity identified by these authors is the use of the literature. As discussed in Chapter 2, there is a deal of confusion about how to use the literature during the grounded theory research process. Overall, there is general agreement that a systematic review of the literature relating to the broad area of enquiry should be avoided. How then to develop your theoretical sensitivity by using the literature? Glaser suggests that you should read 'vociferously in other areas and fields while doing ground theory in order to keep up [your] theoretical sensitivity' (Glaser, 1998: 73). Unfortunately, this statement is not terribly clear about where to draw the line between texts that might force your thinking and texts that might develop it – thus the conundrum discussed earlier. Strauss (1987) and then Strauss and Corbin (1990) are much more liberal and direct, recommending grounded theorists to raise their theoretical sensitivity by reading the literature. Through the comparison of theoretical concepts with coded data, the literature can potentially become a source of data in itself (as discussed in Chapter 5) if it earns its way into the developing grounded theory.

In addition to the use of the literature, Strauss and Corbin (1990) originally identified a number of specific mechanisms for enhancing theoretical sensitivity, which they later renamed 'analytic tools' (Corbin & Strauss, 2008; Strauss & Corbin, 1998), once again superficially removing the direct link to theoretical sensitivity. The aim of analytic tools, however, remains to increase the grounded theorist's sensitivity to potential theoretical constructs in the data, and as such are included here rather than in Chapter 6 where we discuss data analysis. Box 4.3 lists the suite of analytic tools that these authors suggest can be used to develop your theoretical sensitivity, should you choose to use them. Making a decision about including such strategies in your research design will hinge upon how you have positioned yourself philosophically and methodologically.

BOX 4.3 ANALYTICAL TOOLS TO INCREASE THEORETICAL SENSITIVITY

- The use of questioning
- Making comparisons
- Thinking about the various meanings of a word
- Using the flip-flop technique
- Drawing upon personal experience
- Waving the red flag
- Looking at language
- Looking at emotions that are expressed and the situations that aroused them

(Continued)

> *(Continued)*
>
> - Looking for words that indicate time
> - Thinking in terms of metaphors and similes
> - Looking for the negative case
> - 'So what?' and 'what if?'
> - Looking at the structure of the narrative and how it is organized in terms of time or some other variable. (Corbin & Strauss, 2008: 69)

Most of the tools listed previously are relatively self-explanatory, although we would direct you to the latest edition of *Basics of qualitative research* cited above to read about each in depth prior to thinking about including them in your research design. However, of particular relevance to our discussion in this chapter regarding positioning the researcher is: drawing upon personal experience, looking at emotions expressed and the situations that aroused them, and waving the red flag. In each of these three analytic tools, Corbin and Strauss (2008) identify the need for grounded theorists to examine their underlying assumptions about the world on an ongoing basis throughout the research process in order to develop their theoretical sensitivity to the data.

Drawing upon personal experience is a strategy that explicitly recognizes the researcher's history and utilizes it as a conceptual comparison with the data. Instead of bracketing out shared experiences, the researcher is encouraged to use these as comparative cases to stimulate thinking and in turn theorizing. This is similar to recognizing emotions expressed and the contexts that arouse them. Although Corbin and Strauss are overall referring to participants' emotions, they allude to the researcher's emotions also being evoked by certain sensitizing concepts in the data. Using emotions as a cue can lead to analytic breakthroughs regarding the meaning tied to events, which in turn can develop abstract, conceptual theorizing about the phenomena under investigation as well providing a strategy to increase the researcher's reflexivity.

Waving the red flag was one of Strauss and Corbin's (1990) original techniques for enhancing theoretical sensitivity and refers to recognizing when 'biases, assumptions or beliefs are intruding into the analysis' (Corbin & Strauss, 2008: 80). This quote has an echo of a post-positivistic positioning of the researcher as an instrument of data analysis; however, if we substitute unduly influencing for intruding, the statement becomes equally relevant to symbolic interactionist, post modernist and constructivist grounded theorists. We all need to be ready to wave the red flag during concurrent data generation or collection and analysis so that we do not miss developing greater depth and higher levels of abstraction in our grounded theories.

Some of the keywords and phrases that Strauss and Corbin (1990) identify as cues to stop, think and ask another question of either participants, the data or ourselves are: 'Always'; 'Never'; 'It couldn't possibly be that way'; 'Everyone knows that this is the way it is'; or 'There's no need for discussion' (p. 92). Absolutist statements by either participants or our self are never definitive; rather, they should touch a theoretically sensitive nerve that prompts further investigation of why this is considered so.

Regardless of your personal, professional or experiential history, or the extent to which strategies, techniques or tools to raise theoretical sensitivity prove valuable in your research, your theoretical sensitivity will increase with the correct application of essential grounded theory methods. Engaging with, or indeed immersing yourself in, your data will sensitize you to those elements that have meaning, relevance and consequence for your developing theory. Promote development of your theoretical sensitivity through embracing yourself as expert in your own research, use memoing to explicate assumptions and theoretical leanings that must be challenged and acknowledge the grounded theory process as a learning experience in respect of both yourself and your area of study. You may initially question your ability to become theoretically sensitive and must accept this as an important stepping stone to appreciating what you know and becoming conscious of that which you do not.

Conclusion

Becoming a successful grounded theorist requires a high level of self-insight and understanding. Positioning yourself as a researcher means becoming aware of your philosophical preferences and methodological alignments. As discussed previously, essential grounded theory methods remain the same; however, the way you use these methods is shaped by the position that you take. Using techniques to promote a reflexive approach to grounded theory research will assure the quality and ethical integrity of your work through identifying how you and your history are present in the research process. Theoretical sensitivity is intrinsically linked to the position you take and your degree of reflexivity. Developing your baseline theoretical sensitivity during the research process itself will result in a more integrated and abstract grounded theory.

 CRITICAL THINKING QUESTIONS

1   How important do you think it is to consider your position in respect of your research? Do you think that a researcher's position will vary depending on the nature of the study? Consider how different aspects of our multiple selves and different elements of our personal and professional history may come into play at different stages of the research process.

(Continued)

(Continued)

2   Think about the relationship between researcher and participant in the research interview. Is it feasible to consider that power imbalances can be effectively reduced or eliminated? What impact might residual power differentials have in a grounded theory study specifically?

3   Consider the concept of theoretical sensitivity. How might a lack of sensitivity to theoretical concepts in your data impact on your final study? Are you comfortable with the concept? How might you otherwise conceptualize theoretical sensitivity? Is it akin to any other cognitive, professional or methodological concept with which you are familiar?

 WORKING GROUNDED THEORY

Review the 'Working grounded theory' example presented in Appendix A. Note:

- How the researcher positions herself in her study.

- How she was to arrive at this position.

- The process and impact of becoming reflexive for this researcher.

- Evidence of reciprocity in this example.

- How this researcher describes theoretical sensitivity and the process by which she develops this skill.

5 Data generation and collection

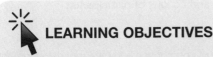

LEARNING OBJECTIVES

This chapter will help you to:

1 Discuss the significance of quality data in the production of grounded theory

2 Identify types and sources of data for use in a grounded theory study

3 Define the term 'theoretical sampling'

4 Distinguish between data generation and collection

5 Describe processes for accessing, generating and collecting data in grounded theory research

Introduction

In previous chapters we presented an overview of grounded theory, provided guidelines for planning a quality grounded theory study and discussed the significance of your position as researcher. In many approaches to research, the next stage of a research project will be the identification of hypotheses or theoretical frameworks as a structure to guide the implementation of a study. In grounded theory, 'everything begins with the data' (Wasserman, Clair, & Wilson, 2009: 358) and the data remains prominent throughout analysis and theory building. The nature of grounded theory research ensures that you will maintain this close relationship with the data throughout your study, rather than undertake data collection as an isolated task as is the case in many other types of research. In this chapter, the generation and collection of data from a diverse range of sources will be examined in the context of grounded theory research processes.

Data in grounded theory research

In grounded theory research, data can take many forms. Glaser (1998) considers that 'all is data' (p. 8), a statement that has drawn criticism for being too vague (Bryant, 2003). It does, however, support a position that embraces the use of a vast array of data sources. Charmaz (2006) asserts that the credibility of your study is determined by the relevance, substance, scope and depth of your data. Among the guidelines she proposes to ensure adequacy of data quality, Charmaz suggests gathering data that:

- Captures a range of contexts, perspectives and timeframes.

- Provides rich detail in respect of the view and actions of participants. .

- Looks beneath superficial layers of data.

- Considers the value of data for the purpose of comparison and category development.

There is enormous diversity in the potential areas of study that can be investigated using grounded theory. Similarly, exploring diversity in the use of data ensures that you do your study justice and produce a grounded theory of value. A summary of examples of the types of data that can be used in grounded theory research are presented in Box 5.1. The sources of this data and the strategies by which they can be generated or collected are discussed later in this chapter.

 BOX 5.1 TYPES OF DATA

- Transcripts of interviews and focus groups
- Fieldnotes, memos
- Journals, diaries, log books
- Questionnaires, surveys
- Governmental and organizational policy documents
- Scholarly literature, novels
- Photographic images, videos
- Artwork, artefacts, architecture
- Music

As grounded theory research often attempts to understand the world of the individual from their particular perspective, participant interviews are the most common source of data. Although frequently used, they should not be considered the standard form of data in grounded theory research. Wales, Shalin and Bass (2007), in an interesting study of the development of naming conventions for an exploratory rover mission on Mars, relied on sources of data other than interviews to produce grounded theory. Data used by these authors included fieldnotes, documentation, scholarly articles, communication exchanges, videotapes and planning printouts. In most grounded theory studies, however, participant interviews will dominate. These may or may not be supplemented by other forms of data as dictated by the individual research situation. Eyles, Walker and Brien (2009) used various methods, in addition to interviews, in a multi-phase study of homeopathic consultations. Caroline Eyles discusses the experience of this approach to data generation and collection in Box 5.2. In this example Eyles also discusses the significance of reflexivity, as examined in Chapter 4, and its influence on the process of data collection.

 BOX 5.2 WINDOW INTO GROUNDED THEORY

Carolyn Eyles on the use of data from multiple sources

As a practitioner of homeopathy, researching homeopathic practitioners' experiences of the consultation, it was important to be constantly aware of my preconceptions and assumptions. This challenge was dealt with by taking a constructivist grounded theory approach which emphasised reflexivity. This reflexivity underpinned and was part of the multi-method approach which I took in this study.

Initially data was collected through face to face in depth interviews. My first and most prominent issue was how to gather and interpret the data without imposing my views as a practitioner. Reflexivity provided a means to reconcile my dilemma as it encouraged tacit understandings to be exposed and the data to be examined more objectively. For example, in one of the first interviews the motivation of one of my participants was questioned by my supervisor, my initial response was to rush to the participant's defence. However a reflexive approach enabled me to also question their motivations and seek clarification in subsequent interviews and discussions with colleagues.

Through development of a core category and saturation of interview data a tentative theoretical model of a UK classical homeopathic consultation emerged. The interview data, though, could not confirm or refute whether the participants behaved as they reported. Therefore in order to capture a truthful representation of the consultation it was necessary to triangulate retrospective interview data with observational data to explore the emerging theoretical model and its categories. As a homeopath I was very apprehensive at the prospect of approaching homeopaths in order to observe their consultations. The consultation is a one to one interaction and the presence of a third party can affect that interaction. The homeopath may change from their normal behaviour and the patient may feel uncomfortable in revealing their symptoms. I was not surprised therefore when

(Continued)

(Continued)

there were only a few willing participants to be observed. This part of data collection also consisted of gathering practitioners' reflective diaries. The purpose of this was to assemble reflections on difficult or challenging consultations experienced during clinical practice as a method of negative case analysis. An additional advantage of the diaries was that they allowed insight into potentially sensitive areas of the consultation relating to behaviour or thoughts that were inaccessible to participant observation and interviews.

In addition I recorded two of my own consultations and also completed a reflective diary. This type of auto-ethnographic data is consistent with a constructivist grounded theory approach and added data relating to my experiential experience as a practitioner. However, the challenge was to be transparent about the boundary between data collected from my consultations and diary and those of my participants, as the data differed as it included my awareness about experiences increasing the subjectivity of the presentation of the data.

The use of multiple data sources in this study was consistent with the principles of grounded theory. The use of reflexivity also lent a transparency to the research process, which together contributed to the robustness of the findings.

The examples of data contained in Box 5.1 have traditionally been discretely distinguished as either qualitative or quantitative, by both grounded theorists and other researchers. In their seminal work, Glaser and Strauss (1967) presented grounded theory as an approach to research that embraced both qualitative and quantitative data sources. In the decades since the publication of this text, the contribution that grounded theory has made to the interpretive sciences has seen it being used most often with data of a purely qualitative nature. Grounded theory can be produced entirely from either qualitative or quantitative data (the latter being reaffirmed by Glaser, 2008). As with any form of research, however, aligning grounded theory methods to only one type of data limits the potential of a study to achieve its aims. Briley, Roberts-Gray and Simpson (1994) demonstrated the value of using both qualitative and quantitative data for generating their grounded theory of menu planning in schools. This study employed a variety of data generation and collection strategies including interviews, weighing and measuring food, observation of food service activities and assessment of local supermarkets and restaurants.

We suggest that you do not get bogged down in debating the relative merits of one type of data over another. Many of the types of data listed in Box 5.1 may be deemed qualitative or quantitative depending on what you do with them (Janasik, Honkela, & Bruun, 2009). Recall from the previous chapter that it is your relationship with the data, how you collect, generate and manage it, that will determine its value to your final theory. As your analysis progresses, your theoretical sensitivity will be heightened, and you will find yourself directed to sources of data that are most relevant to your developing theory through the use of theoretical sampling techniques.

 Activity 5.1

Data in grounded theory research

Review the types of data contained in Box 5.1. Think about your own disciplinary area. What forms of data are most likely to be of value for researching issues that arise in your professional area? Which are least likely to be of value? Can you identify any other potential types of data that you can add to this list?

Theoretical sampling

In previous chapters we have referred to the emergent nature of the grounded theory research process. Theoretical sampling is unique to grounded theory research and is the essential method responsible for making the process emergent. Glaser and Strauss (1967) originally defined theoretical sampling as:

> the process of data collection for generating theory whereby the analyst jointly collects, codes, and analyzes his data and decides what data to collect next and where to find them, in order to develop his theory as it emerges. (p. 45)

This definition remains quite accurate for the contemporary grounded theorist, in spite of the fact that, as Kathy Charmaz suggests, theoretical sampling is interpreted differently by different researchers (personal communication, 23 January 2006). We define theoretical sampling as the process of identifying and pursuing clues that arise during analysis in a grounded theory study. Strategies for raising theoretical sensitivity described in Chapter 4 will make you more attuned to these clues and their significance for your developing theory.

Theoretical sampling is different from sampling strategies used in other types of research. In other research designs, the researcher usually makes decisions in relation to who, what, where, when and how to sample during the planning phase. This is particularly the case when the intention is to test theory or describe phenomena, and sampling is directed at securing a representative data profile. In grounded theory research, the aim is to build theory through the construction of categories directly from the data. Through 'theory-directed' sampling, you are able to examine concepts from various angles and question their meaning for your developing theory (Strauss, 1987: 276). What is obvious? What is notably absent? Is something more obscure being suggested? Questions such as these are raised through the process of constant comparative analysis, as discussed in the following

chapter, and answered by theoretical sampling. Because of these unique characteristics of theoretical sampling, it is not possible to know at the outset of your study:

- The nature or type of data that will be needed to develop your theory.
- How many participants/data sources you will use.
- When, where or how you will generate or collect data.

How then, in practice, do you employ theoretical sampling in your own research?
Initially your sampling will be purposeful. You will identify a source of data that is
relevant to your area of study. You may, for example, conduct an interview with a
participant who is experiencing the phenomenon that is the focus of your research.
Your engagement with the data generated from that interview in the process of
analysis will make you aware of issues that require expansion, clarification or
confirmation. Theoretical sampling provides direction for your next stage of data
collection in a process of concurrent analysis that continues cyclically until categories are fully developed or 'saturated' (a concept that is further discussed in later
chapters).

Theoretical sampling is not just about *what* you do next, it is also about *how* you
do it. Imagine that you are undertaking a study on the adaptation of senior citizens
to technological change. Your initial interview may provide data from an elderly
gentleman who happens to mention that he has a close relationship with his
family, including teenage grandchildren. Your analysis may raise questions about
how senior citizens may cope when they do not have such contact with people who
are younger and therefore likely to be more computer literate. Theoretical
sampling may direct you specifically to seek out older individuals who are relatively
isolated. You would also modify your interview technique to address the issue of
family support. Jacobson, Oliver and Koch (2009) demonstrate the use of theoretical sampling in this way in their study of the phenomenon of dignity and its
relationship to social determinates of health. These researchers purposefully
recruited initial participants from three identified groups through the use of flyers,
word of mouth and invitation. Subsequently, decisions in regard to recruitment of
participants and the nature of interview questions were made in response to
analytical progress.

Charmaz (2006) asserts that theoretical sampling only becomes of value once your
categories have been developed as it enables you to confirm, clarify and expand these
categories. In contrast, we believe that theoretical sampling should be employed from
your first interview or data collection event, as concepts will begin to take shape
even from these earliest stages of analysis. You may then seek broader and more
diverse sources and types of data or alternatively attempt to tease out a specific issue.
You might find the need to follow specific leads that may or may not develop.
However you proceed, you will do so in response to your use of theoretical sampling.

Later in your analysis, theoretical sampling will address gaps identified within
and between your categories up until the presentation of your final theory

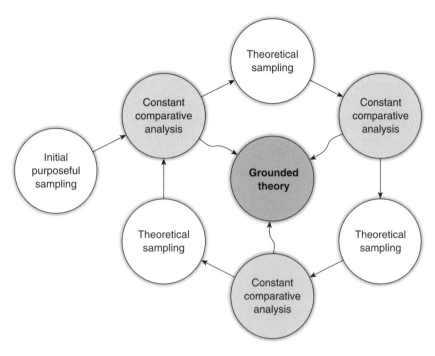

Figure 5.1 Theoretical sampling

(Corbin & Strauss, 2008). Devers and Robinson (2002), in an interesting investigation of after-death communication, described the use of theoretical sampling in the later stages of this study to explore a concept that became evident during analysis. When one participant described their after-death communication experience as 'supernatural' rather than 'spiritual', the data collection became focused on identifying other individuals' explanations for the phenomenon. Theoretical sampling processes are illustrated in Figure 5.1.

Application of theoretical sampling in its purest form would see you undertake a single data generation or collection event, followed by analysis of that data. In reality, this may not always be possible. Geographical constraints, availability of participants and other access issues may limit your ability to conduct analysis intermittently with every episode of data generation or collection. Consider, for example, the researcher who wishes to conduct a study with engineers working on an oil rig, including individual interviews and fieldwork observation. The logistics associated with transport to, and accommodation within, the study setting may reduce opportunities for data analysis between interviews. In unique situations such as this, principles of theoretical sampling can still be applied. While full transcription of interview recordings may be impractical in the study setting, preliminary analysis of interview recordings and fieldwork notes is not only possible, but in fact likely to be more effective, when undertaken within a short timeframe. Allow enough time between each data generation or collection event to consider the meaning of that data. How does it relate to your developing analysis? Does it confirm, contradict, clarify or expand your evolving theory? What direction does it now suggest?

At times, in spite of careful planning and a vigilant adherence to the principles of grounded theory research, circumstances beyond your control may intervene. Neill (2007), for example, found it difficult to access entire families when attempting to undertake whole-family research into the management of acute childhood illness. Practical and ethical issues limited the ability of this author to utilize theoretical sampling in her study. Lack of access to data sources can often impede attempts to employ theoretical sampling, although this is not always the case. Draucker, Martsolf, Ross and Rusk (2007) were unexpectedly inundated with calls from prospective participants in their study of responses to sexual violence. These researchers, in recognizing how difficult it can be for victims of sexual violence to respond to recruitment efforts, had to compromise their planned theoretical sampling approach in order to respond in a timely manner to those who had made contact.

While Corbin and Strauss (2008) suggest that it is sometimes necessary to accept what is available in terms of data, you should make every effort to apply the principles of theoretical sampling and follow the leads generated during analysis. When this is not possible, acknowledge in your published work the limitations that you faced while undertaking your research and the impact this has on your final theory. Think broadly about alternative sources and types of data that might answer questions raised during analysis. In the later stages of theory development, consider how advanced coding, as discussed in Chapter 7, may assist in addressing gaps in your analysis.

 Activity 5.2

Practical issues in theoretical sampling

Think about a grounded theory study that you may be about to embark upon, or a research topic of interest to you that could be investigated using grounded theory.

- How would you access your initial sources of data?
- What problems do you anticipate?
- How might you overcome issues that arise as you attempt to employ theoretical sampling in your study?

In your reading of published work claiming to be grounded theory, you will often struggle to find evidence of theoretical sampling in a given study. Theoretical sampling is one of the most overlooked essential methods. Often a researcher may not appreciate the significance of theoretical sampling in grounded theory research, or perhaps they are entrenched in sampling techniques drawn from another paradigm. In some instances, it is for purely practical reasons that a researcher may choose not to employ theoretical sampling. The security of knowing how you will be undertaking data collection, when and with whom, and what resources will therefore be required, may be reassuring in the short term. Generating and collecting data upfront, then analysing it separately, however, contradicts grounded theory principles. Your analysis and consequently your grounded theory will suffer in the long term.

Be confident in your ability to employ theoretical sampling in your study. Familiarize yourself with the essential grounded theory methods and plan your study meticulously using the guidelines contained in Chapter 2. Grounded theory is a self-correcting approach to research. Any errors in your data collection and analytical processes will eventually be extinguished if you employ the essential grounded theory methods correctly and consistently.

Data generation or data collection?

In the previous chapter we discussed the position of the researcher in relation to their grounded theory study. The position of the researcher impacts upon the entire research process from conceptualization to presentation of the final theory. It is most evident, however, in the relationship that the researcher has with the data. In reading published research you will probably usually see reference made to the *collection* of data. In grounded theory, we refer to both data generation and collection to acknowledge the different roles that the researcher has in relation to the process of data acquisition. Data generation involves the researcher directly engaging with the data source (for example, a participant) to produce materials for analysis. Conversely, the researcher has limited influence on the data source in the process of data collection. This distinction is arguably arbitrary but is convenient for the purpose of discussing the acquisition of data in grounded theory and the role of the researcher in this process (as illustrated in Figure 5.2).

In the remaining sections of this chapter, we will discuss strategies and techniques for data generation and collection. Techniques used in gathering data in grounded theory are similar to those used in other forms of research. There are, however, some important factors that must be considered when generating and collecting data with the intent of producing theory. In the following discussion we will emphasize the grounded theory difference in relation to the gathering of data. We assume that readers of this text will have a beginning level of pre-existing knowledge about research methods. Should you wish to increase your basic knowledge in support of the following discussion we would refer you to a general research text (for example, Nagy et al., 2010).

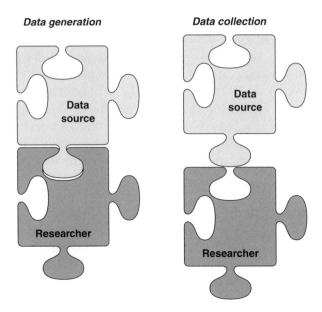

Data generation   *Data collection*

Figure 5.2   Data generation versus data collection

Strategies for generating data

When generating data in grounded theory, the researcher is actively involved in the production of material that will be analysed using the methods described in the following chapter. The researcher may work directly with participants for this purpose by conducting interviews or facilitating focus groups, or may personally generate data in the form of fieldnotes and memos. The dynamic nature of theoretical sampling in grounded theory is best supported by the active nature of these strategies. You will therefore see one or more method of data generation used in most grounded theory studies.

Interviews

The value of interviewing in grounded theory research is evidenced by the extensive number of studies that rely on it as the principal mechanism for the generation of data. Techniques of interviewing in grounded theory research are similar to those used in other interpretive research studies. You should, however, pay particular attention to your approach to interviewing when your intention is to generate theory. You may have extensive experience in interviewing for other reasons. Health care professionals interview patients for assessment and counselling purposes; market researchers interview consumers; and senior staff in a diverse range of industries interview people for prospective employment and promotion. While the skills you may have developed in interviewing for such purposes will serve you well in establishing rapport and communicating effectively with your participants, do not assume that they will be effective in achieving the aims of interviewing in grounded theory research.

As with many other aspects of grounded theory research, the emergent nature of the process will require you to be flexible in your use of interviews as a data generation strategy. What you ask a participant, and how you ask it, will vary both between and within interviews. Remaining attuned to what each participant is saying, being theoretically sensitive to what this means for your developing theory and directing or following the interview accordingly can be very demanding. Prepare for your interviews by pilot testing your technique with a trusted colleague or supervisor. Seek constructive feedback and allow your skills in interviewing for the purpose of your research to develop. Most importantly, once you commence interviewing for data generation you will no doubt find that things go wrong from time to time. Learn from your mistakes through techniques such as reflecting on the experience and memoing. Where possible, returning to earlier participants for a second or subsequent interview enables you to follow up on leads that arise as the research progresses (Charmaz, 2001). Alternatively, make sure that you secure consent from your participants to follow up with them (for example, via telephone or email) any seemingly innocuous comments made in the interview that may later prove significant.

In most instances interviews are conducted in person; however, logistical issues may necessitate conducting interviews by telephone or via video conferencing, as will be discussed later in this chapter. Ruppar and Russell (2009), in conducting a study of medication compliance in kidney transplant patients, employed telephone interviews exclusively with their geographically diverse participants. Note that if you are unable to interview in person, there are some pitfalls of which you should be aware. Subtle non-verbal cues can be missed or misinterpreted when interviews are conducted at a distance (Nagy et al., 2010). Given that in grounded theory interviews, we often rely on the direction provided by the participant, the absence of these cues could be significant and greater attention to verbal communication may therefore be required.

Interviews may be highly structured or completely unstructured. The grounded theory interview is dependent upon the ability of the researcher to travel a path through the interview with the participant. The greater the level of structure imposed, the less able the interviewer will be to take the optimal route. Less structure is better from the perspective of following where the conversation takes you. This is not to suggest that the interviewer should be passive in the interview process; the interviewer acts as coordinator of the conversation with an aim of generating fodder for the developing theory (Corbin & Strauss, 2008; Gubrium & Holstein, 2001). You can use an interview guide or aide-memoire, but expect that it will evolve as your study progresses. Bahora et al. (2009) demonstrated this in their study of binge drinking in the United Kingdom. You will find, as these researchers did, that it is necessary to modify the interview guide as concepts develop during analysis.

Finally, you must give some consideration to how you will make a record of your interview. Commonly, interviews conducted for research are audio recorded and transcribed for purposes of analysis. Anyone who has engaged in this process will tell you that it is extremely time intensive. Interview transcriptions do, however, when combined with your fieldnotes, provide a rich data set. Glaser is strongly opposed to the taping of interviews in grounded theory research (having devoted an entire chapter to its limitations in his 1998 text) arguing that taping the interview is inefficient, detracts from the focus of early category delimitation, and generates mounds of superficial data.

Certainly it is not necessary always to tape interviews. In the study of after-death communication by Devers and Robinson (2002) referred to above, notes were taken in some instances where the setting did not support taping of interviews. We recommend the taping of interviews where possible in grounded theory research, particularly for the novice researcher. Whether you choose to transcribe for the purpose of coding, or retain it only as a back up for later reference, having an audio recording provides additional security for your valuable data. You also have access to verbatim quotations that can be used to defend your coding and illustrate your final theory. You may find that your reliance on audio recording of interviews will diminish as your study progresses, countering Glaser's (1998) contention that your skill development will be hindered by taping.

An alternative to audio recording is video recording. We caution against the indiscriminate use of video recording in grounded theory as the advantages do not necessarily provide justification for the adoption of additional technology that may prove intrusive and impact on your performance and the responses of your participants. In some instances, however, it may be appropriate to video-record your interviews. Hohl (2009) undertook an interesting study examining participants' experiences of an interactive facility that enabled visitors to listen to international radio stations while walking across a dynamic world map. Interviews were video recorded in the setting itself as participants experienced the software within the unique, specialized environment.

Focus groups

Focus groups are an extension of the standard interview in which two or more participants engage in a specified area of discussion led by the researcher. Focus groups have some specific advantages that make them useful in grounded theory research. The assembly of people with like interests is effective in engendering conversation as each participant responds to and feeds off the others. Different perspectives and a broad range of experiences are highlighted through the use of focus groups (Lambert & Loiselle, 2008) making them valuable for category development in grounded theory, as discussed in the following chapter.

Focus groups may be the only means of data generation in a study, such as was the case in an unusual study by Nordvik and Broman (2009). These authors employed three focus groups to generate responses to computer-generated images of wood. Alternatively, focus groups may follow individual interviews as was the case in Melendez's (2008) study of black football players attending a predominantly white college. Focus groups may also be used to generate initial concepts for later follow-up in individual interviews. This approach was used by Hill, Hanton, Fleming and Matthews (2009) to explain why poor performance in sport may occur under stress-ful conditions. You may choose to use the same participants in focus group and individual interviews, as these authors did, or you may choose to use different participants or a mixture of each, depending on your purpose and the accessibility of participants.

When using focus groups, the general principles of conducting interviews apply. You should be aware, however, of some specific issues that can impact on the effec-tiveness of focus group processes. While some individuals may feel more comfort-able in a group, rather than one-on-one situation, this is not always the case and participants who are a little more reserved may withhold valuable data that could be significant for your theoretical development. In most instances, however, the inter-action between participants produces valuable data. This interaction is somewhat dependent on the establishment of rapport between the researcher and the partici-pant group, which limits the potential value of telephone or video focus group interviewing.

Once again, the less structure imposed on the process of focus group interview-ing, the better. Your skills in group facilitation will be called upon, however, and you may find that it is difficult to maintain the focus of the discussion, particularly in larger groups. Your ability to follow theoretical leads that arise may be reduced. The greater level of activity that is natural with the use of focus groups can also make recording the interview problematic, whether through the use of notes, audio or video means. Novice grounded theorists are therefore advised to use focus groups with caution, and as directed by theoretical sampling in their particular study. Should you choose to include focus groups as a means of data generation, awareness of these potential problems in advance can help you plan accordingly to minimize the impact of these issues.

Fieldnotes and memos

Undertaking fieldwork is an important component of grounded theory studies, given the attraction that this approach to research has to those investigating phenomena with a sociological and human element. Most grounded theorists will undertake work in the field, even if it is only to interview participants in their own environment. Fieldwork can include a broad range of data generation activities that include observation and informal conversations, in addition to formal interviews. Kotabe, Parente and Murray (2007) used grounded theory methods as part of a multiple case study design exploring modular automobile production in Brazil. This research employed fieldwork in the form of site observations, in addition to interviews and other materials, in order to build theory.

The researcher on entering the field will not be aware of when, where or how opportunities for gathering data will occur. It is necessary therefore to undertake concurrent data analysis to facilitate theoretical sampling within the field. What do your observations reveal? Are there subtle differences in activities undertaken by the same individuals at different times? What can policy manuals or organizational documents reveal about roles and responsibilities? Are these reflected in the day-to-day running of the organization?

Observations made in the field are recorded in the form of fieldnotes. Notations made in the field are important contemporaneous records of events, activities and your responses to them. Fieldnotes are important in grounded theory studies, regardless of whether you use a single means of gathering data or employ several. Fieldnotes should be made after you conduct interviews to retain details of the physical environment, to record your immediate responses to the interaction and to capture participant non-verbal behaviour that will not be revealed through transcription. You will write fieldnotes on observations made in the field and informal conversations that you have with those in the research setting. Fieldnotes build on earlier fieldnotes as your exposure in the research setting continues. A word of caution: fieldwork can be unpredictable and wonderful opportunities for the gathering of data can occur serendipitously; be sure to secure approval from your institutional review board or ethics committee to ensure that all data that you gather can legitimately be used in your developing theory.

In Box 5.3, Yvonne Eaves discusses the use of fieldnotes in her own grounded theory research. Note how, for Eaves, this writing has an emotional component, reflective of the nature of her study.

 BOX 5.3 WINDOW INTO GROUNDED THEORY

Yvonne Eaves on the use of fieldnotes

My experience has taught me to record fieldnotes as soon as possible after an interview in order to increase their accuracy. I am aware of four factors that affect the accuracy of my fieldnotes.

First, waiting more than 24 hours before writing fieldnotes imposes on my recall and memory of what happened during the interview. When conducting research of an emotive nature, as was the case in my own research, this may prove difficult, as illustrated in the following excerpt from a fieldnote:

> I was supposed to sit down and write fieldnotes right away, most times I could not. It was as if once I walked back into my own apartment, my own world, I had escaped the harsh realities I had experienced a few hours earlier, and to sit down and write fieldnotes about the experience would only bring it all back to the forefront of my mind.

Second, because I travel long distances to rural areas I often conduct two to three interview or observation sessions in one day. I learned that if I conduct more than this number, I tend to get the details of the sessions mixed up because my mind becomes overloaded with information.

> Third, I have attempted to audio-record my fieldnotes in the car while en route to another interview or while driving home after a day of data generation and collection. While this helps to immediately document fieldnotes, I have learned that I am not as open and honest about my reflections with this mode. I unintentionally include a reflective component in my fieldnotes as it helps me to cope with the stress of fieldwork and allows me to 'see' the world from the perspective of my research participants. I find this easier to achieve through the use of pen and paper.
>
> Finally, as a novice qualitative researcher I learned that I have a subconscious safety valve in my mind that turns itself on when I hear traumatic information that I cannot digest in real time. I usually realize this after the fact, such as when I am checking the accuracy of a transcript against the interview recording. When this occurs, I go back and add a 'late entry' to previously documented fieldnotes.

In Chapter 3, we discussed the importance of memos to the grounded theory process. While serving a number of purposes, your memos will prove particularly significant in advancing your analysis, as discussed in the following chapters. Memos contain insights into your data and your analysis of that data. As the level of your analysis is raised, your memos will build on the content of earlier memos. Your earlier insights, when raised to a higher conceptual level in this way, are essentially data in themselves. At this point we restate the advice from Chapter 3 that your memos should clearly distinguish what is raw data and what are your analytical abstractions (Glaser, 1978). For this reason, it is also prudent to keep your fieldnotes and memos separate. While you can theorize within your fieldnotes, it is not recommended as confusion may arise where a document may contain data at different stages of theoretical abstraction (Corbin & Strauss, 2008; Glaser, 1978; Montgomery & Bailey, 2007).

Techniques for collecting data

In addition to generating data through interviews, focus groups, fieldnotes and memoing, the grounded theorist can collect data from other sources. The literature and other documents that are already in existence may be drawn upon, or materials can be obtained from participants. The following discussion will focus on the unique role of the literature as data in grounded theory research, documents as data, elicited materials, and non-traditional data sources. These types of data are best used in combination with data generated through the means discussed above. Theoretical sampling in grounded theory is an active process; therefore the use of data from static sources is of limited value in isolation as the researcher has minimal, if any, opportunity to follow leads that arise in the collection of data.

Literature as data

In Chapter 2 we discussed the use of the literature in the initial stages of a grounded theory study. Here we are referring to what Corbin and Strauss (2008) classify as technical literature, that being published research reports and scholarly discourse of a theoretical or philosophical nature. In many other forms of research, scholarly literature is used to provide a theoretical framework for the ensuing analysis. As a source of data in grounded theory research, where the intent is to generate theory, scholarly literature is used in a different way. Published literature and existing theory are not revered in grounded theory research; they are data and should be treated the same as data from any other source that has relevance to your developing theory (Glaser, 2008). You will go into the literature when your theoretical sampling directs you to do so, and your subsequent analysis of that literature will direct you to other sources of data necessary to further your analysis. Your use of the literature may therefore increase as your study progresses (Dick, 2005). In Box 5.4, Stella Walsh provides an example of how the literature became an important source of data as her study progressed. Note how her movement between participant interviews and the literature was directed by the principles of theoretical sampling.

 BOX 5.4 WINDOW INTO GROUNDED THEORY

Stella Walsh on the literature as data

I feel it is important at the outset to clarify I am a fan of grounded theory (GT) approaches and consider that without the use of GT the project I undertook could never have developed and the richness of the data would not have been uncovered. GT allowed flexibility, which I recognised and appreciated throughout the research process.

I was researching older working-class women and interviewing them in their own homes to explore the factors that influence their current food choices and shopping patterns. These older women are a marginalised group within the community and also in research. In the UK there are large quantities of annually recorded quantitative data on food choices but there is less qualitative data and therefore a lack of understanding of the everyday experience in relation to food choices and consumption patterns.

The GT approach allowed flexibility and development of themes rather than the testing of a pre-determined hypothesis. GT proved to be a flexible research tool as it allowed the development of the combination of differing but complementary perspectives within the study. I combined feminist perspectives and historical studies to yield detailed complex data of the everyday and the 'ordinary' in domestic situations uncovering women's voices and perspectives. At the outset feminist perspectives of interviewing were investigated to clarify the importance of considering the influence of personal, social identity in interview situations. This is an area not highlighted in traditional GT literature, but was of significance and importance to the study.

A further strength of GT was that it allowed for unexpected themes to be developed and captured. There has been controversy over the role of literature in GT. However, if the stance taken by Charmaz is considered, that of an 'interrupted literature review', it makes sense. Two examples may help to explain, namely the need to understand oral history methodologies and the role of gossip, which both required me to delve into the literature during the study.

In the initial interview, the women immediately reflected on their past. These past recollections became a key theme and required an understanding of the historical and oral history methodologies, which I did not have. It had never been the intention to collect oral histories but it became necessary due to the manner in which the women described their lives, including details of the past.

The interviews also captured the continued importance of gossip to older women. I was surprised that at age eighty years women would be influenced by gossip, but they were. A return to the literature was required when this theme arose. Other methodologies would not have provided the flexibility to use the literature in this way and allow absorption and understanding of the data in this manner. GT therefore enhanced the study and led to a better understanding of the current context of domestic food choices for older working-class women.

The extent to which you rely on the literature as a source of data will vary depending on the nature of your study. Lee (2009), in a study of Korean–American girls' understanding of romantic love, used the literature to clarify themes arising from interview data as part of her use of constant comparative analysis. A study by Olson, Daggs, Ellevold and Rogers (2007) into the processes of communication used by paedophiles relied entirely on the literature as data. Reliance on the literature as the sole source of data can be considered appropriate given the sensitive nature of this study. The judicious use of grounded theory methods by these researchers ensured the generation of a theory that explains predators' luring communication strategies.

 Activity 5.3

The literature as data in grounded theory

Obtain a selection of articles that report research described as grounded theory. You may wish to return to those used in the activities in Chapter 2. How many of these articles discuss the use of the literature as data? How

(Continued)

(Continued)

is this use described? Is there evidence that the literature has been theoretically sampled or used gratuitously? Compare the use of the literature in grounded theory with its use in other approaches to research with which you are familiar. What differences are most evident? How do these reflect the philosophical underpinnings of the varying methodologies?

Documents

Various documents in the form of published and unpublished materials can be used as sources of data in grounded theory research. These may include:

- Newspapers and magazines

- Government reports and policy documents

- Organizational policy and procedure manuals

- Personal diaries, journals, log books and letters

- Biographies, non-fiction books and novels.

The means by which you locate these materials will vary depending on the type of document you are seeking. The establishment of online databases and records of library holdings over recent decades has simplified the process of locating documents that may otherwise prove difficult to acquire. In some instances, specialized libraries may need to be accessed in order to locate the required data. Meadus (2007) provides an example of this in producing a grounded theory that explained the process by which adolescents cope with a mood disorder. Data for this study included medical records of some of the participants, which were analysed in conjunction with unstructured interviews and fieldnotes.

   Depending on the aims and focus of your study, documents can prove extremely valuable in your research. As with any other source of data, you will use documents such as those listed above only when directed to do so by your progressive analysis. You may be led to less accessible sources of data, such as historical documents and diaries held in private collections. While these may prove more difficult to acquire, they may have great significance to your research. Be aware of their potential, and plan accordingly to seek them out as guided by your analysis.

Elicited material

Charmaz (2006) defines elicited texts as those produced by participants at the request of the researcher. These may include common data collection mechanisms such as questionnaires and surveys, along with less common approaches such as diaries, logs and personal histories. She distinguishes these from extant texts that already exist, such as documents and the literature as discussed above. Although the researcher initiates data production when eliciting material, the process involves minimal researcher interaction with the participant and the resultant data as it is being produced. The researcher poses questions in a questionnaire, or provides instructions for the completion of a diary or log, yet does not otherwise affect the construction of the data (Charmaz, 2006). Lösch (2006), for example, employed an anonymous questionnaire as the mechanism for the collection of data in her study of behaviour and relationships in e-reverse auctions. Although the sole reliance on this elicited text may bring into question the quality of her resultant theory, an additional aim of this researcher was to demonstrate the use of quantitative methods in the generation of theory in the area of information systems.

Used in conjunction with data generated through other means, texts elicited from participants can add value to a grounded theory study. Often even an extensive in-depth interview does not allow time for consideration of all the issues of relevance and concern to the participant. The ability to reflect on these matters before, during and after a formal interview may render further data. In the study by Lee (2009) referred to above, participant children made notes and drawings both during and outside of interviews that served as supplemental data to aid the process of analysis.

Non-traditional data sources

Less common sources of data suitable for use in grounded theory include visual media (such as film and photographs), artwork, music and artefacts (including any and all articles to which an individual or group may assign meaning). These data sources are traditionally associated with methodologies such as ethnography and may be derived directly from the research field or accessed elsewhere. The ability to create, store and disseminate data sources such as these in digital form has seen them become more accessible for use in all forms of research (Knoblauch, Baer, Laurier, Petschke, & Schnettler, 2008). You may find that your research directs you to sources such as these, depending on the specific aims of your study. While there are data management software programs that will enable you to import non-traditional types of data, you should be aware that these will eventually need to be translated into textual form to facilitate analysis. The stage at which this occurs will depend on the nature of data you collect and its place within your study.

Secondary data sources in grounded theory research

The amount of data generated and collected for the purpose of research on a global scale is colossal. Often, only a fraction of this data is used for the purpose for which it was collected. Increasingly, researchers are choosing to work with data that has been collected in the past for another purpose, either by themselves or (most often) other researchers. The use of secondary data sources in grounded theory was originally proposed by Glaser and Strauss (1967) in relation to the use of quantitative data, a position that has been maintained by Glaser (2008). The collection of data for secondary analysis need not be limited to quantitative material, however, since data generated for an earlier qualitative study can also be subject to secondary analysis. There are numerous advantages to using data that has been accumulated for prior research. These include savings in respect of time, money and other resources, and the ability to focus more on the important stages of analysis (Glaser, 2008; Goulding, 2002).

Boslaugh (2007) makes the distinction between primary and secondary data on the basis of who collects the data versus who analyses it. She proposes that data is *primary* when it is analysed by the person who collected it, while data is deemed *secondary* when it is analysed by someone else. Grounded theory processes are quite unique and are implemented with the specific aim of generating theory. We therefore define secondary data in grounded theory as *any* data collected in the past for purposes not originally related to the current study. Defining secondary data in this way highlights a significant disadvantage for its use in grounded theory. Consider the discussion in the previous chapter regarding the position of the researcher in relation to the data. Working with data collected by others removes you from the generation and collection processes. The philosophical perspective and aims of the original researcher will have influenced the nature of data they have gathered and how they approached processes of data generation and collection. Your own philosophical position and its relationship to your study will no doubt be different, a situation that will impact on how you interpret the available data. Even in cases where you choose to use data that you have personally gathered for an earlier study, your purpose and perspective at that time will likely have been different, and will therefore have implications for your use of that data in your current study.

The greatest obstacle that you will face when using data from secondary sources is the inherent limitations this has for theoretical sampling. While it is not impossible for you to sample theoretically within data that has already been collected, as you can, to some extent, work with concepts as they become evident in the data (Corbin & Strauss, 2008), the flexibility necessary for true theoretical sampling will be absent. During the analysis process, questions in relation to your current research purpose will be raised, to which you may have difficulty finding answers. Leads will be generated and attempts to pursue these may be stymied by the restrictions of the available secondary data set. Gaps may subsequently exist in the theoretical constructions that defy your attempts to generate cohesive theory.

Our purpose in pointing out these problems is not to put you off using data from secondary sources; rather, we are alerting you to the potential pitfalls in what can otherwise be a valuable exercise. Using data that has already been gathered can be of value in your grounded theory study, for all the reasons we have already presented. Most importantly, you will be ensuring that the work of earlier researchers, and perhaps yourself, is capitalized upon, as data that would otherwise lay dormant can be used to the advantage of your research (Glaser, 2008). Attention to the application of essential grounded theory methods in your treatment of secondary data will minimize the potential disadvantages. Ensure that the data has relevance for your study before commencing. Remember that your primary purpose is to generate theory. Work with and beyond the data, where possible, to achieve this. If necessary, return to the field to gather absent data, or be prepared to accept any resultant gaps in your theory (Corbin & Strauss, 2008).

Does secondary data analysis have relevance for your grounded theory study? Perhaps you have stumbled across a data set that you would like to subject to grounded theory analysis, or maybe theoretical sampling of your original data has led you to existing data sets of which you were unaware. Perhaps you are working with limited resources and the cost and time advantages of secondary data analysis are attractive to you. If this is the case, where do you find the data to use in this way? Boslaugh (2007) suggests that secondary data sets can be located through activities such as searching online databases and databanks relevant to your discipline, reviewing websites that publish statistical data (for example, government census and surveys) and making contact with other researchers. Regardless of the means by which you obtain access to secondary data, be sure to secure permission from the original researcher, and any relevant institutional bodies, to use this data in your study.

Information and communication technology in data generation and collection

Information and communication technology offers abundant opportunities for accessing individuals and resources that will make a vital contribution to your developing theory. It is quite likely that you will use information and communication technology at one or more stages of your grounded theory study. At the very least you will probably rely on the internet to search and obtain documents and literature in support of your study. Communication with participants and with colleagues and supervisors will be established and maintained through electronic means. As discussed in Chapter 3, the internet can be a source of resources and practical support as you undertake your research.

Information and communication technologies can be used specifically for the purpose of data collection. The online environment can be used to access participants, as was done by Christianson and Everall (2009), who recruited counsellors to participate in their study of teenage suicide through list servers and websites. If you are using questionnaires, surveys or diaries, you may choose to make these accessible to participants online, as was done in the study by Lösch (2006), referred to above. This is particularly appropriate if you know your participants to be computer literate and/or more comfortable with this medium. Note that collection of data through asynchronous, static mechanisms such as these have the same disadvantages as those that are paper based, in that the ability to follow up on comments made by participants is limited. Synchronous communication technologies such as video conferencing or Voice Over Internet Protocol (VoIP) (for example, Skype) provide opportunities to conduct interviews with participants whose geographic location may make them otherwise inaccessible. The greatest advantage offered by information and communication technologies, from the humble telephone, through email to synchronous video conferencing, is capitalized upon when the researcher is able to maintain contact with participants for the purpose of clarification, expansion or elucidation.

The internet is now an established part of life in most societies, particularly among younger generations. There are a vast number of social networking sites, web logs (blogs) and discussion boards that address various topics and that may be of value for use in a grounded theory study. While the contents of these sites should be treated in the same way as any other textual data used in your research, you should be aware that specific ethical issues may be raised, particularly as the contents are often of a sensitive nature and the contributors may choose to be anonymous. Williams and Reid (2007), for example, drew data from pro-anorexic websites in order to explore the phenomenon of anorexia nervosa, having sought only default consent from the website administrators. While these researchers did not include any potentially identifying information in the reporting of results, they relied on the premise that those who posted material on the site were aware that they were doing so in the public domain, raising the question as to whether this amounts to consent for inclusion in research.

Information and communication technologies provide a wealth of resources and you will no doubt rely on them heavily either to support your research activities or to source data for use in your grounded theory study. Be conscious of the potential that these resources have for your research but also be aware of the limitations. Information posted to the online environment may not always be trustworthy, nor may it be suitable or appropriate for use in your research. Be prudent in your use of these technologies and they will serve you well in your study.

Conclusion

Undertaking research to produce a theory that is grounded in the data places high priority on that data and the mechanisms by which it is generated or collected. Application of theoretical sampling principles throughout the research process ensures that the data sought out and acquired will serve the construction of a grounded theory that reflects logical analytical processes. This chapter has described various mechanisms for data generation and collection that can be used individually or in combination, as directed by the evolving analysis. In the following chapters we will explore analytical techniques that are used in the production of a quality grounded theory.

CRITICAL THINKING QUESTIONS

1 Reflect on your understanding of the use of data in research generally. Has your perception of the role of data changed as a result of what you have learned from reading this chapter?

2 Consider the concept of theoretical sampling. Do you believe that theory could effectively be built without the application of theoretical sampling principles?

3 Think about the distinction between generating and collecting data. Can you effectively reconcile your position as a researcher with this distinction? What implications does an appreciation of your relationship with the data have for your own research efforts?

 WORKING GROUNDED THEORY

Review the 'Working grounded theory' example presented in Appendix A. Note:

• The strategies employed by this researcher to promote the generation of quality data.

• The types and sources of data used in this example.

• Issue encountered by this researcher in undertaking theoretical sampling.

6   Data analysis in grounded theory

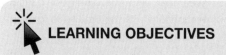

LEARNING OBJECTIVES

This chapter will help you to:

1 Compare and contrast concepts, codes and categories in grounded theory research

2 Describe the process of constant comparative data analysis

3 Distinguish between initial, intermediate and advanced stages of coding

4 Discuss the concepts of properties and dimensions in relation to category development

5 Explore strategies and tools that may aid analytical processes

6 Outline the sequence of analytical processes used in grounded theory research

Introduction

In the previous chapter we discussed the importance of quality data in the development of grounded theory. We will now turn our attention to essential grounded theory methods related to data analysis. In this chapter, the reader will be taken through the process of conceptual development, which includes the tasks of coding and categorization. The importance of concurrent data collection or generation and analysis in ensuring the final theory is grounded will be emphasized throughout this chapter. Strategies and tools that can enhance the process of analysis will be examined and discussed. This chapter will provide you with important directions for initial and intermediate data analysis while preparing you to move into the final phases of theory development discussed in the following chapter.

Understanding terminology

Often the most confronting and confusing issue for those attempting a grounded theory is the need to grapple with terminology relating to analysis. The numerous books and articles written on the topic often do not assist in overcoming this problem; in fact, for the novice researcher, they can add to the confusion. The following discussion will help you to develop a foundational understanding of common terminology related to grounded theory analysis as a precursor to the discussion of analytical methods that follows.

Concepts

There are two rules in grounded theory data analysis. The first of these is that everything is a concept, which is very similar in its intent to the dictum that all is data (Glaser, 1978). Holloway (2008) defines a concept as a descriptive or explanatory idea, its meaning embedded in a word, label or symbol (p. 43). Differences between how concepts operate in a grounded theory relate to their function in the analytical process and levels of sophistication, both of which are interconnected. The second rule is that data analysis needs to proceed in relation to the research question, aims and unit of analysis planned for in the initial research design (see Chapter 2). In order to maintain focus and develop analytical depth and integration, the substantive area of enquiry should be kept in mind at all times. In any study with a qualitative component, generating large amounts of data for analysis is inevitable. Because of the inductive nature of the grounded theory process, it is easy to be distracted and sometimes lose sight of your research question. Doing so will slow you down and possibly result in what Clarke (2005) refers to as analytical paralysis, a condition where you feel totally overwhelmed by the data and your seeming inability to develop a theory from it.

Overall, grounded theory analysis is categorical in its intent. The language used by different grounded theorists can seem confusing until you realize that the terms 'concepts', 'codes' and 'categories' generally mean the same or similar things. The grounded theory road begins to divide between Glaser (1978; 1992), Strauss (1987) and Strauss and Corbin (1990; 1998) when it comes to elucidating methods of theoretical abstraction. In order to aid understanding, Table 6.1 maps out the conceptual language used by seminal grounded theorists to describe the different stages of data analysis. The various concepts have been chosen as umbrella terms under which we have classified seminal texts and the language used to describe methods of grounded theory analysis.

In earlier chapters we challenged you to think about your methodological position in relation to deciding how to use essential grounded theory methods. The complexity of Table 6.1 makes evident a major source of confusion for beginning grounded theorists who have not already positioned themselves and their research design.

Table 6.1 Map of conceptual terminology

	Concepts				
	Codes	**Categories**	**Properties and dimensions**	**Core category**	**Methods of theoretical abstraction**
Glaser and Strauss (1967)	Coding incidents	Categories	Properties	Systematic substantive theory	Common sociological perspective
Glaser (1978)	Open coding that moves to selective coding of incidents once the core variable is identified	Categories which are interchangeably referred to as concepts	Properties and typologies	Core variable that explains a basic social process	Theoretical codes
Strauss (1987)	Coding paradigm: conditions, interactions, strategies, tactics, and consequences. Open, axial and selective coding	Categories	Properties and dimensions	Core category	
Strauss and Corbin (1990)	Coding paradigm: cause, context, action/interactions, and consequences. Open, axial and selective coding	Categories and sub-categories	Properties and dimensions	Core category is a central phenomenon	Storyline and the conditional matrix
Strauss and Corbin (1998)	Coding paradigm: conditions, actions/interactions and consequences. Open, axial and selective coding	Categories and sub-categories	Properties, dimensions and coding for process	Central category	Storyline and the conditional/ consequential matrix
Clarke (2005)	Codes	Categories	Seeking variation in the situation of enquiry through: situational maps, social worlds/ arena maps and positional maps	Multiple possible social processes and sub-processes	Situational maps, social worlds/arena maps and positional discourse maps and associated analyses
Charmaz (2006)	Initial, focused and axial coding	Categories	Properties	Theoretical concepts	Theoretical codes

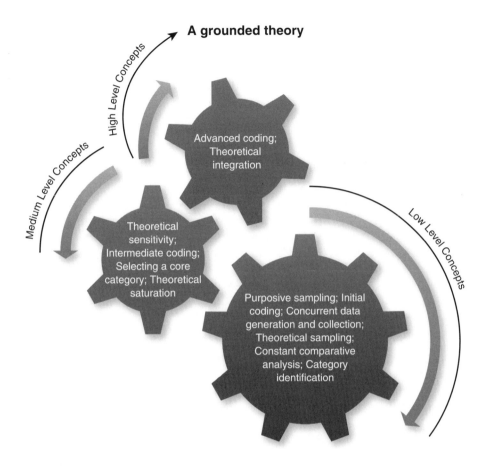

Figure 6.1   Conceptual ordering of essential grounded theory methods

Regardless of the choices that you make, the use of essential grounded theory methods results in the development of concepts that are initially low level and subsequently developed to a higher level as your analysis progresses. Conceptual ordering is a common thread throughout all of Strauss and Corbin's writing about grounded theory (Corbin & Strauss, 2008; Strauss, 1987; Strauss & Corbin, 1990; 1998) and provides a useful heuristic to think about the essential grounded theory methods of data analysis illustrated in Figure 6.1. Each of the cogs in this figure, which you will recognize from previous chapters of this text, have been relabelled to indicate the conceptual output that each of the essential grounded theory methods produces. These outputs range from low-, to medium-, to high-level concepts.

In Box 6.1, Barry Gibson writes about his experience of supervising novice grounded theorists who are beginning to grapple with the essential methods of grounded theory analysis, all of which include the identification of concepts. Some of the processes he discusses in relation to coding and catagorization are explained further on in this chapter.

BOX 6.1 WINDOW INTO GROUNDED THEORY

Barry Gibson on concepts in grounded theory

One of the most frustrating things to try and teach about grounded theory is 'what is a concept?' What is the best way to teach this aspect of grounded theory? I honestly don't know. But it is something that the community of researchers that do grounded theory should think about. I often get students coming to me with a theory that doesn't say anything. They have hundreds of names for concepts but there doesn't seem to be anything going on with those concepts.

I always think this is the converse of what Glaser and Strauss meant by grab. There is nothing that grabs you about their concepts. At this stage you have a very eager student telling you about their concepts and yet you cannot see what it is that is so exciting about them. This is not because they don't know what they are doing. It is simply because there is nothing grabbing about the words they are using to describe their emerging theory.

A common problem in this respect is that students tend to open-code without enough comparison between emerging concepts. Sometimes there is an amazing amount of energy that goes into producing words or labels that re-describe other words but these words are not compared to each other. Often you can have twenty different fledgling codes that are describing the same thing. Like a kind of inverse coding where the words being used to describe what the data is saying are actually more than the sum of the data.

So what to do? Having articulated what unit of analysis the theory is about, start open-coding. Compare incident-to-incident and most importantly code-to-code. Try to compare the words you are using to describe what is happening. Look to see if they are in fact talking about the same thing. There will be several codes that seem to be articulating something about similar aspects of the problem being processed. Group them together and when you get sick of reading data, sit with these codes and write memos on how they are related. Try new words to group these words together. Use a dictionary and thesaurus to help you achieve this. Often this way of working can produce new insights. As you regroup words and try out new labels you will find that you are getting 'conceptual pick up'. This is a fancy way of describing that your new concept is describing more than just one incident and that it is multi-dimensional rather than uni-dimensional.

I think what I am trying to say is that conceptualisation is more than simply redescribing data with other words (coding). It is about learning how to handle emerging concepts, set them in the context of your unit of analysis and sort out priorities for further coding and data collection. You need to be sensitive to the direction a particular coding strategy will take you and to make sure you control your concepts and that they don't control you. This can be very difficult for the novice. A clear focus on the unit of analysis should help you achieve the level of control you need. Finally, what is a concept? A concept is a word or category that describes how the data varies with respect to the unit of analysis. Always keep the unit of analysis in mind when conceptualising as hopefully it will save time.

Codes

In Chapter 5 a large number of potential sources of data in a grounded theory study were discussed. These included textual material and a range of non-traditional sources: for example, photographic images, videos, artwork, artefacts and music (for an extended discussion on analysing visual work see Clarke's (2005) work on mapping visual discourse). Regardless of the type of data that has been either generated or collected, the process of analysis remains the same in that data is initially analysed for incidents, an umbrella term for recurring actions, characteristics, experiences, phrases, explanations, images and/or sounds. Reading transcripts or fieldnotes, listening to recordings of interviews, or observing visual artefacts, results in the researcher identifying the concepts that underlie incidents in the data and it is these concepts to which a code can be applied. Codes are a form of shorthand that researchers repeatedly use to identify conceptual reoccurrences and similarities in the patterns of participants' experiences. Groups of codes representing a higher level concept form a category. Quite often the label assigned to a code is elevated to become the name of a category because it has inherent conceptual grab (Glaser & Strauss, 1967) for the researcher.

Coding is an active process drawn from the substantive area of investigation, the researcher's knowledge and experience, and extant theory. Substantive codes (Glaser, 1978: 55) are taken from the language of the data and generally assume the form of either gerunds and/or *in vivo* codes. Charmaz (2006) argues for the use of gerunds (verbs used as nouns that always finish with 'ing') when coding as a way to identify process in the data as well as focusing on the participant's experiences as a source of conceptual analysis. Examples of the use of gerunds as codes that eventually morphed into categories are 'seeing things in a different light' and 'becoming different' (Birks, Chapman, & Francis, 2009). The term '*in vivo*' is Latin for 'within the living' and this type of code captures participants' words as representative of a broader concept in the data. Two examples of *in vivo* codes that are also gerunds are 'walking with another' and 'getting to know a stranger' (Mills, Francis, & Bonner, 2008). The researcher's previous thinking about extant theory, professional experience and knowledge, and lay experience and knowledge can also influence the identification of codes. Codes derived from extant theory have a specific use in later stages of theory development, and will be discussed in Chapter 7.

Constant comparative analysis

Concurrent data collection or generation and analysis using codes and categories are essential methods that differentiate grounded theory from other predominantly interpretive research designs. From the time of their initial foray into the field, grounded theorists are analysing data. Constant comparison of incident with incident in the data leads to the initial generation of codes. Future incidents are then compared with existing codes, codes are compared with codes, groups of codes are collapsed into categories with which future codes are then compared and categories are subsequently compared with categories. It is the constant comparison of the different conceptual levels of data analysis that drives theoretical sampling and the ongoing generation or collection of data. Ultimately it is this iterative analytical method of constantly comparing and collecting or generating data that results in high-level conceptually abstract categories rich with meaning, possessive of properties and providing an explanation of variance through categorical dimensionalization.

Decision making when constantly comparing data relies on a combination of inductive and abductive thought. Inductive thought is defined as 'a type of reasoning that begins with study of a range of individual cases and extrapolates patterns from them to form a conceptual category' (Bryant & Charmaz, 2007: 608), whereas abduction is defined as 'a type of reasoning that begins by examining data and after scrutiny of these data, entertains all possible explanations for the observed data, and then forms hypotheses to confirm or disconfirm until the researcher arrives at the most plausible interpretation of the observed data' (Bryant & Charmaz, 2007: 603).

Originally, grounded theory was promoted as an inductive research method that generated theory grounded in the data while challenging 'doctrinaire approaches to verification' (Glaser & Strauss, 1967: 7). Strauss (1987) later clarifies this as a mistaken impression, arguing that grounded theory analysis requires three activities: induction, deduction and verification. In a more recent treatise on this topic, Reichertz (2007) examines the logic of grounded theory and concludes that grounded theory researchers use a combination of inductive and abductive thought that accounts for the conceptual leaps of analysis that occur to move a grounded theory away from being a qualitative descriptive account and towards being an abstract conceptual framework.

Analytical methods

As with the terminology relating to concepts, seminal grounded theorists use different language to describe the different stages of analysis. To facilitate our discussion on these processes, we will refer to these phases as *initial*, *intermediate* and *advanced* coding (Birks, Chapman, & Francis, 2006; as modified from Boychuk-Duchscher & Morgan, 2004; and Heath & Cowley, 2004). Note that these analytical processes directly relate to the level of conceptual abstraction the researcher is

Table 6.2 Phases of coding

	Initial coding	Intermediate coding
Glaser and Strauss (1967)	Coding and comparing incidents	Integrating categories and properties
Glaser (1978)	Open coding	Selective coding
Strauss and Corbin (1990; 1998)	Open coding	Axial coding
Charmaz (2006)	Initial coding	Focused coding

developing at the time. Initial, intermediate and advanced coding procedures corre-late with and feed into low-, medium- and high-level conceptual development. Initial coding processes power grounded theory analysis by fuelling low-level conceptual analysis. Once you begin the work of integrating your grounded theory by explicating the links between and within categories through intermediate coding, your level of conceptual analysis will increase. A fully integrated grounded theory is a high-level conceptual framework that possesses explanatory power supported by advanced analytical processes. The following discussion will focus on initial and intermediate phases of coding (Table 6.2), with advanced analysis being discussed in detail in Chapter 7. Note that the recursive nature of grounded theory sees the researcher alternate between phases of coding throughout the study as they concurrently generate or collect data and analyse these, the iterative process of which is illustrated by a dotted line in Table 6.2.

Initial coding

The process of initial coding of data is the first step in grounded theory analysis. Initial coding is synonymous with that of the same name used by Charmaz (2006) and 'open' coding referred to by Glaser (1978) and Strauss and Corbin (1990; 1998). Despite the revolutionary nature of *Discovery*, Glaser and Strauss (1967) provide limited practical direction in respect of grounded theory methods. We can, however, distinguish their discussion of coding and comparison of incidents, within the context of constant comparative analysis, as their approach to initial coding. In the first instance, initial coding is used to fracture the data (Glaser & Strauss, 1967) so as to compare incident with incident, name apparent phenomena or beginning patterns and begin the process of comparison between the codes applied. With initial coding, the researcher moves swiftly to open up the data by identifying conceptual possibilities.

Initial coding is a particularly reflexive activity (Strauss & Corbin, 1990) whereby the researcher needs constantly to interrogate themselves about the early analytical decisions that they make. In a grounded theory study about they ways in which lesbian couples undertake home making activities, Bailey and Jackson (2003) discuss the difficulties faced in trying to code data in a purely inductive manner uninfluenced by their theoretical preconceptions. They resolved this conundrum by framing their theoretical history as a series of sensitizing concepts, relying on the work of Charmaz (2000) to support their position. Taking a reflexive approach to data analysis assists the researcher to avoid subconsciously applying pet theoretical codes (Glaser, 1978) during initial coding, while at the same time appreciating and developing their theoretical sensitivity (see Chapter 4).

Initial coding is often undertaken by analysing transcriptions or fieldnotes line by line (Glaser, 1978) or using short segments of data. Huberty et al. (2008) illustrate this in their use of line, sentence and paragraph analysis of focus group interview data in their study of factors that influence women's adherence to exercise. Such a concentrated approach is recommended in the first instance, as it requires the researcher to examine the data in minute detail while at the same time asking questions of the data. Glaser (1978: 57) poses three questions to be asked of the data in the following list, with Charmaz (2006: 47) adding a fourth:

1   What is this data a study of?

2   What category does this incident indicate?

3   What is actually happening in the data?

4   From whose point of view?

Strauss and Corbin (Strauss, 1987; Strauss & Corbin, 1990; 1998) also advocate questioning the data during early stages of coding; however, their questions are based on a coding paradigm (see Table 6.1) that clearly reflects Strauss's pragmatic concern with structure and process (Corbin, 1991). In the most recent edition of *Basics of qualitative research*, Corbin and Strauss (2008) have simplified the original coding paradigm and renamed it 'the paradigm', which has three broad components for researchers to think about when they are analysing data:

1   There are conditions – why, where, how and what happens?

2   There are inter/actions and emotions.

3   There are consequences – of inter/actions and emotions.

This departure from the more prescriptive coding paradigm offered previously aims to prevent novice researchers from becoming too rigid in their thinking about the required outcomes of data analysis, which may in turn have the potential to force the data into a preconceived framework.

Any coding paradigm is vehemently rejected by Glaser (1992) as a useful adjunct to analysis as he perceives it will force data into a theoretical framing of the researcher's making as opposed to allowing theory to emerge inductively from the data. At this juncture the decision you make about the type of questions you ask of the data is based on how you position yourself methodologically and any analytical concerns you may hold.

Initial coding proceeds until categories begin to form. Line-by-line coding is a technique that is most useful in the very early stages of analysis, eventually becoming redundant as the researcher gains a sense of conceptual control over the data. Caution, however, needs to be exercised in moving too quickly towards an 'overview approach' (Glaser, 1978: 58) to data analysis as there is a risk of missing important concepts that may only be identified after prolonged and intense engagement with the data. The significance of this phase is illustrated by Heath and Cowley (2004) in their study of professional development needs of nurses in practice. These researchers found the narrowing of focus that naturally accompanied initial coding gave direction to further data collection and aided progression of the analysis.

 Activity 6.1

Initial coding

Browse your local or national newspapers over a period of a few days and collect news articles that relate to a specific contemporary issue. Using the techniques described above, code each article. Be sure to work with short segments of the data and use constant comparative processes to generate codes that reflect the major issues evident in the text. How many codes did this process generate? Retain the products of this initial coding session as we will return to it again later in this chapter and the one that follows.

Intermediate coding

As stated above, coding processes in grounded theory have a natural progression that reflects the varying levels of conceptual analysis attained (see Figure 6.1); therefore intermediate coding follows on from initial coding. Glaser and Strauss (1967), in discussing the integration of categories and their inherent properties, identify intermediate coding in its earliest form. For Glaser (1978), open coding is followed by 'selective coding', where attention is turned to generating codes around an identified core variable. Charmaz's (2006) 'focused coding', in which existing significant codes direct analysis, is a similar process. 'Axial coding', defined by Strauss and Corbin (1990: 96) as 'a set of procedures whereby data are put back together in new ways after open coding, by making connections between [and within] categories', while elevating the level of conceptual analysis, is the most developed form of intermediate coding. This definition acknowledges that the identification of patterns and relationships during the process of category development is inevitable.

The result of concurrently generating and analysing data is a large number of codes that require continuous organizing and about which memos need to be written (see Chapter 3). It is the grouping of codes that leads to the formation of categories as the researcher begins to identify explanatory, conceptual patterns in their analysis. Grounded theory categories are multi-dimensional and may consist of a number of sub-categories that together explain the broader concept. Bowen (2008) provides a clear example of this form of conceptual ordering in his study of stakeholder collaboration in anti-poverty projects in Jamaica. Under the category 'working together' are the sub-categories of 'matching resources to requirements', 'getting the job done' and 'showing tangible results'.

Categories and their sub-categories also have properties that need to be identified in the data and explained fully in order to develop conceptual depth and breadth. Strauss and Corbin (1998) define a property as a 'characteristic of a category, the delineation of which defines [the category] and gives it meaning' (p. 101). Properties of categories and sub-categories should be considered in terms of their dimensions, or the range of variance that the property demonstrates. Dimensions of properties can also be linked to the conditions that they operate under. As a very simplistic example of this analytic process, consider the category 'walking the dog'. Properties of this category might be 'time', 'enjoyment' and 'energy'. Each of these properties can be dimensionalized; take for instance 'time'. Participants might identify that the time they take walking the dog varies from short to long and that they are influenced by the weather in making this decision. If it is raining, they usually only spend a short amount of time walking the dog, as opposed to a sunny day when they spend a long amount of time walking the dog. Techniques to raise theoretical sensitivity (see Chapter 4) can be very helpful in fully developing the properties and dimensions of categories and their sub-categories.

One of the key tasks of intermediate coding is the linking together or integration of categories. Using the familiar principles of constant comparison of data, categories and their sub-categories are compared with each other while the researcher questions the relationships between these medium-level concepts. Again, gaps and holes will be identified, and more questions will be raised that require further data collection/generation and analysis in order to find a satisfactory answer. One outcome from this type of coding can be relational statements that operate at a conceptually high level to link together or integrate categories (Strauss & Corbin, 1998) and explain the action or process apparent in the burgeoning grounded theory. You will find that you will explore and develop relational statements in your memos as an aid to analysis. In the reporting of findings, relational statements can be either implicit or explicit and historically have been explicitly expressed as hypotheses or propositions (Glaser & Strauss, 1967).

Returning to Figure 6.1, you can see that through intermediate coding, the analytical work of the researcher has moved into the realm of medium-level concepts. As we stated earlier, the development of categories is based on the generation of large amounts of low-level conceptual codes. Working then to group codes into categories and possibly collapse a number of early categories to become

sub-categories of stronger medium-level conceptual categories creates the foundation of your eventual grounded theory. Refining categories by defining properties
and their dimensions while considering the conditions they operate under will
quickly identify the gaps and holes in your data. At this point, the essential
grounded theory method of theoretical sampling (see Chapter 5) really comes into
its own, as a means of addressing the series of questions that are raised following
the analytical work of category development and integration. You will continue to
sample theoretically throughout your research, including through more advanced
stages of analysis as discussed in the following chapter, until theoretical saturation
is achieved.

Theoretical saturation is the term introduced by Glaser and Strauss (1967) to
describe the criterion for when to stop theoretically sampling for data pertinent
to a category. As will be discussed in the following chapter, theoretical saturation
is a necessary factor in the integration of the final theory. Strauss and Corbin
(1990) define theoretical saturation as occurring when there are no new codes
identified in later rounds of data generation or collection that pertain to a
particular category, and the category is conceptually well developed to the point
where any sub-categories and their properties/dimensions are clearly articulated
and integrated. In more recent times the option of reporting decision making
about theoretical saturation of categories in the findings, as a method of ensuring accountability and quality, has been suggested. Bowen (2008) argues that
types of evidence provided can include a high percentage of interviews reflecting
the conceptual categories, and member checking participants' level of resonance
with the final categories. Neither of these propositions hold up in relation to
grounded theory research, with Morse (1995) having laid the groundwork
against counting the frequency of a code as an indicator of theoretical saturation
early in the piece. Rather, as she states, 'researchers cease data collection when
they have enough data to build a comprehensive and convincing theory. That is,
saturation occurs' (p. 148).

Member checking involves the researcher returning their analysis of qualitative
data to participants to check and comment upon with the aim of validating
findings. Sandelowski (1993; 2002) questions an overreliance on member checking, claiming participants' beliefs and understandings about their world are not
static entities, but rather are subject to change and influenced by the context of the
day, making them inherently unreliable. We would argue that the process of
concurrent data generation or collection and analysis subsumes the strategy of
member checking in grounded theory analysis. Charmaz (2006) concurs that
grounded theory methods make member checking redundant as a source of verification for conceptual analysis. Pragmatically, though, she does suggest that the
term 'member checking' can be included in grounded theory research proposals
to institutional committees as a mainstream term that will provide for re-entry to
the field should your theoretical sampling strategy determine that it is required to
facilitate category saturation.

Activity 6.2

Intermediate coding

Refer back to the initial coding you completed for Activity 6.1. Moving your analysis to the level of intermediate coding, compare codes to identify relationships that may indicate a higher level category. As categories are developed, compare these with other codes and categories to identify possible relationships. Which categories may be subsumed beneath other categories? Can you discern properties and dimensions of developed categories? If you feel inspired, you may wish to write a memo to assist you in answering these questions.

Identifying a core category

A central idea in early seminal grounded theory texts (Glaser, 1978; Strauss, 1987; Strauss & Corbin, 1990) is identifying a core category or concept that encapsulates the process apparent in the categories and sub-categories constructed. Strauss and Corbin (1990) define a core category as 'the central phenomenon around which all the other categories are integrated' (p. 116). In later works (Charmaz, 2006; Clarke, 2005), the importance of selecting a core category appears to have lessened, with a broader approach being taken that describes how categories and their sub-categories integrate together to form an abstract grounded theory of a substantive area of enquiry.

Glaser places developing a strong, conceptually abstract core category at the heart of grounded theory analysis. For Glaser (2007), a core category is generalizable: 'it has grab; it is often a high impact dependent variable of great importance; it is hard to resist; it happens automatically with ease. Researchers tend to see their core category everywhere' (p. 14). Glaser (1978) had earlier discussed the relationship between the core category and a basic social process, which he defines as theoretical in nature, reflecting and summarizing the 'patterned, systematic uniformity flows of social life' (p. 100). He further points out that while a core category may be a basic social process, this is not always the case. Strauss and Corbin (1990) and Charmaz (2006) reassert this, with both of them taking a more widespread approach in identifying the core category as a particular phenomenon. Clark (2009), in producing a grounded theory of resilience in marriage and family therapists, selected the core category 'integration of self with practice'. This author acknowledges that her selection of this category was a constructivist process and that a different phenomenon may have resonated with another researcher working with the same data.

The point at which a core category is selected occurs when the researcher can trace connections between a frequently occurring variable and all of the other categories, sub-categories and their properties and dimensions. The precise use of essential grounded theory methods means the researcher moves between initial and intermediate coding, the specificity of which is directed by theoretical sampling.

Once a core category is selected, theoretical sampling becomes delimited to the generation or collection of data that will theoretically saturate the core and related categories and sub-categories. In this way the researcher is able to shape their grounded theory, refine and fully integrate each theoretical component, while developing the overall level of conceptual abstraction. At this stage, the researcher is naturally progressing to the advanced analysis stage, as discussed in the following chapter.

Tools and strategies to aid analysis

Computer software

In Chapter 3 we introduced the potential use of computer software to assist in the management of data in grounded theory studies. The use of computer software to aid in the coding process is now mainstream for grounded theorists. While Glaser (2005) describes the use of computers as 'burdensome and terribly time taking' (p. 38), most researchers today are generally computer literate and less likely to encounter such difficulties. It is nonetheless worth noting that the use of computers to aid specifically in the analytical process is an acquired skill, developed with experience and through exposure to training programmes and texts that are beyond the scope of this chapter. We encourage you to seek out opportunities to explore the potential of software programs that aid in the management of research data and, if possible, find a mentor who is familiar with their use. At this stage we will, however, reinforce the importance of treating software for the analysis of qualitative data as an adjunct tool for analysis rather than an analytical solution in itself. You may find, as many (particularly novice) researchers do, that a combination of manual and computerized coding processes is most effective. In Box 6.2, Andrea Gorra provides an example of this in her description of how she managed the practical aspects of coding and categorizing data in her grounded theory study on the relationship between individuals' perceptions of privacy and mobile phone location data.

 BOX 6.2 WINDOW INTO GROUNDED THEORY

Andrea Gorra on the use of computer software

Using the qualitative analysis software NVivo helped me to organise, re-arrange and manage a considerable amount of interview data. Initially I formatted the interview transcripts in Microsoft Word to facilitate importing them into NVivo. This meant, for example, that interview questions were assigned a 'Heading 1'

(Continued)

(Continued)

format. When importing the transcript into NVivo, this resulted in the questions being displayed in the content panel in the NVivo explorer. Hence when selecting a question, it was possible to jump to this section in the interview transcript. In addition, meaningful information about the interview was placed into the first two paragraphs of each transcript. This enabled this information to be automatically put into the properties of the interview document when importing the interview into NVivo. As well, different sets of interviews could be assigned different colours in NVivo for easy identification.

Another valuable feature of NVivo was that the software keeps a log of all data entered, which means codes and memos are automatically assigned a date and time stamp. This feature helped to trace the development of codes when writing up my chapters.

However, despite the numerous advantages of using software to code interviews, this did not prove to be the most beneficial approach to help my grounded theory analysis. When I used NVivo to code the first interviews, over one hundred codes were assigned to four short interviews. In addition, it seemed that some of the codes and categories were 'forced upon the data', as Glaser and Strauss would call it. In other words, some codes resembled themes from the literature and were not explicitly mentioned by the interviewees. I realised that I had to adopt a different approach for coding to extract meaning from my data.

After setting aside several months for a survey data collection, I adopted a different and more suitable approach to my interview analysis. This time I did not devise interview codes on screen but worked through paper copies of each of the transcripts and used line-by-line coding and took note of themes and phenomena on the margins. Codes were not devised strictly microscopically and some more abstract categories came into view; some codes were very close to the interviewees' accounts and others were more abstract or conceptual. Keywords and phrases were noted on differently coloured Post-it notes and stuck on to a blank A2 flip chart sheet. The Post-it notes were arranged in a logical order on the paper sheet. As more and more interviews were coded, this sheet started looking less like a random collection of labelled Post-it notes and more like a brainstorm map or a tree where branches of thought grew from certain categories. Memos were written throughout this exercise to keep track of thoughts and ideas regarding the data analysis.

This system of creating codes, combined with reflection, was maintained for coding all interviews. At the end of this coding exercise, three A2 sheets were covered with Post-it notes containing categories and codes. In addition, I used a matrix in Microsoft Word to sort all codes, properties and dimensions, as well as some comments and quotations. This list of codes was revised continuously as more interviews were coded. The codes were modified and verified by being applied to further interview transcripts but stayed alike for the most part. Only at this point did I enter the codes into the NVivo software to allow for searching of the interviews, re-sorting of material and consistent redefining of codes in order to support the analysis process.

In reflection, the NVivo software proved to be a useful tool when dealing with codes that were already finalised but I felt that it was rather cumbersome to use and stifled creativity when developing new codes.

Figure 6.2 illustrates the different techniques that Andrea Gorra refers to in the example in Box 6.2.

Diagramming

Producing diagrams that conceptually map analysis throughout the process of undertaking a grounded theory study is very important. However, because adults have preferred modes of learning, namely visual, auditory and kinaesthetic (Russell, 2006), diagramming does not appeal to everyone. Diagramming receives varied amounts of attention among the seminal grounded theorists. Glaser (1978) limits a discussion of diagramming to constructing typologies during theoretical coding, whereas Strauss and Corbin (1990) advocate the use of diagrams from the commencement of a study in tandem with the writing of memos.

 Activity 6.3

Preferred learning style

Think about the types of words you use to communicate in a learning situation. If you respond to people using 'the way I see it', you most likely enjoy using images and pictures to understand concepts. People who use words like 'I hear what you are saying' often prefer to talk their way through the processes of comprehension and understanding. If you are a 'less talk, more action' person, you probably enjoy learning through the experience of physically doing something.

Identify if your preferred mode of learning is visual, auditory or kinaesthetic. Ask yourself how you can capitalize on this insight during the process of undertaking a grounded theory study. In particular, what sort of strategies could you plan to use during the concurrent data generation or collection and analysis of your study to make the most of your preferred style of learning?

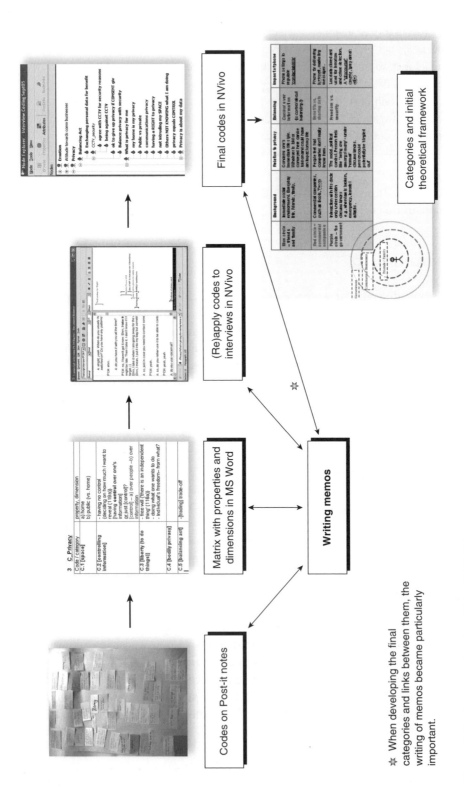

☆ When developing the final categories and links between them, the writing of memos became particularly important.

Figure 6.2 An example of coding processes

Diagramming while concurrently generating or collecting data and analysing this encourages you to map and connect various codes in the first instance. Initial coding will result in a long list of codes that can make the novice researcher feel quite overwhelmed. Organizing and diagramming these early coding lists is very messy, but it will go some way to restoring calm to the chaos that seems to have exploded in your office. If you choose to keep on diagramming as your analysis progresses, your diagrams will change to reflect the developing levels of conceptual analysis (see Figure 6.1). Generally, initial coding results in messy and intricate diagrams, which will evolve into neat and simple diagrams as you move into intermediate and advanced coding stages.

Remember our discussion of abduction earlier in this chapter? Diagramming is *the* creative tool to use when operationalizing the logic of abduction. You can diagram to identify the properties and dimensions of categories and their sub-categories. By default, therefore, diagramming will also assist you to find the gaps and holes in your developing theory that will further direct theoretical sampling. Identifying points of connection, intersection and overlap by diagramming categories and their sub-categories is also important. This is particularly so when overlaps exist, as visually recognizing these will challenge you to think critically in order to resolve them through the further refinement of categories and their component parts. A diagram that contains mid- to high-level conceptual analysis can be a useful starting point to use in participant interviews or focus groups. Asking participants to feed back on your verbal explanation of a diagram in lieu of an open-ended question focuses the generation of data towards theoretical saturation of the developing theory.

When diagramming, there is only one rule: keep a record of what you have created and throw nothing away. Do not feel constrained, embarrassed or frightened to begin diagramming. Not everyone is an artist and diagramming allows you to express yourself as best you can.

If your preferred learning style is kinaesthetic, consider using computer software to diagram. Inspiration 9 and MindGenius are examples of software programs that allow you to import in and export out of Microsoft Word to create lists of codes that *you* organize hierarchically. These lists can be converted to flexible diagrams that you can then work with on your computer screen. Consider having your final diagrams enlarged and possibly laminated to enable you, along with your supervisors and participants, to draw on in order to reflect and record insights and creative analytical exchanges.

For researchers who are predominantly visual, consider the example provided by Andrea Gorra (Figure 6.2) where she used sticky notes to organize her codes in the first instance, creating a 'movable feast' of concepts to work with. As these concepts became more refined, she changed over to using computer software to map categories and their sub-categories.

Experienced grounded theorists, such as Merilyn Annells (personal communication, April 2005), have their favourite strategies such as keeping a large artist's block close at hand to use with students so they can diagram concepts together during supervision sessions. Electronic whiteboards are another tool effectively to capture

LIVERPOOL JOHN MOORES UNIVERSITY
LEARNING SERVICES

grounded theory diagrams in a retrievable format. Flip charts also work well, but you need to photograph the resultant diagrams in order to create a manageable visual record. Let loose your creative energy with a rainbow variety of coloured pens of varying thickness in order to differentiate between concepts and illustrate various relationships.

Whatever you use to diagram your work, ensure it is labelled and dated and electronically filed securely. Alternatively, convert it to A4 format, print it and file it chronologically in a plastic sleeve within a ring binder. Adele Clarke (personal communication, May 2009) shared this tip with us when chatting about effective supervision of students engaged in a grounded theory study. By storing your diagrams in this way, you are able to flick through pages that trace the development of your grounded theory over time. This has two purposes: firstly the researcher will get a sense of accomplishment from seeing their analysis develop before their eyes; and secondly an accurate record is created that provides evidence for the audit trail of decision making regarding analysis (as discussed in Chapters 3 and 9).

Analysing contextual conditions

The idea of analysing grounded theory data for structural or macroscopic conditions is a controversial one. Closely tied to the coding paradigm, Strauss (1987) introduced the notion of specifically coding for contextual conditions in the first text he wrote about grounded theory after publication of *Discovery* (1967). In the 20 years that transpired between these two seminal works, Strauss had developed his thinking about methods of grounded theory analysis in line with his philosophical position of pragmatism and symbolic interactionism whereby 'while actors act towards their environment they are also both socially and materially a part of their surroundings … subject, cognition, knowledge and theory all need to be conceptualized as a dynamic process resulting from activity relating actors with environment' (Strubing, 2007: 595).

In the first edition of *Basics of qualitative research*, Strauss and Corbin (1990) developed an analytical framework they called the conditional matrix, which along with its associated conditional paths was designed 'to protect researchers against the untenable assumption of two contrasting realms of the macroscopic and microscopic, falsely thought by many to be either independent of each other or needing somehow to be related to each other' (Strauss, 1993: 64). It is this reaction against the predominantly dualistic thinking of the time that provides a foundation for a conditional matrix that centres on action and identifying the salient structural conditions (Clarke, 2005) of this action. The conditional matrix includes the following levels: (8) international, (7) national, (6) community, (5) organisational and institutional, (4) sub-organizational, sub-institutional, (3) group, individual, collection, (2) interaction, (1) action pertaining to a phenomenon. In concert with the coding paradigm, this matrix of conditions guides the researcher in the questions that they ask of the data at various points during the process of analysis. There are various iterations of the conditional matrix; however, we concur with

Clarke (2005) that a later version amended to place the individual at the centre of conditional analysis (Strauss & Corbin, 1998) is not reflective of Strauss's concern with action as the centre of analysis.

Using the concept of a conditional matrix as a stepping-off point, Clarke's (2005) project of pushing grounded theory around the postmodern turn argues for a reframing of data analysis to consider that 'everything in the situation *both constitutes and affects* most everything else in the situation in some way(s)' (p. 72). The research design of a situational analysis study uses essential grounded theory methods and combines them with three different types of situational maps and analyses:

1 **Situational maps** as strategies for articulating the elements in the situation and examining relations among them

2 **Social worlds/arenas maps** as cartographies of collective commitments, relations, and sites of action

3 **Positional maps** as simplification strategies for plotting positions articulated and not articulated in discourses. (Clarke, 2005: 86)

Actively analysing data for contextual conditions of the substantive area of enquiry is premised on the philosophical and methodological position assumed by the researcher. The inclusion of strategies advocated by Strauss, Strauss and Corbin, and Clarke in a grounded theory research design needs to be carefully considered in relation to questions of human agency and discourse (Mills, Chapman, Bonner, & Francis, 2007). If you are clear about how you understand the world ontologically and epistemologically (see Chapter 4) then you will also be clear about the possibilities for either the coding paradigm/conditional matrix or situational analysis mapping in your work.

Coding secondary data sets

We have made the point above that analytical processes in grounded theory remain the same regardless of the type or source of data. As the use of secondary data sets is a growing trend in research, it is worth taking some time to discuss this as a source of data for analysis in grounded theory. Secondary data was defined in Chapter 5 as a 'data set collected by someone else for some other purpose' (Boslaugh, 2007: 1). The advantages of using secondary data sets are their low cost and ease of access, particularly when facilitated by specialist databanks such as ESDA Qualidata (University of Essex/University of Manchester, 2006) in the United Kingdom.

Secondary data sets can be analysed in the same manner as primary data using essential grounded theory methods. Glaser (2008) supports the analysis of both quantitative and qualitative forms of secondary data and posits that because grounded theories are 'conceptually abstract of time, place and people', the traditional limitations of secondary data analysis posed by the nature of archival data (Corti, Witzel, & Bishop, 2005) are less of a problem.

Whiteside (2010) used secondary data in her grounded theory study of empowerment in the context of Indigenous Australians' lives. Collecting this type of data set to address research questions about vulnerable populations is beneficial because it reduces the level of impact the researcher has on participants themselves. As long as the original ethics approval includes written consent for the use of participant data in future research, secondary data can provide a rich resource for grounded theory studies. In Box 6.3, Mary tells of her research experience and in particular the challenge of theoretical sampling without the option of interview as a method to generate additional data.

 BOX 6.3 WINDOW INTO GROUNDED THEORY

Mary Whiteside on secondary data analysis

The focus of my PhD was to develop a grounded theory of empowerment in the context of Indigenous Australia. The rationale for this study lay with the well-documented research gap in relation to empowerment as a social determinant of health in society in general, and for Indigenous Australia. This gap exists in part because of methodological challenges, including access to participants. I had consent to draw upon very rich data in the form of personal stories of Indigenous Australians, documenting their personal transformation following participation in an Indigenous Family Wellbeing (FWB) empowerment program implemented in multiple sites. This evaluation data provided an opportunity to examine the concept of empowerment in the context of Indigenous Australia and contribute to the evidence base for this issue.

In determining a methodology I was drawn to the systematic methods associated with grounded theory, and the stated assumption that all is data, however I could find little in the grounded theory literature about the use of existing data sets. So, to some extent, I entered unchartered waters with my research design. In doing so I encountered a number of challenges, including how to theoretically sample when I was unable to undertake additional interviews.

In practice, the application of grounded theory in this study involved a number of phases. First, I undertook a series of brief literature reviews on empowerment and related concepts and the historical and the social context of Indigenous health and wellbeing. These reviews helped to locate and determine the relevance and importance of the study, provided direction for theory development and connected the study to disciplinary practice.

I then put this information aside to focus on grounded theory processes of theoretical sampling, coding, categorising and building theory from the data. I was not aiming to approach the grounded theory process as a 'tabula rasa' or blank slate, but I did seek to avoid imposing preconceived ideas on the work.

I found the data to be complex and the analytic process all consuming, making prior knowledge less likely to be a major influence.

Initial sampling occurred on the basis of accessing the richest data for theory building. I commenced with the site where FWB was most comprehensively implemented and evaluated, assuming this was where the richest data lay. I coded and categorised data from this site until data saturation was reached. After coding and writing summaries of the first ten interviews in this first site, I stopped to reflect on the story that the codes and initial categories were telling me. This helped to gain a sense of the theory that was emerging.

Having access to data from multiple sites, which varied in relation to location, size and gender make-up, provided opportunities for theoretical sampling whereby I would compare the categories and their properties across context and condition. Would the emerging theory hold true in these different sites? I repeated the process of coding and categorising until data saturation was reached in each of the other sites and found only minor differences, reflective of context. At this stage I returned to the literature to locate the theory and consider the theoretical contribution of the study.

There were additional challenges associated with this methodology. One of these was that I was a non-Indigenous researcher studying an Indigenous issue. To counter this limitation I sought ongoing feedback from an Indigenous mentor. Also, being open to the data risked replicating the program evaluation rather than developing the resultant grounded theory of empowerment. I needed to ensure the research question remained the focus of analysis in order to break new theoretical ground. However, despite these and other challenges, this methodology provided a means for building much needed and authentic evidence about the lived experience of Australian Indigenous people.

Progressing to advanced analysis

Before we conclude this chapter, it is worth spending a few moments addressing some issues that you may face in progressing your analysis to the advanced phases discussed in the following chapter. Figure 6.3 represents the early stages of a grounded theory study. The interaction between initial and intermediate coding, concurrent data collection/generation and analysis, and theoretical sampling is cyclical as opposed to a linear research design. Your activities during these early phases will generate a large body of data and a proliferation of codes and categories will occur. It is at this point that novice grounded theorists can become 'stuck', finding it difficult to move beyond description to the development of medium- and high-level concepts, which are the hallmark of grounded theory studies.

Reflecting on the range of essential grounded theory methods and accounting for these in the implementation of your research design can be helpful in progressing

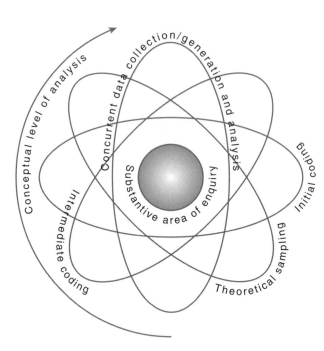

Figure 6.3 Early stages of grounded theory analysis

your analysis forward. Key to maintaining analytical momentum is understanding how intermediate coding assists the researcher to develop categories fully and link these together. Consciously working to raise theoretical sensitivity, critically interrogating categories prior to declaring them theoretically saturated, and selecting a core category that encapsulates the developing grounded theory will also move you out of the mire of potentially descriptive, thematic analysis, therefore positioning you to move your analysis to the advanced phase discussed in the following chapter.

Conclusion

Analysis is perhaps the most daunting aspect of grounded theory for the beginning researcher. Despite the need to ensure diligence in the application of essential grounded theory methods, this approach to research is inherently flexible. In this chapter we have examined data analysis methods in relation to diverse methodological positions and have discussed tools and strategies to enhance their application in your own research. In the following chapter we move into the advanced phase of analysis and explore techniques for integration of your final theory.

CRITICAL THINKING QUESTIONS

1 What are the key points of difference between Glaser and Strauss in the publications that followed *Discovery* in relation to data analysis? Reflecting on your own philosophical and methodological position, how might these works influence your grounded theory research design?

2 Describe how you would identify if your level of conceptual analysis has progressed in line with the initial and intermediate stages of coding described in this chapter.

3 Consider how you might account for context in your own grounded theory research design.

 WORKING GROUNDED THEORY

Review the 'Working grounded theory' example presented in Appendix A. Note:

- How this researcher struggled with major concepts of analysis in the early stages of her study.

- Her use of constant comparative analysis and its contribution to code identification and category development.

- The approach used in initial and intermediate stages of coding.

- The method used to express properties and dimensions of each category.

- Tools employed by the researcher to advance the analysis.

7 Theoretical integration

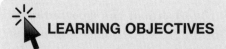

LEARNING OBJECTIVES

This chapter will help you to:

- Discuss the importance of integration as the final phase of grounded theory generation

- Describe factors necessary for theoretical integration

- Outline techniques of advanced coding in grounded theory research

- Employ the storyline technique as a mechanism of theory integration and presentation

- Identify theoretical coding as a strategy for enhancing explanatory power and reach in grounded theory research

Introduction

Earlier chapters in this text have aimed to guide you through the use of essential grounded theory methods in undertaking research that aims to generate theory. To this point you have learned to generate, collect and analyse data as the basis of your developing theory. In this chapter we will discuss the significance, purpose and mechanisms of theoretical integration. Within this context we will present advanced coding strategies for the production of a theory that is both grounded in the data and demonstrates explanatory capacity, factors that are critical for ensuring credibility in your own research.

Defining theory

Before we explore the concept and processes of theoretical integration, it is worth pausing to consider what we mean by the word 'theory'. We define theory as an explanatory scheme comprising a set of concepts related to each other through logical patterns of connectivity. A number of other definitions exist that largely reflect the philosophical roots of their proponents; positivists, for example, seek to observe relationships with the aim of explanation and prediction while interpretivists aim for increased understanding through theory development (Charmaz, 2006). Glaser and Strauss (1967) originally defined theory as that which has explanatory or predictive ability. While we question the positivist intent of prediction as reflective of the goal of generalization, it is clear that the high level of abstraction achieved by grounded theory lends explanatory power. Symbiotically, it is the existence of an overarching explanatory scheme that adds cohesion to the theory (Corbin & Strauss, 2008). Bryant (2009) asserts that original grounded theories need not be speculative or universally explanatory; rather, they are contextually constrained, awaiting further development (such as to the level of formal theory, as discussed in Chapter 9).

 Activity 7.1

The concept of 'theory'

What comes to mind when you hear this term? Consider some examples of theories that direct your professional life or that are universally accepted. What purpose do these theories serve? How might theories of this nature differ from your perception of grounded theory?

In evaluating published research, you will find that many studies claiming to be grounded theory do not actually generate theory. As we have discussed previously, and will explore further in Chapter 9, this is often the result of studies not rising above the level of description. In other words, such studies do not demonstrate the capacity to *explain* phenomena that are the focus of the research. We believe that this failure is most often a consequence of the researcher struggling with the critical stages of advanced coding and theoretical integration. This later stage of analysis involves processes that are intellectually and emotionally demanding. You will undoubtedly find that integration, or the pulling together of your final theory, is the most difficult part of your research (Strauss, 1987). Take heart in the fact that the associated challenges render the reward of a unique and original theory that contributes to knowledge in your own discipline and beyond.

Certainly, not all studies aim to generate theory, but those that go beyond descriptive analysis have the potential to add further to what we know of the world and improve our understanding of it (Corbin & Strauss, 2008). Grounded theory is not just a collection of categories that are assembled into a theory (Glaser & Strauss, 1967). Theoretical integration requires the application of advanced analytical strategies in order to raise your analysis to the highest conceptual level possible.

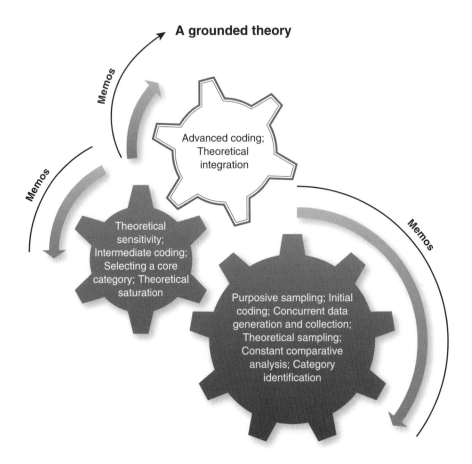

Figure 7.1   Advanced coding and theoretical integration

Factors necessary for theoretical integration

When does theoretical integration commence? In reality, your construction of theory begins with your first piece of data. Through the application of your theoretical sensitivity (as discussed in Chapter 4), your analytical focus will be directed towards theory development, albeit in an embryonic form, from the earliest stage. Then, as relationships are being formed between categories during intermediate coding, your study 'begins to fulfill its theoretical promise' (LaRossa, 2005: 849). Eventually there will come a time when advanced coding techniques, as described below, can be effectively employed to pull together your theoretical scheme into the final grounded theory. This stage represents the final phase of grounded theory production, as indicated in Figure 7.1.

Glaser and Strauss (1967) speak of theoretical criteria being necessary to guide the final stage of theoretical development, yet do not make clear what constitutes these criteria. We propose that there are three factors necessary for the integration of a grounded theory:

1   An identified core category.

2   Theoretical saturation of major categories.

3   An accumulated bank of analytical memos.

In the previous chapter we discussed the significance of the core category in grounded theory research. Because of its centrality in relation to all concepts, the core category is analytically powerful and therefore has the ability to explain the phenomena under study (Corbin & Strauss, 2008). During later stages of analysis, the core category is the hub of the developing theory. Without it, relationships between concepts within the theory are fragile and theoretical elaboration is stunted. You may well enter the stage of advanced analysis having identified a core category during intermediate coding. At times, however, it is necessary to employ techniques of advanced analysis before your core category crystallizes.

The second element necessary for integration of theory is saturation of major categories. As discussed in Chapter 6, theoretical saturation occurs when further data collection fails to add properties or dimensions to an established category. Dey (2007) compares a saturated category with a sponge that has absorbed as much water as it can. In the same way that nothing further is gained by adding more water to the sponge, neither can a category be enhanced once all its dimensions and properties have been explicated. Theoretical saturation is dependent on correct application of theoretical sampling principles to ensure a diverse range of data (Glaser & Strauss, 1967). Dey (2007) points out that saturation should not be at the expense of refinement of categories. While it is arguable whether this state can ever be truly achieved, saturation must be viewed in abstract terms, as being represented by a pattern or theme that makes sense to the researcher (Morse, 2007). Saturation can therefore be defined as a 'judgment that there is no need to collect further data' (Wiener, 2007: 306). As analysis in grounded theory continues until formation of the final theory, theoretical saturation will probably not be truly achieved until your study is complete. Once categories are saturated they are theoretical abstract yet substantively grounded (Charmaz, 2006), thereby functioning as the link between the data and the final theory.

In Chapter 3 we spoke extensively about the significance of memoing in grounded theory research. Memos are not just produced as a mechanism for recording analytical insights, they are functional tools that will serve as a reference through-out your use of essential grounded theory methods. Glaser (1978) aptly describes memoing as 'the bedrock of theory generation' (p. 83). It is during these later stages of analysis that your investment in memoing provides its greatest return. At the integration stage you will actively sort memos to aid the final formation of your grounded theory. Glaser (2005) emphasizes the importance of sorting memos, considering this a critical element in his advanced (theoretical) coding stage. Corbin and Strauss (2008) also discuss reviewing and sorting memos as a key element of integration, although as integration of theory commences during their axial coding phase, they acknowledge the greater complexity that is associated with sorting during later stages of analysis.

Sorting of memos has traditionally been done by hand, and Glaser (2005) maintains that this is the only way to remain 'creatively conceptual' (p. 39). Conversely, Corbin and Strauss (2008) suggest that computers can assist in managing the increasing density of the memos and evolving theory as analysis progresses. Revisiting and sorting memos, even at the later stages of analysis, invariably results in the generation of more memos. Possession of a management strategy is therefore particularly important at this stage.

Your purpose in sorting memos is to aid the integrative process through the identification of relationships and unifying concepts not previously evident (Corbin & Strauss, 2008). Memos should be organized according to the categorical scheme that has resulted from your earlier phases of analysis. Charmaz (2006) suggests that you should not be afraid to experiment with this process. Her practical advice is to sort memos by category, compare category with category and ultimately aim to produce a logical scheme that reflects the studied experience. She suggests that you may choose to print your bank of memos and sort them (and any that are subsequently generated as a result of this process) manually as you commence integration of your theory. Alternatively you may find that you revisit your memos periodically within a computerized data management program throughout your analysis. We find this latter approach to be a progressive strategy that you will tend to undertake naturally as you apply essential grounded theory methods in your research.

Advanced coding

The previous chapter examined the use of initial and intermediate coding in a grounded theory study. Application of essential grounded theory methods as you undertake coding through the initial and intermediate stages will see you eventually progress to the point of advanced coding. Table 7.1 summarizes the coding phases including strategies that constitute advanced coding for the major grounded theorists.

Advanced coding is at the heart of theoretical integration. It is through these processes that data ultimately become theory. As can be seen from Table 7.1, Strauss and Corbin (1990; 1998) originally discuss advanced analysis and theoretical integration within their definition of selective coding. The storyline technique is introduced as a mechanism to aid this process. In the later edition of their work

Table 7.1 Phases of coding

	Initial coding	Intermediate coding	Advanced coding
Glaser and Strauss (1967)	Coding and comparing incidents	Integrating categories and properties	Delimiting the theory
Glaser (1978)	Open coding	Selective coding	Theoretical coding
Strauss and Corbin (1990; 1998)	Open coding	Axial coding	Selective coding
Charmaz (2006)	Initial coding	Focused coding	Theoretical coding

(Corbin & Strauss, 2008), the reference to selective coding is dropped and less attention is paid to the use of storyline as an aid to theoretical integration. For Glaser (1978; 2005) advanced analysis is reliant on techniques of theoretical coding. Charmaz (2006) also employs theoretical coding in the advanced stages of her analysis.

As has been stressed throughout this text, grounded theory processes are not linear; your progress will be recursive and you will find that analytical phases will continue to overlap (once again represented by the dotted lines between coding phases in Table 7.1). Even during the advanced stages of theory development, you will need to return to fundamental theoretical sampling and coding activities at various points to ensure that your theory remains grounded. Charmaz (2006) speaks of the need to be tolerant of ambiguity during coding; as your analysis moves towards theory we caution you that such ambiguity becomes more pronounced and the need to stay focused and precise in your use of grounded theory methods will be amplified. You will find that both the storyline technique and theoretical coding are important strategies that will assist you during advancing analysis and theoretical integration. We have written about these techniques previously (Birks, Mills, Francis, & Chapman, 2009) in an attempt to extend the application and reach of these important aids to the production of grounded theory. The following discussion builds on and develops our earlier work.

Storyline

Storyline as an aid to analysis in grounded theory reflects the sociological roots of this approach to research. It was not, however, addressed as a specific methodological strategy in *Discovery* (Glaser & Strauss, 1967). An extensive description of the use of storyline was originally presented in Strauss and Corbin's (1990) text. This work generally, and storyline as a grounded theory technique specifically, drew harsh criticism from Glaser (1992) in his subsequent rebuttal. Glaser (1992) was critical of the over reliance by Strauss and Corbin (1990) on storyline, considering it a framework to be imposed on the data. Such an approach was posited as being inconsistent with grounded theory's emphasis on allowing the data to direct how the story develops (Glaser, 1992). The criticism attracted by these authors may explain in some measure the reduced attention paid to the use of storyline in the second (Strauss & Corbin, 1998) and third (Corbin & Strauss, 2008) editions of their text.

What is storyline?

Stories are not a new concept in research, being commonly used in a number of interpretive methodologies. Narrative analysis, for example, uses stories as a source of data, while ethnography employs storytelling as a mechanism to convey research findings. In studies employing grounded theory methods, stories may also be a source of data, most often generated through in-depth interview processes. Dent-Brown and Wang (2006) asked participants to create a fictional story to identify personal and subjective elements in their study of how such a process could be used in therapy. Some grounded theory researchers also present their findings in the form of a story. Grounded theories are in fact stories, whether explicitly stated or not, and some researchers do recognize the story inherent in the theory they produce. Wishart (2006), for example, generated grounded theories in the form of life stories as the foundation for memorial services. Smolander and Rossi (2008: 24) produced an 'explaining story' in their grounded theory study of the development of information and communication technology (ICT) architecture.

Stories and storytelling have quite specific purposes in these examples that are different from the use of storyline as a technique for theoretical integration. Strauss and Corbin (1990) define *story* as 'a descriptive narrative about the central phenomenon of the study' and *storyline* as 'the conceptualization of the story … the core category' (p. 116). The difference between the two terms is important in this context as we see the extended term *storyline* as inherently suggesting coherence and continuity. Storyline has a dual function in grounded theory in that it assists in production of the final theory and provides a means by which the theory can be conveyed to the reader. As a tool for integration, storyline aids in constructing and formulating the final theory. As a mechanism for presenting findings, it enables the researcher to bring to life a theory that may otherwise be dry and unpalatable. For the grounded theorist, therefore, storyline is both a means and an end in itself.

Most researchers do not capitalize on the advantages that storyline has for the *process* of theory construction or in presenting the *outcome* in the form of an integrated grounded theory. We believe this results from the limited attention that has been given to the use of storyline as a mechanism for constructing and conveying grounded theory. The full potential of this essential grounded theory method has therefore been largely untapped by both early grounded theorists and those who have followed.

Writing your storyline

Through the use of storyline you are writing your theory; you are explicating the relationships between the concepts that make up your theory. Storyline is the *explanation* of your theory, which in turn provides an explanation of the phenomenon under study. To achieve this you will rely on the strategies that you have employed throughout your analysis. Memos and diagrams, as discussed in previous chapters, will assume greater significance as your theory takes shape. Your earliest drafting of a storyline can be done in the security of a memo. Corbin and Strauss (2008) suggest that your first attempt at writing your storyline need only be a few sentences that will subsequently be built upon until your storyline is formed.

In producing your storyline, a number of strategies can be used to ensure it is an accurate reflection of the data within which it is grounded. These guiding principles can be remembered through the use of the mnemonic 'TALES' as summarized in Box 7.1.

BOX 7.1 GUIDING PRINCIPLES OF STORYLINE

- **Theory takes precedence**
- **Allows for variation**
- **Limits gaps**
- **Evidence is grounded**
- **Style is appropriate**

Theory takes precedence

Grounded theory in its written form is different from other manifestations of qualitative research in that the emphasis is on the theory as a product of analysis (Charmaz, 2006). When writing the final storyline the theoretical constructs (categories and their relationships) that form the foundational framework are given precedence (Strauss, 1987). The required focus can become problematic when the writer becomes so caught up in producing a readable storyline that all semblance of theory is lost. As has been emphasized throughout this text, a study is not grounded theory if it does not reach a high level of conceptual abstraction that is beyond the level of description. Theoretical integrity must be evident in the presentation of the final product in order for it to be judged accordingly.

A balancing act is required to ensure that a researcher's theory is translated into a storyline that remains both digestible for the reader and reflective of the analysis. Charmaz and Mitchell (2001) caution that a strong emphasis on analysis can impact negatively on the readability of the final work, with Charmaz consistently arguing that it is possible to write an interesting, imaginative, inspired grounded theory that presents theoretical constructions reflective of the data (Charmaz, 2000; 2006; Charmaz & Mitchell, 2001). Ultimately, as will be discussed in the following chapter, the writer does not necessarily have to sacrifice creativity for the sake of maintaining theoretical precedence.

 Activity 7.2

Theoretical precedence

Collect a selection of research articles that are described as grounded theory research or draw from those you have collected for activities in previous chapters. Can you clearly discern theoretical elements in the way the findings are presented in these articles?

Allows for variation

In writing the storyline it is not possible, nor indeed necessary, to account for every piece of data. Adequate variation will be evident where data have been generated from broad and diverse sources in accordance with the principles of theoretical sampling. Concepts derived from the data are linked by relational statements that are generally applicable to all those in the specific situation under study (Corbin & Strauss, 2008). As a technique of advanced analysis, the use of storyline raises the conceptual level of the analysis, and the aim of producing theory in the form of a 'conceptually abstract narrative' (Holton, 2007: 285) can be achieved.

There are times when cases appear that do not seem to fit the overall theoretical scheme. You may, for example, observe a situation that is contrary to what is expected or hear statements from a participant that are inconsistent with what other participants have said, producing what are known as 'negative cases' (Morse, 2007). Charmaz (2006) asserts that when negative cases come directly from the data they encourage refinement of the developing theory. Incorporating variation will not work against the storyline, rather such variants add depth and further dimension to the developing theory as expressed in the storyline, much like an unusual character adds dimension to a fictional story. Strauss and Corbin (1998) further argue that building variation into the final theory increases its reach and explanatory power.

Limits gaps

One advantage of the use of storyline is the resultant ability to identify gaps in the developing theory. Integration both facilitates and is achieved by the development of the storyline. Stories of any description rely on logical structure, consistency and flow. Holes, gaps and inconsistencies in a grounded theory will be highlighted during construction of the storyline. This process will make obvious such limitations as would pages torn from a novel make that story incomplete.

Careful attention to analytical processes throughout your research will ensure that gaps and limitations in the evolving theory are identified as analysis progresses. Charmaz (2006) considers that it is the identification of such gaps and limitations that characterizes the element of discovery in grounded theory. You may find, however, that in spite of diligent work, gaps in the theory are made evident through the writing of your storyline. In such cases, it will be necessary for you to return to the data and possibly even the field in order to sample theoretically for data to complete the theory (Corbin & Strauss, 2008). Avoid the temptation to use poetic licence to fill in the gaps that are made apparent by the use of storyline. Charmaz (2006), for example, argues for creativity in the writing of a grounded theory 'without transforming it into fiction' (p. 172).

Evidence is grounded

The use of storyline as a grounded theory method has its greatest influence during theoretical integration. As discussed earlier in this chapter, theory development begins from the earliest stages of a grounded theory study. So too you should be conscious of the developing storyline from your first interaction with the data in order for it to be fully grounded in participants' experiences of the substantive area of enquiry.

Note, however, that the form a storyline takes will vary at different stages of the study. During the early phase of data generation, your storyline will germinate as you compare data with data, and data with developing categories (Glaser, 1978). This process of constantly re-grounding your developing theory in the data is critical. Although you need to be sensitive to the developing storyline from the earliest stages of the research, the storyline should not be constructed in isolation of the data. In other words, avoid producing a storyline that is then imposed on the analysis. Any story that exists in the data will become evident through the correct application of analytical processes and procedures (Glaser, 1992). Once again it is attention to the detailed use of analytical procedures that will reduce the potential for misinterpretation of meaning, or the presumption of unsubstantiated relationships, that may bring the validity of the storyline into question.

In Box 7.2, Goldsmith (2007) discusses her use of the storyline technique as a tool for theoretical integration in her own research. Of importance in this example is Goldsmith's reliance on storyline to identify her core category and achieve theoretical saturation as she moves recursively through the stages of analysis.

 BOX 7.2 WINDOW INTO GROUNDED THEORY

Laurie Goldsmith on the use of storyline

Identifying and committing to a central category for my analysis was one of the hardest things I had to do in creating my grounded theory about access to health care. I knew that this central category would pull the rest of my analysis together by serving as the core around which the multiple sources and types of variation in my data could operate as coherently as possible. Identifying this central category required a leap of faith and the ability to trust myself and my immersion in the data to be able to see 'what seems to be going on here' (Strauss & Corbin, 1998: 148; see also Glaser, 1978). Attempting to pin down the key story in the data – a technique Strauss and Corbin (1998) call 'writing the storyline' (p. 148) – eventually led me to the ultimate central category of 'achieving balance'.

That's not to say the using the storyline technique was easy or produced immediate results. Far from it. Writing my storyline – the storyline of *my* data – demanded time, anguish, and mental gymnastics. I needed to try out a few storylines before I found one that fit.

My first approach used was to think of categories that were obviously key categories and try to use those as the basis for the storyline. It was clear that

(Continued)

(Continued)

elements of the doctor–patient relationship and the 'good doctor' were key categories. But trying to use any of these categories as the central category did not capture process or categories that were not related to the health care system. I knew I needed to capture process to be true to grounded theory. And I knew that my storyline needed to incorporate the importance of non-health care system issues, as such issues were clearly important parts of my participants' stories of getting and using health care.

My second approach posited two parallel processes: the care process and the system process. While this second approach dealt with the earlier problems, I eventually rejected the second approach as it still did not adequately capture the story I was hearing in my data.

And so I returned again and again to the original data, trying to answer the following questions: 'What is the main issue or problem with which these people seem to be grappling? What keeps striking me over and over? What comes through, although it might not be said directly?' (Strauss & Corbin, 1998: 148). After reading one particular interview for what felt like the hundredth time, I was captured by the participant's description of the precariousness of the illness experience as 'living on the edge'. This image, with its association with falling and tipping, helped me to see that my participants were describing access to health care as a process of achieving balance. This realization sparked a flurry of memo writing and new coding. This idea of access as achieving balance was a new category. And it was quickly accompanied by other new categories: seeking balance, maintaining balance, and balance upsets. Thankfully, much of this new way of thinking about my data was a reworking of old ways of thinking about my data rather than necessitating starting all of my coding from scratch.

I then revisited each individual's interview to ensure that the portion of the life story that each individual had told to me could be accommodated by the process I explicated in my nascent theory, using any negative cases to revise the theory and the definitions of the major categories. For example, when a participant with an unresolved back injury simultaneously belonged in the seeking balance phase and the maintaining balance phase – a feat my instincts and my storyline said should not be possible – I took that as a cue to refine my definition of balance.

I continued to use these and other selective coding techniques until I felt I had done justice to the story there was to tell about my data. Doing justice to the story also meant that my theory was 'conceptually dense' (Strauss, 1987: 17) and that I was confident that I had reached theoretical saturation.

Did you detect in Goldsmith's account the application of the guiding principles for the use of the storyline technique? Her emphasis on theoretical precedence is clear, as is her attempt to allow for variation by addressing issues relevant to her participants and also through the use of negative cases. By generating new categories she was able to limit gaps that became evident as her storyline took shape. Furthermore, by returning to her raw data she was ensuring that her rendering of theory through this process was grounded.

Style is appropriate

What should your completed storyline look like? Presentation of a grounded theory as a series of concepts linked by statements of logic may be technically correct; however, entrenching these within a narrative enhances their cohesion and digestibility (Dey, 2007). Your storyline should ideally be 'lucid, understandable and … compelling' (LaRossa, 2005: 850). While Dey (2007) refers to storyline as an abstract or overview of a study that does little more than allude to the bigger picture, we suggest that storyline can in fact be used to produce a comprehensive rendering of your grounded theory. In Chapter 8 we will explore in greater detail options for presenting your final grounded theory. As will be discussed in that context, the style and format of your presentation will depend on a number of factors. Whether you choose, or are directed by convention, to present your theory as a fully developed storyline or simply as a mechanism for summarizing your findings, the principles outlined in this chapter remain relevant.

 Activity 7.3

Use of the storyline technique

Go back to the coding exercise undertaken in the previous chapter. Take the concepts developed through your intermediate coding stage and write a storyline about what you see. Don't be too worried about writing conventions or technical accuracy. Write a storyline from your analysis so far, while attempting to adhere to the guiding principles summarized in Box 7.1.

Theoretical coding

Theoretical coding is employed in the later stages of grounded theory analysis for the purpose of moving 'your analytic story in a theoretical direction' (Charmaz, 2006: 63). Theoretical codes are advanced abstractions that provide a framework for enhancing the explanatory power of your storyline and its potential as theory. Despite the significance of theoretical coding, Glaser (2005) acknowledges it is with this aspect of a grounded theory study that researchers most often have difficulty.

Glaser (1978) is the strongest proponent of the use of theoretical codes, originally describing 18 sociological constructs known as 'coding families'. He would later identify many more, while acknowledging that these lists were far from exhaustive (Glaser, 2005). Strauss and Corbin (2008), although not referring to theoretical coding or coding families specifically, use a coding paradigm with similar intent during their intermediate coding phase (as discussed in Chapter 6). Kelle (2007) suggests that this paradigm reflects many of the key elements of the original coding families yet proves an easier option, particularly for novice researchers.

In Box 7.3, Fei (2007), a proponent of the Glaserian approach to grounded theory, discusses the use of theoretical codes in his own research.

 BOX 7.3 WINDOW INTO GROUNDED THEORY

Foster Fei on Theoretical Coding

Researchers who use grounded theory methods often overlook theoretical coding as a crucial research procedure. I have seen examples of where the notion of theoretical coding was wrongly interpreted as coding theories, such as one would do when coding the substantive data in a grounded theory study. This interpretation is incorrect and obviously contrasts with the purpose of theoretical coding as proposed by Glaser which is to 'conceptualize how the substantive codes may relate to each other as hypotheses to be integrated into a theory' (1978: 55).

My own research examined change initiation by managers in a UK subsidiary within each of two multinational corporations (Fei, 2007). The theoretical code that emerged in this grounded theory was *interaction of effects on a global–local continuum*. This code was derived from the interactive family, which includes *mutual effects, reciprocity, mutual trajectory, mutual dependency, interdependence, interaction of effects* and *covariance* (Glaser, 1978). My theoretical code of *interaction of effects on a global–local continuum* functioned to organise those substantive codes that described changes initiated by the managers, the challenges they experienced and their responses to these challenges. Through my own research experience, I see the use of theoretical code as a way of ensuring that substantive codes 'hang together' conceptually.

How you use theoretical coding will be determined by your approach to coding in the intermediate phase. Your reliance on theoretical coding will be greater if you delay the process of identifying relationships between concepts in your theory to the advanced stages of analysis. As we have stated in the previous chapter, however, these conceptual relationships will become evident as you move from initial to intermediate coding. When essential grounded theory methods are applied correctly, the original integrating scheme will itself be derived from the data (Glaser & Strauss, 1967) and while theoretical coding is not always explicit, it is always there (Glaser, 2005). In the production of a storyline you are implicitly applying your theoretical sensitivity at its most advanced level to produce an abstract explanation of the findings of your research.

Glaser (1992; 2005) believes, however, that theoretical codes are most effective when made explicit, providing their use is dictated by the developing grounded theory. The researcher must avoid applying an external theory until after their own theory has been developed (Glaser & Strauss, 1967). We concur with this directive given the potential for such extant codes to be used as a preconceived framework that the inductively constructed grounded theory is forced to conform to. For this reason we position extant theoretical codes outside of the storyline. Within the storyline itself, the extent of description and explanation of the researcher's interpretations are limited to the products of analysis. There is therefore no confusion as to which concepts have arisen from the data and which have been imported in order to add explanatory power. Cutcliffe (2000) believes that theoretical codes function to 'provide the full and rich understanding of the social processes and human interactions which are being studied' (p. 1482). Our position is that such theoretical concepts are more effective in achieving this outcome when they are superimposed on the theory as rendered through storyline. The researcher is then able to go on to position their theory in the context of broader disciplinary knowledge.

Most of the theoretical codes proposed by Glaser (2005) derive from sociological theory, although he does suggest that those from other disciplines can be used. He further acknowledges that more than one theoretical code may prove relevant to a developing theory, in which case a combined approach may prove appropriate. We strongly encourage the use of theoretical frameworks derived from your own discipline where these prove relevant in explaining your grounded theory and discussing the contribution it makes to knowledge in your professional area. In reality these are the theoretical constructs with which you are most familiar, notwithstanding Glaser's (2005) advice that the researcher should be continually open to learning as many theoretical codes from as many sources as possible. We suggest that while you should seek opportunities to expand your repertoire of knowledge, you should use what is available to you as long as it 'fits'. Through applying the work of others to your storyline, you are able to augment, support and validate existing theories and in so doing explain and reinforce the value of your own contribution. As Glaser (2005) points out, using theoretical codes in this way ensures that the process is a reciprocal one, with the shared aim of expanding a knowledge base.

 Activity 7.4

Theoretical coding

Refer back to the storyline you wrote in Activity 7.3. From your existing knowledge base, consider what theoretical frameworks could be used to enhance the explanatory power of your storyline. For example, news articles about recovery from a natural disaster may suggest theoretical codes that explain grief, loss and/or adaptation. Stories that discuss the impact of a visiting rock band may invoke theories of mass hysteria and mob mentality. Think broadly and beyond your own discipline to identify potential theoretical codes to explain your analysis.

Metaphors as theoretical codes

Metaphors are figures of speech that can be used as theoretical codes where there is a sufficient fit between a metaphor and the grounded theory. Metaphors help to explain a theory by clarifying relationships and providing labels for various components. You are advised to be cautious in their use; as with any type of theoretical code, metaphors must only be used as and when indicated by your theory in the later stages of development. Carpenter (2008) warns that 'misuse of metaphors can create an inaccurate portrayal, casting shadows on the experiences re-presented in the data' (p. 279). This includes mixing metaphors in one analysis, using metaphors that have a poor fit with the data and not following through with a metaphor introduced earlier in a presentation. Glaser (1978) specifically expresses concern at the use of metaphor in grounded theory because of its potential to distract the reader from the phenomenon at hand.

In spite of the potential pitfalls in using metaphors, there are several examples of where metaphor has been effectively used in a grounded theory study to increase its explanatory power. One of these is a grounded theory study of American Indians receiving haemodialysis. Walton (2007) used the metaphor of 'Prayer Warriors' (p. 380) to capture the core category/basic social process of a study that had as its substantive area of enquiry 'spirituality'. Prayer Warriors experience a four-stage process of honouring spirit, suffering, healing old wounds and connecting with community. The metaphor of a warrior was used to 'describe a fierce commitment to prayer … praying was not casual, lighthearted, or joyful; it was hard work and often involved long hours of sweating, fasting, chanting, and pain while praying for others' (p. 380).

In Box 7.4, Ann Bonner tells us about her experience of using metaphor in another grounded theory study that is coincidently also concerned with renal failure, this time from a nurse's perspective. Bonner's (Bonner & Greenwood, 2005; 2006) study of nephrology nursing expertise acquisition used metaphor to explain a core category also identified as a basic social process.

 BOX 7.4 WINDOW INTO GROUNDED THEORY

Ann Bonner on the use of metaphor in grounded theory research

Metaphors are used in everyday speech, to compare one thing to another although this comparison is not literally applicable, in order to suggest a resemblance. A metaphor involves two concepts that are not the same but which assist our understanding of one conceptual domain in terms of another conceptual domain. For instance, we use body parts as metaphors to represent clearly and succinctly the parts of other material objects: 'leg of a table', 'head of a pin', 'eye of a needle' or 'foot of a mountain'. Conceptual metaphors typically employ a more abstract concept as target (e.g. base [of mountain]) and a more concrete or physical concept as their source (e.g. foot). We use metaphors just as we use non-metaphoric concepts to help group together or categorise information into manageable chunks. Essentially the use of metaphors is a means by which people can think about and interpret their world.

Metaphors are also seen in both quantitative and qualitative research and can be an important and useful analytic device for grounded theory research. For instance metaphors can assist in: moving from raw data to more generalised concepts; identifying patterns in data by placing them into larger contexts; and stimulating researchers to connect the categories in an emerging grounded theory.

In my doctoral studies, I sought to discover the process of expertise acquisition and its exercise by nephrology nurses. The properties of the core category emerged during concurrent data collection and analysis quite easily. However, labelling of the core category was problematic; I found that ordinary language failed to provide a label for the core category that would adequately subsume the sub-categories, properties and dimensions as well as explain the theoretical relationships between them. Eventually, several months later, an orchestral metaphor of expertise acquisition and exercise emerged (Bonner & Greenwood, 2006). The core category or source metaphor of producing the magnum opus reduced all of the data into one overarching theory to explain the highly complex target process of expertise acquisition and exercise. The orchestral metaphor encapsulated and accounted for most of the data and was both exciting and a relief to discover.

Some words of caution too. There are possible problems with relying too heavily on metaphors in grounded theory analysis and I recommend several strategies to avoid these problems. For instance resist searching for overarching metaphors too early, avoid incomplete or mixed metaphors, and do not force a metaphor on the data. Instead metaphors once explained should readily fit the data and illuminate the grounded theory.

As an analytical device in grounded theory studies, metaphors can facilitate the emergence of the core category and also assist with understanding the theoretical relationships between categories in the theory. The relationships become clearer and more coherent. Metaphors create images, clarify and add depth to meanings and, if used appropriately in grounded theory studies, can capture data at highly conceptual and abstract levels.

Conclusion

Producing a grounded theory is a result of the interaction between you as the researcher and your data. Through concurrent generation or collection of data and its analysis as described in the previous chapter, the foundations of your theory are constructed. The quality of the final product of your research is reliant on your ability to move your conceptual renderings from these processes to the level of an integrated grounded theory. Techniques of writing a storyline and theoretical coding discussed in this chapter will serve as the bridge between analysis and theory. In the following chapter, we will discuss the various mechanisms and options for presenting your final grounded theory.

 CRITICAL THINKING QUESTIONS

1 Theoretical integration, as discussed in this chapter, is often the most difficult phase of grounded theory research. Why do you think this is? To what extent do you believe ingrained models of knowledge development influence the ability of the researcher to grasp principles of advanced coding?

2 Think of how you might describe storyline in grounded theory as compared with the use of stories and storytelling in other research methodologies if asked to explain the distinction to a colleague.

3 Consider the concept of implicit theoretical codes and their role in theoretical integration. Did you recognize any in the storyline that you produced in Activity 7.3? What are the sources of these codes?

 WORKING GROUNDED THEORY

Review the 'Working grounded theory' example presented in Appendix A. Note:

- How this researcher approached the process of theoretical integration.

- Mechanisms of advanced analysis employed in this study.

- The reliance of this researcher on storyline to achieve integration and facilitate presentation of her final theory.

- The use of a discipline-specific theoretical coding to enhance the explanatory power of this grounded theory.

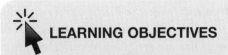

8 Presenting a grounded theory

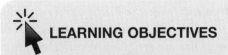
LEARNING OBJECTIVES

This chapter will help you to:

- Discuss the principles of presenting grounded theory findings

- Identify the range of options for reporting a grounded theory study

- Use illustrative modelling as a technique to aid in the presentation of grounded theory findings

- Implement strategies to maximize the impact of your grounded theory findings

Introduction

This chapter addresses the practical aspects of preparing a grounded theory for dissemination. General principles of presenting a grounded theory are identified and discussed. Options for the formatting of research findings, including postgraduate theses/dissertations, reports, journal articles and oral presentations are outlined. The use of illustrative models of grounded theory, including situational maps, is also explained in this chapter. Finally, strategies are suggested that will maximize the impact of recommendations arising from your grounded theory study.

Writing in grounded theory research

Using essential grounded theory methods demands that you begin to write from the very beginning of your study. Generating memos of varying levels of analytical and conceptual sophistication, and writing a storyline of your developing theory, puts you 'in the box seat' when it is time to present your findings in the shape of a grounded theory. As discussed in the previous chapter, reviewing memos in tandem with writing a storyline during the process of integrating a grounded theory results in a foundation for the various publications and oral presentations that are vehicles for dissemination.

When planning this chapter, thoughts turned to writing about writing, and writing about qualitative research in general. Wolcott (1990) speaks of two types of researchers, those who prefer to read and those who prefer to write. A grounded theory research design will suit a researcher who prefers to write with the aim of generating new theory, rather than a researcher who prefers to read about and then test existing theory. Writing and thinking are inextricably intertwined in the construction of a grounded theory, with Sullivan (2009) likening this nexus to being 'the same … as thrashing your arms around is swimming. One is the material expression of the other' (para 1). Richardson and Adams St Pierre (2005) consider writing a method of enquiry as opposed to a task that is undertaken at the end of the study, which is an ethic grounded theorists live out every day. Writing lubricates the cogs that otherwise might grind together in the moving forward of a grounded theory analysis. With generous amounts of memoing, cogs move more smoothly, sliding soundlessly around each other as the researcher also moves fluidly between the data and the field in the process of concurrent data generation or collection and analysis. Writing is thinking – driving analysis, directing theoretical sampling, with the product a conceptually abstract, elegant and integrated grounded theory. Stanley (2008) believes that we should be motivated to learn through the process of writing. For grounded theorists writing is a fundamental act of enquiry as valuable, if not more so, as generating or collecting, reading and coding data. Glaser (1978) encourages this same approach, believing that through writing researchers evolve in their relationship with the data. Writing copiously develops not only the analysis but also the researcher, even though sometimes it does feel as though you sit at a keyboard to open a vein (Smith, cited in Wolcott, 1990).

However, there comes a time when the purpose of writing ceases to be about enquiry and begins to be about communication. With regard to this, Wolcott (1990) again provides some pithy advice sharing 'a writing tip borrowed from Lewis Carroll's *Alice's Adventures in Wonderland:* When you come to the end, stop' (p. 13). Nothing is ever perfect and sometimes it can be hard to say 'stop' when it comes to ending a love affair with your data. Seek advice from your mentors, supervisors and/or colleagues in making the brave decision to accept that your grounded theory is as complete as you can make it and ready for presentation. Strauss and Corbin (1990) write about the 'logic of letting go' (p. 236) as being where you come to an understanding of your analysis as always being a work in progress, open to future critique and reformulation.

Principles of presentation

When presenting a grounded theory, there are four general principles that you need to consider:

1 Identify your audience.

2 Decide what level of analytical detail is required.

3 Choose an appropriate style of writing.

4 Present your grounded theory as a whole.

Identify your audience

A piece of advice often provided to new writers is to determine who their audience is before metaphorically putting pen to paper. Different audiences require different modes of presentation with reference to: their prior understanding of the substantive area of enquiry; their level of understanding of the different aspects of a grounded theory research design; the language that they prefer to use when communicating; and their motivation for reading and understanding the findings and subsequent recommendations. Of these points the most important one is that which relates to a reader's motivation for engaging with a grounded theory. If you were to compare a policy maker's motivation with a professor's motivation it is likely that the former is interested in recommendations for implementation while the latter is concerned with the methodological congruence and rigour of the study as a whole. Both motivating factors are as important as the other; however, for the researcher to meet each reader's needs, the grounded theory has to be presented in very different ways in order for it to be both palatable and sensitive to the target audience (Strauss & Corbin, 1990). As well as working out what each audience considers to be important, the researcher needs to decide upon what they would like in return, as this will influence the presentation's content and the emphasis placed on various aspects. If the aim of the presentation of findings is to get someone to implement your recommendations, how do you 'sell' your grounded theory in a package that will provoke a 'yes, we can do that' moment from the audience? If the aim is to achieve a pass for your thesis/dissertation, how do you signpost your findings so that your grounded theory is transparently rigorous and able to be judged worthy of the accolades that you seek?

Corbin and Strauss (2008) provide some clear and pragmatic advice on the task of presenting grounded theory findings to specific audiences. Focus areas for three types of audience, namely colleagues, practitioners and lay readers (p. 290–1), are identified. Table 8.1 reformulates these ideas to include the type of presentation required for each level of analytical detail, separates colleagues into either peer reviewers or examiners and expands lay readers to highlight the place of policy makers. The number of ticks indicates the recommended level of focus for each of these areas in a particular piece of writing; the greater the number of ticks, the stronger the emphasis that is required.

Decide what level of analytical detail is required

An important decision to be made when planning to present a grounded theory is the level of analytical detail to be included. We define analytical detail as the

Table 8.1 Matching audience to presentation

Type of presentation for dissemination of findings	Analytical detail	Implications for methodological/ methods development	Situating findings in relation to extant theory and the literature	Implications for local action	Implications for broader reform
Lay readers including policy makers — Oral presentation, newsletter, report	✓		✓	✓✓✓	✓✓✓
Practitioners — Oral presentation, newsletter, report, journal article	✓		✓	✓✓✓	✓✓✓
Peer reviewers — Journal article	✓	✓✓✓	✓✓✓	✓	✓
Examiners — Thesis/dissertation	✓✓✓	✓✓✓	✓✓✓	✓✓	✓✓

specific labelling of a grounded theory's core category, categories and possible sub-categories, properties and dimensions, in the presentation of findings. The level of analytical detail required varies depending on the audience and the type of presentation planned. Along with other grounded theorists (Charmaz, 2006; Corbin & Strauss, 2008; Strauss & Corbin, 1990), we urge caution in deciding when it is appropriate to include a highly detailed account of each analytical component of the final product. One instance when there is a need for this degree of analytical detail is in the presentation of a thesis or dissertation and the examiner needs to be convinced of your competence in using grounded theory methods. Including analytical detail, however, does not include the use of 'funny words' (Stern, 2007: 122) to rename essential grounded theory methods. All that results from such poetic licence is confusion – just call it like it is, citing the relevant seminal text in the process, to reduce the likelihood of confusing your examiner.

Sandelowski (2007) writes about words, the intent of which should be seen in the reporting of findings, without their necessarily being written. In particular, Sandelowski refers to some authors suffering an 'acute attack of grounded theory-itis' (p. 129) in their inclusion of a multitude of labels for various parts of their presentation. In Sandelowski's opinion, the condition, 'grounded theory-itis' results in an obscuration of findings and in turn their potential usefulness for the reader. Returning to Table 8.1, you will observe a low-level requirement for analytical detail when presenting grounded theory findings in any form of presentation other than a thesis/dissertation. When writing a journal article or report, the inclusion of a grounded theory's 'little logic' (Glaser, 1978: 129) in the form of an abstract of the storyline (Dey, 2007) will suffice to introduce one aspect of the theory to be explored and explained in depth. For oral presentations and newsletter articles, the confines of time and space will usually dictate that you are only able to refer the reader to a fuller explanation of the theory as a whole, before expanding on one point. Nonetheless, these forms of dissemination are very important in trying to get a message out that has implications for either local practice or broader policy development. Hopefully, these particular audiences will later seek out your findings in more detail with a view to implementing change.

Sandelowski's editorial referred to previously is discussed by second-generation grounded theorists in their text reporting on a grounded theory symposium (Morse et al., 2009). In this edition, these researchers appear nonplussed about the idea of labelling versus not labelling concepts as codes or categories in the presentation of a grounded theory. As the group reflects on this, and other critiques of grounded theory, Corbin speaks of Glaser and Strauss's elegant monographs written in a narrative style, while Stern provides a spirited defence of the usefulness of labels to ensure that analytical processes and the organization of a grounded theory are made clear. As Charmaz (2006) states in an earlier work, 'whether the theory remains embedded in the narrative or stands out in bold relief depends on your task and your rendering of it' (p. 173).

Choose an appropriate style of writing

Choosing a style of writing for the presentation of grounded theory findings follows on from previous decisions made about both audience and the matching level of analytical detail. As a rule, the use of plain English to explain the overall findings of a grounded theory works well. Plummer (2009) shares his thoughts about why the researcher as author sometimes attempts to dazzle the reader by the use of overly intricate language:

> Maybe it is the complexity of the ideas which require more complex narratives. Maybe it is the translations from some difficult work of the past. Maybe. More often I think it is more to do with the puffed up pretence – to make our understandings appear more scientific, deep, serious, truly profound – that we dress it all up in a language that obfuscates and obdurately masks what we see and say. (para 5)

However you choose to write about your grounded theory study, the one thing you do not want to do is unintentionally mask your findings with impenetrable terminology. One of Charmaz's great gifts to novice grounded theorists is her body of work (Charmaz, 1991; 2000; 2005; 2006; Charmaz & Mitchell, 1996; Mitchell & Charmaz, 1996) about the importance and possibilities of using different writing styles when presenting qualitative findings. Charmaz often uses the term 'rendering' to describe the process of achieving a particular style of writing when presenting a grounded theory. To render is to translate or make understandable to the reader the researcher's analysis of what is happening in a substantive area of enquiry. Therefore, the way in which you choose to render a piece of writing is again a direct reflection of your audience and what you hope to achieve from the dissemination of your findings in a particular way. Charmaz (2006) discusses a range of techniques to achieve these different outcomes, while 'balancing the logic of exposition with the logic of the theorized experience' (p. 173). Many of her suggested strategies relate to creating a sense of participants' experiences while drawing the reader into the written account. Some examples of these strategies are 'catching experiential rhythm and timing … [providing] unexpected definitions and assertions … and asking rhetorical questions' (p. 173) of the reader.

Choosing an appropriate style of writing when presenting a grounded theory will result in your findings being read by many more people than might otherwise have been the case. As LaRossa reminds us,

> much the same as a newspaper report or novel will have a slant to it, so also research narratives will have a slant. And that slant may make the difference in whether an article or book is read – and, if read, remembered. (LaRossa, 2005: 851)

Producing findings that are remembered may also result in those findings being used to implement change in the substantive area of enquiry. Remember, research is about more than just the process, it is also about making a difference to people's lives.

Present your grounded theory as a whole

The inherent beauty of a grounded theory lies in how each component integrates together. Because of this, there is an imperative always to present your grounded theory findings as a whole, even if it means introducing the overall theory before moving on to explain one part of it in depth. The difficulty in this lies with creating brevity without superficiality; however, a well-integrated grounded theory that demonstrates logic, consistency and its contribution to knowledge can be communicated in an interesting and succinct manner.

When presenting a grounded theory Glaser (1978) argues for a funnel-down approach where a grounded theory's core category is introduced using an outline approach prior to the researcher focusing on a specific component in depth. When focusing on a specific component, however, the explanation needs to remain at a conceptual level, using select data fragments to provide supporting evidence. Strauss and Corbin suggest asking the question 'do I need this detail in order to maximize the clarity of the analytic discussion and/or to achieve maximum substantive understanding?' (p. 247) prior to including data fragments in the presentation of a grounded theory.

We recommend that findings of your grounded theory study be presented in isolation of both extant theory and the contemporary literature and then discussed in relation to each. This can be achieved using storyline as discussed in the previous chapter. The subsequent use of theoretical codes will consolidate your grounded theory and enhance its explanatory reach. In any form of reporting, an explanation of the substance of the storyline can then be discussed in the context of the current literature to explain its relevance and contribution to existing knowledge.

Options for reporting

Postgraduate thesis/dissertation

Studies undertaken at graduate level to secure an academic award such as a Masters degree, Doctor of Philosophy, or other professional doctorate, usually culminate in the production of a report in the form of a thesis or dissertation. Often the distinction between a thesis and a dissertation is unclear with the terms used interchangeably to describe a student's research report submitted for examination. The term used often depends on your country of origin and the course of study in which you are enrolled. The word *thesis* can be defined as a sustained argument; this is the defining element of a research report that aims to demonstrate a student's capability to conduct independent research.

Whichever term is used, the emphasis in the reporting of grounded theory research as a graduate student is on presenting a consistent, logical and substantial argument. Ultimately you will be required to demonstrate how you employed grounded theory methods to produce theory from your data. Most theses and dissertations follow a similar structure in order to demonstrate an understanding of the substantive area of study, broader theoretical knowledge and, significantly, methods and methodological principles and procedures. We concur with Clare (2003), who suggests that production of a research thesis or dissertation is often shrouded in mystery. She considers that this situation can best be overcome if the desired outcome is viewed as a collection of essays, each serving a specific purpose and that, when linked together, form the finished product. We have adapted her recommendations to suggest a structure relevant to the presentation of a grounded theory study in Table 8.2.

The structure outlined in Table 8.2 is subject to adaptation and will no doubt be tailored to your unique study situation. It provides a good starting point, however, and is a useful framework to have in mind from the outset of your research.

Clare's (2003) description of chapters as a collection of essays is supportive of the option of completing a research thesis or dissertation by publication. When we refer to the completion of a thesis by publication, we are describing a process in which the research is undertaken in a traditional way, and chapters, or extracts of chapters, are published as the research progresses. We are not referring to the compilation of previously published related articles submitted as a means of obtaining an award (a process often referred to as a 'rubber band' thesis).

Francis, Mills, Chapman and Birks (2009) describe a number of advantages to producing a thesis or dissertation by full or partial publication. These advantages include early dissemination of findings, the development of writing skills and

Table 8.2 Recommended thesis/dissertation structure

Chapter	Topic	Content
1	Introduction	Impetus for study discussed
		Significance of study introduced
		Research question, aims or unit of analysis defined
		Philosophical/methodological position established
		Structure of thesis presented
2	Background	Position of study in broader context established
3	Research paradigm	Philosophical position established
		Methodological underpinnings discussed
		Study design described
		Rational for research approach defended
4	Findings	Research findings (storyline) presented
		Theory elaborated
5	Discussion	Significance of findings discussed in the context of existing knowledge
		Relevance and contribution of theory described
6	Conclusion	Limitations of study identified
		Recommendations for application of findings explored
		Potential areas for further study discussed

confidence, and maintenance of a professional profile. Further, these authors assert that the feedback provided from the peer review process strengthens the products of the research and ultimately promotes completion of the project. As data collection and analysis in grounded theory research is concurrent and continues until theory development, the production of papers relating to findings and the developed theory will be delayed until the final stages of the study. Nevertheless, the potential remains for the early publication of papers that relate to the background and study design, as discussed below. Options, requirements and policies for the production of a thesis by publication vary between academic institutions. While most universities will permit this approach, specific guidelines will determine whether papers have to be in manuscript form, under review, or published before the thesis or dissertation can be submitted.

Reports

Reports are usually a summary of research produced to satisfy the requirements of a specific organization. Often this will be a body that has an interest in your research, perhaps a funding or regulatory organization such as an institutional review board or ethics committee. You may also be required to produce a report in support of an oral presentation such as those described below.

The organization for which your report is to be produced will often prescribe its structure and content, and therefore its focus. Where no such guidelines exist, the agenda of the target organization or committee will provide some direction. A funding body, for example, will require a report of expenditure and seek some evidence that this money was well spent. Your emphasis will therefore be on the impact of your research and any published papers or presentations, completed or planned, that will assist in disseminating your work. Conversely, an institutional review board or ethics committee will be concerned with issues that may have arisen in your research in relation to the well-being of your participants and the security and confidentiality of the data generated or collected in your study. Do not be afraid to provide supportive organizations with feedback relevant to their particular areas of interest as future students, participants and other stakeholders will benefit from your experience of these processes.

Journal articles

The most effective means of disseminating your grounded theory research is through publication in professional journals. While the principles for presentation of your grounded theory discussed above remain relevant, often these will be predetermined by your selected journal. Your audience will be specific to the journal, and often guidelines are prescribed in respect of article length and style, factors that may impact on the level of analytical detail you can include and your ability to provide a comprehensive description of your theory. It is therefore important that you select your target journal carefully as this will determine the level of control you have over the final published work.

Meeting journal requirements in regard to the length of manuscripts for submission can be difficult. Focusing on selecting and shortening verbatim quotes to reduce the word count of a manuscript is a useful strategy to consider. Often new grounded theorists find it hard to use only succinct and strong fragments of data to support their argument (Margaret Kearney, personal communication, February 2010). However, lengthy quotations can often detract from the researcher's analysis, which should always be the main focus of the manuscript, so that the researcher can make the 'utility of stories explicit' (Sandelowski, 2004: 1377).

You are probably already familiar with those journals that publish work in your disciplinary area and these are likely the ones most relevant to the subject matter of your research. Do not be afraid to look beyond the journals specific to your disciplinary area. A number of publications address broad topic areas that may increase the reach of your research. Seek out peer-reviewed journals that can provide feedback on your manuscripts and reflect the quality of your study should they be accepted for publication. Select journals based on impact factors to reinforce further the credibility of your work. If your goal is wide dissemination, consider choosing online journals, particularly those that are open access, to expand your potential audience.

Activity 8.1

Publishing a grounded theory

Access the websites of journals relevant to your discipline. If you lack familiarity with these journals, conduct an internet search using the name of your discipline along with the word 'journal'. Note the requirements indicated for each publication. How prescriptive are these guidelines? Do the journals indicate an impact factor? Is the journal available online and to whom is it made available? What specific guidelines (if any) does it provide for studies employing a grounded theory design?

Finally, do not limit the published products of your research to articles that present the final theory. Review or methodological papers discussing your research experience are also of value to the broader research and disciplinary community. Think about issues that have arisen in the process of data collection and analysis. Perhaps there are tools, strategies and techniques that you have developed in the process of undertaking your study. In what ways may you have contributed to the evolution of essential grounded theory methods? What have you learned from using a grounded theory research design that might be of value to researchers embarking on their own study? Furthermore, your background research may contribute to broader knowledge in the area. Often you may gather data in the process of your research that proved extraneous to your theory as it was developing. Such material makes excellent fodder for articles that will enhance your profile and extend the reach of your research activity.

Oral presentations

Most research students will be required to give an oral presentation at some stage of their candidature. Often the need to demonstrate the ability to undertake research is required in the early stages through confirmation of candidature seminars or colloquia. Later in their candidature, a student may be required to present an oral defence of their thesis or dissertation. Oral presentations are also a feature of many research seminars where students have the opportunity to present an overview of their project at various stages and obtain feedback from colleagues and supervisors. On completion of a study, dissemination of research findings through conference presentations provides an opportunity for interested individuals to hear your personal account of your study and ask questions of you in an open forum.

As a grounded theory researcher, you will therefore need to develop skills in the conduct of oral presentations. There is a vast number of resources to assist you with this and experience is an important factor in developing the necessary skills. We will, however, make some important points that have relevance to the presentation of grounded theory research. Be aware that in undertaking an oral presentation of your research, you are likely to face many of the same issues that we discussed in Chapter 2 in respect of the production of a written proposal. Those more familiar with other approaches to research may have difficulty understanding the inherent rationale of essential grounded theory methods. We recommend that you employ the same strategies that were suggested in relation to developing a proposal. Most importantly, be confident in your use of grounded theory as the research design for your study. Demonstrate an understanding of the rationale for concurrent data collection and analysis and the principles of theoretical sampling. Be sure to accept feedback on the weaker areas of your study and seek to address these as your research progresses.

On completion of your research, the approach you use to present your findings will be influenced by the principles of presentation discussed earlier in this chapter. Once again, your audience will determine the content and style of your presentation. The presentation of your grounded theory requires particular attention. As discussed in the previous chapter, the use of storyline is a means by which theory can be made more palatable, and this is particularly the case in presenting your research orally. Illustrative examples and descriptive stories can make an oral presentation more meaningful and memorable for the audience (Corbin & Strauss, 2008). The extent to which these are used will be determined by the overall purpose of your presentation. Be aware, however, that they should at all times remain a true reflection of your research.

 Activity 8.2

Oral presentation of grounded theory

Imagine that you need to prepare an oral presentation of a grounded theory study. How might you vary the structure and content of this for the purpose of an oral presentation:

- of your proposed study to a potential funding body?
- to provide evidence to an academic panel that you have required skills to undertake the research?
- in defence of your final thesis or dissertation to a university review board?
- at an international research methods conference?
- to a conference of professional colleagues seeking to improve practice in their professional area?

Illustrative modelling

In Chapter 6 we discussed the use of diagrams in grounded theory. The difference between a diagram and a model in grounded theory is that the former is a strategy for analysis, while the latter is a strategy for presentation. More generally a *model* can be defined as an abstract representation of reality that is not real (Pearson, Baughan, & Fitzgerald, 2005). Think of a model aircraft; it is an abstract representation of something much larger that we fly in from country to country. A model aircraft is not real in that it does not have the same capacity as that which it represents, but we can look at it and understand some of the component parts of larger aircraft. In the same way, illustrative modelling is used visually to represent the component parts of a grounded theory and, because of this, an explanation of the model needs to accompany it in the form of an abstract of the storyline or previously constructed outline.

When designing an illustrative model it is important to remember the various types of learning styles that readers bring to their assessment of your work, which can result in either an easy comprehension of your model, or the judgment that it is indecipherable (Birks et al., 2009). Strauss and Corbin (1998) argue that any visual representation of a grounded theory should contain minimal labels, lines and arrows, rather focusing on abstraction, logic and flow. If the core category of your grounded theory is a basic social process, then try to use shapes and positioning that meaningfully encapsulate a sense of flow.

The use of illustrative models is a relatively new strategy for the presentation of grounded theory findings, with the first- and second-generation grounded theorists focusing instead on diagramming as a method of analysis. Increasingly, however, grounded theorists are using models as a summative visual representation of their findings. A clear example can be found in Drury et al.'s (2008b) study of rural mature-aged students' experiences of becoming registered nurses. This grounded theory clearly delineates a three-step process: taking the first step; keeping going; and letting go and moving forward. The accompanying illustrative model (Figure 8.1) uses a simple shape and different colours to represent each step. Each of these design elements adds visual impact, while in the journal article the accompanying abstract from the researchers' storyline adds explanatory power.

 Activity 8.3

Differentiating between diagrams and models

Refer to the collection of journal articles you have used in previous activities. Do any of them purport to present a grounded theory model? Is the picture presented a model of the author's substantive grounded theory or is it really an analytical diagram? Is it accompanied by a succinct abstract of the storyline that explains how the component parts fit together?

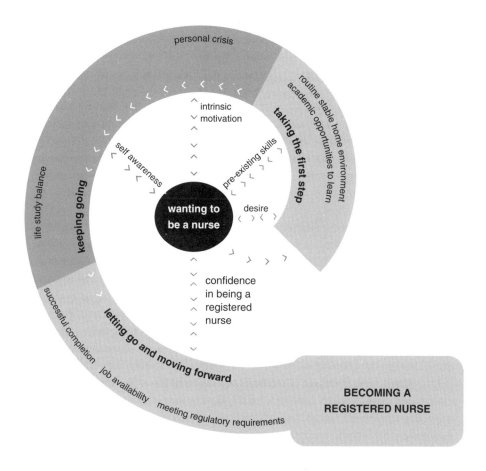

Figure 8.1 Becoming a registered nurse

Source: Drury, V., Francis, K., & Chapman, Y. (2008). Mature learners becoming registered nurses: a grounded theory model. *Australian Journal of Advanced Nursing, 26* (2), 39–45. Reprinted with permission of the *AJAN*.

Grounded theory studies that use techniques of situational analysis also use a type of illustrative modelling in the form of situational, social world and positional maps to present findings. It is important to consider, though, that given the postmodern positioning of researchers who fully integrate situational analysis methods into a grounded theory study, the intent of such visual representations is to be a work in progress as opposed to a 'final' product. In this case, situational mapping in all its forms is both a technique for analysis and a form of presentation. In Box 8.1, Perez and Cannella (In Press) relate their experience of using situational analysis mapping in a study of young children, charter schools and public education in New Orleans, post Hurricane Katrina.

BOX 8.1 WINDOW INTO GROUNDED THEORY

Michelle Perez and Gaile Cannella on the use of situational analysis

The use of situational analysis to construct maps as an activity in itself can sometimes feel binding and have a permanent sense, which is something that we wanted to avoid since the methodology is to be used as a post-modern tool. We wanted our maps from our work in New Orleans to serve as one point within an ongoing reflexive process that would be thought of as continuous, even at the 'conclusion' of the study. In other words, we did not intend the maps to serve as a final product, but rather provide representations of the discourses that could be considered as fluid and ever changing.

Since 'researcher as instrument' was an integral part of the map making process, living in New Orleans for two years (attending meetings, volunteering, participating in grassroots organizations, and being part of everyday life) allowed for our bodies to become immersed in the map making process.

Our 'messy maps' allowed us to bring together all of the aspects within, surrounding, and impacting the situation. This was an important aspect of our study as it gave us the flexibility to discuss and represent topics that would not necessarily become part of the primary focus of the situation but clearly had a profound impact on it.

The 'ordered maps' helped to create a larger view of the topics from our messy maps. This more detailed look into the discourses led us to multiple streams of information. We also found that a reworking of some of the major headings/sections in the ordered maps was necessary to communicate the power structures that were becoming more prevalent in the discourses.

Our 'social worlds/arenas map', which we renamed 'social spheres/power arenas map' to fit the context of our study, helped to communicate the organizations, individuals and groups that functioned as domains of power, and the way in which these arenas of power interacted with and marginalized particular organizations, people, and groups. It felt more fluid and less structured than our ordered map as it allowed us to communicate degrees of dominance and marginalization (and how these interacted) with the use of various shapes and lines.

Our 'positional map' was initially created in a two dimensional form but morphed into a three dimensional map. It represented the positions present in the situation on the face of the map (both positions that were dominantly and marginally present in the discourses). The three dimensional aspect allowed us to illustrate the positions that were left out of the conversation, or one could say that were present and impacting the situation, but not part of the discourses analysed.

Overall, our experience with mapping allowed for a way to work with the data, much like an artist might use various tools and methods to communicate and fashion their work. We were especially drawn to the use of situational analysis as a post-modern tool so that our creations would not be considered as concrete representations of the discourses but allow for an unveiling of power that could serve as one point of analysis and discussion.

Maximizing impact

Grounded theorists who work in the academy are cognisant of the current trend for reporting the impact of their research to their employers, governments and other funders of research. There is an ongoing dialogue in the literature that considers the questions of what constitutes impact, and how we measure it, with Morse (2006) and others (Cheek, Garnham, & Quan, 2006; Lather, 2004; Sandelowski, 2004) calling for reworking of the measures of scientific evidence (see Chapter 10). Cheek (2002) cites the work of Boyer in a treatise on the concept of scholarship and what that means for researchers in the academy. Rather than using scholarship as a 'catch all' title for the work of academics, Cheek uses Boyer's framework to articulate four defined areas that are useful when considering the production and presentation of findings. These areas are: the scholarship of discovery; the scholarship of integration; the scholarship of application; and the scholarship of teaching. Grounded theorists, like all researchers, have an ethical obligation to engage in each domain of scholarship in order to maximize the impact of their findings and subsequent recommendations. Discovery is just this first step of the research process, for unless findings are integrated into disciplinary knowledge they will not be applied in the form of recommendations or taught to future generations as theoretical advancement in the field. Charmaz (2006) believes emphatically that essential grounded theory methods have the potential to change the world for the better; however, this change can only occur if findings are presented in such a way that they can make an impact (Sandelowski, 2004).

Attracting attention is a very important aspect of disseminating a grounded theory with the aim of it being either directly applied to practice or taught for future application. Stern (2007) provides clear advice on the importance of developing a 'read-me title' (p. 121) that can capture the reader's notice. As a reader will often scan very long lists of results from an electronic search of a database, a read-me title is more easily spotted. Consider some of your *in vivo* codes during the process of naming a potential journal article to assist coming up with something appealing. In addition to the substantive area of enquiry, include the words 'grounded theory' in either the title or the keywords of your writing so that the reader is aware that this is the research design used.

At the end of a research study, one of the most challenging tasks is coming up with a comprehensive series of recommendations. This task becomes challenging not only because of the difficulty of writing such constructs, but because at this point the researcher is often quite close to being burnt out and exhausted. We suggest that you alleviate this by compiling a list of recommendations as these occur to you during the process of analysis. Often you will find that this is when these ideas are most likely to occur to you. Glaser (1978) suggests that it is useful to conclude the report of a grounded theory that has application for a discipline's practice with a series of recommendations. Wilson, Hutchinson and Holzemer (2002) provide an excellent example of how researchers can situate clear and useful recommendations in the context of contemporary literature and extant theory in their grounded theory of HIV medication adherence and symptom management.

Recommendations included a strong focus on health professional activities and possible outcomes that could result from a change in practice.

Conclusion

Presenting grounded theory findings in a way that increases their accessibility to potential readers is important in making a contribution to knowledge while developing a personal scholarship that has integrity and value. Adopting the principles of presentation described in this chapter will ensure dissemination of your grounded theory with maximum impact. The value that your research ultimately has in application will be determined by its quality. In the following chapter, this concept will be addressed as we discuss the evaluation and application of grounded theory.

 CRITICAL THINKING QUESTIONS

1   Consider your own experiences as a reader of research. By what means (for example, conference, journal publication, etc.) do you find you are most easily able to access findings? What are the implications for your own grounded theory research?

2   In what ways would it be possible to measure the impact of a grounded theory? How could you report on the impact of your study to an outside body?

3   Revise the principles of presenting a grounded theory. How would you incorporate these into a publication/presentation schedule for your grounded theory?

 WORKING GROUNDED THEORY

Review the 'Working grounded theory' example presented in Appendix A. Note:

- The means by which the research in this example was reported and presented.

- The relative reliance of this researcher on narrative presentation and illustrative modelling.

9   Evaluation and application of grounded theory

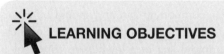

LEARNING OBJECTIVES

This chapter will help you to:

- Review arguments relating to evaluating quality and rigour in the conduct and presentation of research

- Outline traditional and evolved criteria for evaluating grounded theory research

- Describe the salient features of a quality grounded theory study

- Employ flexible criteria to evaluate grounded theory produced by self and others

- Devise strategies for the application of grounded theory research

- Discuss the concept of formal grounded theory and its relationship with substantive grounded theory

Introduction

Throughout this text we have described the essential grounded theory methods and discussed their use and application for the purpose of developing quality grounded theory. In this chapter, we will discuss evaluation of research generally and examine specific criteria for appraising grounded theory. While you will find the concepts discussed in this chapter useful for evaluating existing studies, we also encourage you to use the chapter to review the products and processes of your own grounded theory research. In this chapter we will also consider the application of grounded theory to your own disciplinary area, once the worth of such studies has been established. Finally, we will consider how the reach of grounded theory can be enhanced through the production of grounded theory at the formal level.

Current debates in evaluating research

In most instances, the only opportunity to evaluate a research study is on the basis of what is presented in published articles and summary reports. Many generic textbooks provide guidelines for the critique of published research studies, with most of these focusing on whether methodological strategies and techniques were correctly applied by the researcher when conducting the research. This is particularly the case in studies using quantitative data. The prescriptive objectivity required of the traditional scientific method provides a similarly structured framework for the evaluation of studies in which numerical data is the unit of analysis. The perceived value of objectivity by those who subscribe to a positivist paradigm has resulted in a devaluing of research that employs qualitative data sources. The debate over how research with a qualitative component can and should be evaluated has raged for decades. It is not our intention to rehash the substance of these debates, but as most grounded theories employ data of a qualitative nature, it is worthwhile briefly to review current arguments surrounding the evaluation of research.

The main premise of the positivist position is that research outcomes can be deemed accurate only if they are produced in situations and through methods and processes that are rigidly controlled. Measures to ensure that the results are valid (that is, they reflect the study variables accurately) and reliable (in that they are likely to be consistently accurate) are central to the issue of control. How rigidly various control measures are implemented will determine the extent to which we can rely on the research results. Often these concepts are reflected in *levels of evidence* tables that present guidelines for interpreting evidence within a hierarchical structure (Nagy et al., 2010). Levels of evidence tables are commonly used in disciplines where perceived reliability of research is critical. Evidence-based medicine and health care, for example, use levels of evidence tables to determine the value of research-derived interventions in practice. Invariably, systematic reviews and randomized control trials sit at the top of the hierarchy (CEBM, 2009; Joanna Briggs Institute, 2008; NHMRC, 2009). Positionality of evidence within these tables is arbitrary, however, as it is the research question, rather than the methodology, that ultimately determines what value is placed on research outcomes within such frameworks (Nagy et al., 2010; Sandelowski, 2008).

The suggestion that quantitative methods are superior due to greater attention to issues of validity and reliability implies that the treatment of qualitative data lacks rigour. The perception that qualitative research is not rigorous results from the lack of concrete procedural rules and predetermined processes and criteria (Goulding, 2002) and a belief by some that postmodernist approaches in particular are simply a relaxation of the scientific rules (Rolfe, 2006a). As a result, there is a tendency for research using qualitative data to be judged on the basis of a one-way comparison with quantitative data, with researchers subsequently apologising for any perceived shortcomings that are in fact simply differences between the two paradigms (Sandelowski, 2008). Rolfe (2006b) has argued that it is not constructive to dichotomize qualitative and quantitative research traditions for the purpose of evaluating the quality of a study. Perhaps this is no more evident than in the conduct of grounded theory research where it is ultimately processes that determine the relevance and value of data.

 Activity 9.1

Distinguishing qualitative and quantitative research

Ryan-Nicholls and Will (2009) assert that some researchers believe that qualitative and quantitative research methods are not mutually exclusive as characteristics of one are evident in the other. What do you think these authors mean by this statement? Can you identify any features of qualitative research that are evident in quantitative research? What relevance does this distinction (or lack of it) have for grounded theory studies?

Throughout this text we have reinforced the importance of being aware of your own philosophical position and its relevance for the ontological and epistemological foundations of your study. Some will argue that it is these very concepts that distinguish qualitative and quantitative research traditions, yet this distinction is not so clear cut (Rolfe, 2006b). It is therefore critical that you articulate these important perspectives on the world and your research, in order to demonstrate the quality of your research, regardless of whether qualitative, quantitative, or both types of data are used.

Evaluating grounded theory research

The above discussion confirms that the debate surrounding the evaluation of research, particularly that with a qualitative element, is alive and well. It is worth noting that it is these very concerns about quality in research that were the impetus behind the development of grounded theory methods. Through the publication of *Discovery*, Glaser and Strauss (1967), and later Strauss and Corbin (1990), proposed rigorous processes that would ensure the survival of approaches to research that did not fit a positivist model (Fielding, 2005; Wasserman et al., 2009).

In discussing the evaluation of grounded theory, we reassert our non-partisan approach to the conduct of this type of research and remind you that it is the quality of your data and how you apply grounded theory methods in its collection, generation and analysis that will determine whether your research will be deemed a quality study. When you attempt to judge the quality and value of grounded theory produced by others, or indeed when others evaluate the theory generated by you, certain specific criteria can be applied to aid in this process. In the following section we will discuss three approaches to evaluation that can assist you in judging the worth of a grounded theory: prima facie evaluation; evaluation using classic criteria; and comprehensive evaluation. Whether you are evaluating a grounded theory as a scholarly exercise or for the purpose of practical application (as discussed later in this chapter), you will find these guidelines will assist you. You need not apply them in a rigid or ordered manner; their value will be determined by the specific nature of the research and its intent (Corbin & Strauss, 2008). Draw from the following discussion what you need to enable you to appraise critically a grounded theory for your specific purpose.

Prima facie evaluation

Before we discuss more formal approaches to evaluation, it is useful to examine the assessment of grounded theory on the basis of face validity. From your own experience, you will be aware that your approach to reading and reviewing research and other published work is dependent on your reason for doing so. Some articles may require a cursory review of the abstract, while others require a thorough critical appraisal. This is also the case with the evaluation of grounded theory. Prima facie evaluation may be undertaken as a precursor to more formal evaluation, using approaches such as those described below, or you may use it to make a preliminary judgement about the value of a given study before investing further time in its review. Either way, you will find prima facie evaluation useful in that it will give you an overall feel for the quality of a piece of grounded theory research, either your own or that of another researcher.

Research that has been peer reviewed is, of course, likely to be more reliable than that which has not, yet do not assume that simply because a paper is published, it is credible. Notwithstanding publication limitations, a lot can be gleaned from assessing the overall quality of writing and expression. A lack of attention to detail in presentation can suggest similar failings in the actual conduct of the research. As we discussed in Chapter 2, a large number of published articles described as grounded theory research cannot legitimately make this claim. Most often, while the researchers may have employed grounded theory methods, there is a clear failure to move beyond a fundamental description of phenomena.

 Activity 9.2

Prima facie evaluation of grounded theory

Conduct a search of the literature for a study claiming to be grounded theory research, or refer to one you may have already collected. What is your initial perception of the value of this research? Does the general style and tone suggest a quality piece of work? On the face of it, do the stated aims seem appropriate to a grounded theory study? Do the researchers present a final theoretical scheme or at least indicate intent to generate theory? Is explanation of phenomena a key objective of this study or do the researchers simply state that their intention is to describe and/or explore?

Classic criteria

Glaser and Strauss's (1967) intent to address the perceived lack of rigour in research aiming to generate theory is evident in their identification of specific criteria for the evaluation of grounded theory. In this seminal text, these authors question the value of existing criteria for judging the credibility of theory generated directly from the data. Holton (2007) has more recently identified grounded theory as 'occupying its own distinct paradigm on the research landscape' (p. 267). Recognition of this fact has seen evaluation criteria evolve with the work of grounded theorists in recent decades. The most commonly cited approaches to judging grounded theory are summarized in Table 9.1.

Glaser and Strauss (1967) discuss evaluation in broad terms in their original work. Their emphasis on judging credibility, as is the case throughout the text, is on rigour in the application of strategies, techniques and methods for the purpose of producing theory that is accurately grounded in the data. Presentation of a clear, integrated theory that draws the reader in and provides evidence of logical conclusions and their relationship to the data is seen by these authors as the key element of a credible grounded theory. Glaser and Strauss (1967) do, however, acknowledge the difficulty that the researcher often faces in presenting a theory that can

Table 9.1 Classic approaches for judging grounded theory research

Glaser and Strauss (1967):	Glaser (1978):	Strauss and Corbin (1990):	Charmaz (2006):
Fit	Fit	Data quality	Credibility
Understandable	Work	Research process	Originality
General	Relevant	Empirical grounding	Resonance
Control	Modifiable		Usefulness
	Glaser (1992):	Strauss and Corbin (1998):	
	Fit	Data quality	
	Work	Theory quality	
	Relevant	Research process	
	Modifiable	Empirical grounding	
	Parsimony		
	Scope		
		Corbin and Strauss (2008):	
		10 basic criteria	
		13 additional criteria	

withstand critical appraisal within the limitations of standard publication parameters. They believe that the onus rests with both the researcher and the readers to use appropriate judgement to ensure that an accurate appraisal of published research is possible.

Glaser and Strauss (1967) discuss the criteria presented in Table 9.1 in the context of the application of grounded theory. As the practical applicability of grounded theory research is the ultimate measure of its value, appraisal in this context is appropriate. These authors suggest that the theory should demonstrate *fit* with the field of its intended use, should be *understandable* by those who work in the area, be *general* enough that it can be flexible in application while allowing the user *control* over its use. Glaser (1978) speaks of the need for grounded theory to have *fit* with respect to the theory fitting the data and states that the theory must also *work* in that it should possess explanatory and predictive power, therefore demonstrating *relevance*. These three criteria were presented in the first chapter of *Discovery* although not addressed in the level of detail that Glaser (1978) later devotes to their discussion. The criterion of *modifiability* was also added at this stage to accommodate later variation and ensure the continued relevance of a theory. In Box 9.1, Fei (2007) discusses the use of these criteria in ensuring quality in the conduct of his own research. This example reinforces the importance of being conscious of the concept of quality evaluation through the grounded theory research process, as discussed in Chapter 3.

 BOX 9.1 WINDOW INTO GROUNDED THEORY

Foster Fei on applying classic grounded theory evaluation criteria

My area of research interest has evolved from management education and learning in the classroom setting to management learning in the workplace. Such a change resulted from my own observation that many management theories taught in the classroom had no relevance to the field of practice. Like many researchers, I was exposed to an overwhelmingly large amount of extant literature before the fieldwork, as well as a range of research methodologies in social sciences. At that time, I was also quite critical of some of the methodologies, fearing that research conducted by adopting these methodologies would have no relevance for research participants. So at the early stage of my research journey, I was constantly searching for a way in which a degree of relevance could be maintained in both the substantive area of research and my chosen research methodology. Having noticed that some of the management theories taught in the classroom setting were not particularly relevant to practitioners, I was trying to find a way to disregard the existing literature and maintaining relevance in a methodological way. I then came across grounded theory and found it compatible with my past and present approaches to research, both substantively and methodologically. Thus, I attended the seminars and did my reading while doing the research and was determined to do an orthodox grounded theory study, using it as a full methodological package.

I was also aware of other versions of this methodology and their critiques. It was a conscious choice of mine to maintain research rigour by doing an orthodox grounded theory study and adhering to its tenets and procedures. It was important to me that those who would judge my work would find that it met the classic criteria of evaluation: relevance, fit, workability and modifiability. I began without any specific focus, but a general area of research interest in management learning in the workplace. I also made sure that the research problem and questions had reflected the main concern of the research partic-ipants, as well as how it was constantly resolved. By fit, it meant that the core category – 'resourcing change' as well as its categories and dimensions had adequately expressed the pattern in the data. Participants' main concern was how to deal with challenges in their initiation of changes as learning at work. I then listed a number of challenges facing managers in one UK subsidiary within each of two multinational corporations and their resolutions, compared them with the existing literature and conceptualised them at a more abstract level. In doing so, it was intended to attain workability – the core category, categories, dimensions and the theoretical discussions that followed suffi-ciently accounted for the continual resolution of their main concern. During the iterative process of data collection and analysis, I demonstrated evidence of modifiability by comparing emergent concepts and theory with new data and subsequently modifying them towards a more abstract and conceptual direc-tion. My attention to these elements was intended to ensure that they would be evident in the final theory, allowing it to withstand evaluation using Glaser's (1978) classic criteria.

Strauss and Corbin (1990) provide a comprehensive discussion of evaluation in their initial text. These authors identify *data quality*, the *research process* and *empirical grounding* of the final theory as being key elements for judgement, with several specific criteria being provided in relation to the latter two points. This discussion did not escape critique from Glaser's (1992) rebuttal, in which he restated his earlier four precepts as the essential criteria for evaluating grounded theory. He also included concepts of *parsimony* and *scope* in explanatory power as additional criteria, elements that had also been touched on in a broader context in earlier work.

In the follow-up edition of *Basics of qualitative research*, Strauss and Corbin (1998) expand little on their previous work in relation to evaluation, adding the additional criterion of making judgements about the theory itself and expanding the discussion of empirical grounding to include the need for the theory to stand the test of time. It is interesting that Juliet Corbin's treatment of the issue of evaluation in the third edition of this text (Corbin & Strauss, 2008) is different from that of the earlier versions when Strauss was at the helm. Greater attention is given to the concept of

LIVERPOOL JOHN MOORES UNIVERSITY
LEARNING SERVICES

quality in research, particularly in respect of process and researcher attributes. New criteria are presented for judging grounded theory research and the lists of criteria presented in the first and second editions are combined to form additional criteria. While it is not clear what distinction exists between these two lists, we can perhaps consider the basic criteria as being of value in appraising the theoretical outcome (the sum of the parts), with the additional criteria being useful for judging issues of structure and process (the parts themselves).

Charmaz (2006) reasserts the importance of applying evaluation criteria in accordance with purpose and context. She simplifies the issue of evaluation by reducing the process to four criteria: *credibility*, which reflects logic and conceptual grounding; *originality*, including reference to the significance of the study; *resonance*, which considers the need for the theory to have meaning and scope for all those for whom it may be relevant; and *usefulness*, in relation to knowledge development and practical application. Of these, Charmaz (2006) considers that credibility and originality spawn resonance and usefulness. Ultimately, as she points out, the outcome of any evaluation is enhanced through quality articulation and presentation of the final theory.

Comprehensive evaluation

In reading the preceding section you have seen that traditional grounded theorists have emphasized either the applicability of a grounded theory, or the processes by which it was derived. We suggest that a comprehensive evaluation will go beyond these elements to include factors identified in Chapter 3 as being critical to quality in grounded theory research (Figure 9.1). To assist you in applying these criteria, questions addressing each domain are presented in Table 9.2. Your use of these questions will be modified in accordance with the purpose of your evaluation and the nature of the study you are examining. A study purporting to have generated grounded theory, for example, will have a greater obligation to respond positively to the questions posed than one that employs grounded theory methods in the context of a diverse study design.

 Activity 9.3

Comprehensive evaluation of grounded theory

Return to the paper you reviewed in Activity 9.2. Undertake a comprehensive review of this article using the criteria presented in Table 9.2. What does your evaluation reveal? Compare it with the prima facie evaluation undertaken earlier. How does your preliminary assessment compare with your application of the comprehensive evaluation criteria?

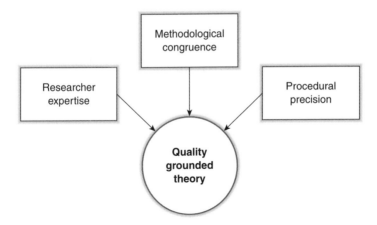

Figure 9.1 Factors influencing quality in the conduct of grounded theory research

Table 9.2 Criteria for evaluating grounded theory research

Domain	Criteria	Yes/no
Researcher expertise	Does the researcher demonstrate skills in scholarly writing?	
	Is there evidence that the researcher is familiar with grounded theory methods?	
	Has the researcher accessed and presented citations of relevant methodological resources?	
	Are limitations in the study design and research process acknowledged and addressed where possible?	
Methodological congruence	Has the researcher articulated their philosophical position?	
	Is grounded theory an appropriate research strategy for the stated aims of the study?	
	Do the outcomes of the research achieve the stated aims?	
	Is a grounded theory presented as the end product of the research?	
	Are philosophical and methodological inconsistencies identified and addressed?	
Procedural precision	Is there evidence that the researcher has employed memoing in support of the study?	
	Has the researcher indicated the mechanisms by which an audit trail was maintained?	
	Are procedures described for the management of data and resources?	
	Is there evidence that the researcher has applied the essential grounded theory methods appropriately in the context of the study described?	

(Continued)

Table 9.2 *(Continued)*

Domain	Criteria	Yes/no
	Does the researcher make logical connections between the data and abstractions?	
	Is there evidence that the theory is grounded in the data?	
	Is the final theory credible?	
	Are potential applications examined and explored?	

Undertaking an evaluation of the work of others is not only necessary when considering the potential application of grounded theory, but is also an important exercise in developing your skills as a researcher. Be constructively critical in your appraisal of the work of others, but also remember that reflective evaluation of your own work is essential to ensure that the grounded theory you produce has merit and potential practical value. While research reports, dissertations and theses often include an evaluation of completed grounded theory, constraints of space in professional journals limit the potential for the inclusion of self-critique in most publications. You may, however, see papers discussing research methods that address the issue of evaluation specifically. One such example is provided by Chiovitti and Piran (2003) who evaluate rigour in their own study of psychiatric nurses' meaning of caring for patients. Through transparent application of evaluation criteria, these researchers demonstrate accountability of themselves and the credibility of their study. Adopt this level of transparency in your own research. Be your own critic first, address the limitations of your work and produce research outputs that are credible and engender respect from others and pride in yourself.

Application of grounded theory

Rarely is grounded theory generated to produce knowledge for the sake of knowledge alone. Theories constructed through the use of grounded theory methods aim to provide understanding of a phenomenon that will ultimately inform practice in a given discipline. When considering application of grounded theory, either one that you have generated or the work of others, you will need to: ensure that the theory is credible; confirm its relevance to your own situation; tailor it accordingly; and develop and implement a plan for sustainable change (Figure 9.2).

The preceding sections in this chapter discuss the evaluation of grounded theory and provide guidance for establishing the quality and worth of published work. The method and focus of your evaluation are likely to be different when appraising a particular grounded theory for a specific purpose, as opposed to when evaluating a study generally. Glaser and Strauss (1967) originally proposed that a good grounded theory will be sensitized to a particular situation, yet would be flexible and open to reformulation in static or changing environments. Glaser (2007) argues that categories in grounded theory are abstract enough to be non-context dependent and are therefore contextualized during application. Do not, however, confuse this

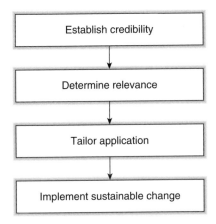

Figure 9.2 Applying grounded theory research

flexibility with broad generalizability. General applicability is a characteristic of formal grounded theory that will be discussed later in this chapter.

A grounded theory may not necessarily be applied in its totality; the insights gleaned from the theoretical renderings of this type of research can spark new ideas, initiate changes and reform thinking. The extent to which you are able to apply the products of any research will be determined by the identification of elements that have relevance and meaning to your specific situation. Your earlier evaluation of a grounded theory may also raise your awareness of specific aspects that are more credible, and your comfort in applying only these outcomes to your own situation may therefore be greater.

Little has been written on the practicalities of applying grounded theory (although Glaser (2007) has identified potential applications of formal grounded theory, as discussed below). While a chapter was devoted to applying grounded theory in *Discovery* (Glaser & Strauss, 1967), this work, as referred to above, essentially focuses on appraising elements of the theory with a view to application. This emphasis reinforces the relationship between evaluation and application. Note that it is possible to evaluate a grounded theory without intention to apply it (such as in the course of an academic exercise); however, application without evaluation is clearly ill advised.

Once you have established that the grounded theory you propose to use is credible, has relevance to your intended area of application and can be tailored for your specific purpose, you will need to develop a practical strategy for implementation. When attempting to apply grounded theory research, you are likely to confront the same issues as are raised in the implementation of evidence-based change generally. Whether your intended application takes the form of policy change, practice change or knowledge development (Corbin & Strauss, 2008), you will no doubt face challenges. Box 9.2 identifies a process for implementing and sustaining evidence-based change from a practical perspective. While these guidelines are developed in relation to research generally, they nonetheless have relevance to the application of grounded theory research.

BOX 9.2 IMPLEMENTING AND SUSTAINING CHANGE FROM GROUNDED THEORY RESEARCH FINDINGS

1 Ensure a need for the change exists.
2 Identify potential barriers and enablers to the proposed change.
3 Explore existing theories, frameworks and models that may have relevance to the proposed change.
4 Develop an implementation plan in consultation with key stakeholders.
5 Implement the plan.
6 Evaluate the outcome. (Adapted from Nagy et al., 2010)

Enhancing applicability: Substantive versus formal theory

As this book is designed for the neophyte grounded theorist, chances are your only experience of this form of research is in the development or implementation of a study that relates to a specific phenomenon in the context of a clearly identified group of individuals. Such research is regarded as *substantive* as it is produced for the purpose of understanding a tangible phenomenon in a clearly defined situation (Glaser & Strauss, 1967). Hypothetically, for example, you might develop a theory of 'immersed socialization of medical interns to the professional role', describing a process of disciplinary adaptation for this particular group. Most of the grounded theories you will uncover through searching the literature will also be substantive grounded theories. *Formal* grounded theory, on the other hand, is theory developed to a higher conceptual level. These types of theories have applicability across a number of substantive areas due to their higher level of abstraction and generalization of concepts (Charmaz, 2006).

Kearney (2007) identifies a number of formal grounded theories produced by Glaser and Strauss, and describes some produced by others, although she employs quite a broad definition of what constitutes formal grounded theory in contemporary terms. Glaser (2007) acknowledges only one formal grounded theory originating from his work with Strauss, that being *Status passage* published in 1971. The concept of 'awareness contexts', derived from Glaser and Strauss's (1965) research into dying in hospitals, is an often cited example of a potential formal grounded theory that was never developed and presented as such (Kearney, 2007). In this research, the potential for awareness contexts to be elevated to the level of formal theory is discussed at length, with examples given of awareness contexts beyond dying in hospitals that include hustling, impersonation, spying and selling cars (Glaser & Strauss, 1965). Reference to awareness contexts outside of the original study is testament to the meticulous application of method and insightful identification of the potential broader application of this research. It is perhaps also an example of ad hoc production of formal theory by less formal means.

 Activity 9.4

Formal grounded theory

You are probably familiar with Elizabeth Kubler-Ross's (1973) theory of stages of dying. This theory has seen wide application beyond its original intended substantive area. Conduct a search of your library to identify how this theory was raised from substantive to formal level by later work of Kubler-Ross and others. Investigate the diversity of other applications of this theory evident in the published literature. Note also that this work has drawn criticism from others. What impact has later contradictory work had on the credibility and status of Kubler-Ross's original research as formal grounded theory?

Both substantive and formal theories have greater value if derived from (and therefore grounded in) data relevant to the intended area of application (Glaser & Strauss, 1967; Mullen, 2006). Glaser and Strauss (1967) suggest that too often a researcher will use language in a single study to imply applicability beyond the substantive area. In your theory of medical interns, for example, you may simply choose to present your theory as 'immersed socialization to the professional role', suggesting a theory that is derived from, and applicable to, professional groups generally. Nothing has been done to extend your theory over and above the substantive area of your study and its applicability to the broader environment has therefore not been established (Glaser, 1978).

While it is possible for a single study to generate formal grounded theory, most examples you will see are derived from existing substantive theory (Glaser & Strauss, 1967). In such cases, the core category of a substantive grounded theory is expanded through additional data (Glaser, 2007). Concepts from existing developed theories, along with new raw data, are identified through theoretical sampling and are analytically compared with the original substantive grounded theory (Glaser, 1978). If you were to develop your theory of 'immersed socialization', for example, you might seek out other studies that address professional adaption among other groups and generate or collect new data as theoretical sampling principles dictate. Through this expanded analysis, the reach of the resultant theory is extended and its value, credibility and applicability are enhanced.

Glaser and Strauss originally identified the need for more attention to the development of formal grounded theory in their early work in *Awareness of dying* (Glaser & Strauss, 1965) and again in *Discovery* (Glaser & Strauss, 1967), with Glaser (2007) lamenting the lack of attention paid to the development of formal grounded theory four decades later. In this later work, Glaser identifies a number of potential uses for formal grounded theory including increasing knowledge and understanding, correcting and extending existing theory and enhancing academic activities. In spite of the solid arguments supporting the value of formal grounded theory presented in these texts, there remain limited examples of grounded theories that have been raised from the substantive to the formal level. Goulding (2002) suggests that the time and costs associated with the generation of formal grounded theory are major barriers to most researchers moving beyond substantive theory generation.

Conclusion

Correct application of essential grounded theory methods is time intensive and intellectually demanding. The end product should therefore justify the resources, time, energy and effort invested in its production. This chapter has provided guidance for the evaluation and application of grounded theory to assist you in ensuring that the outcome of your research will have a positive impact on the individuals and environments to be most likely affected by your work. Evaluation and application of grounded theory are not afterthoughts to be considered on completion of your research; rather, they are goals that must be at the forefront of your thinking during the conduct of your study. Your ability to remain focused on these goals will determine the ultimate worth of your final grounded theory.

 CRITICAL THINKING QUESTIONS

1 Review the discussion above concerning current debate about the evaluation of research. What relevance do you think this has to the contemporary grounded theorist?

2 Consider the criteria proposed by grounded theorists for evaluating grounded theory outlined in Tables 9.1 and 9.2 of this chapter. Note how these criteria have evolved over the decades. What influences do you think have driven this evolution?

3 In this chapter we have identified some barriers to the development of formal theory. What other factors can you think of that have limited the amount of formal theory that we have seen developed from substantive grounded theory?

>> **WORKING GROUNDED THEORY**

Review the 'Working grounded theory' example presented in Appendix A. Note:

- The importance placed by this researcher on the evaluation of her own grounded theory.

- The criteria she employed in evaluating her work and the sources from which these were derived.

- Her reference to the application of the outcomes of her research (both methodologically and substantively) by herself and others.

10 Situating grounded theory in the context of current debate

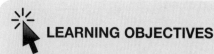

LEARNING OBJECTIVES

This chapter will help you to:

1 Define research evidence in the context of varying methodological positions

2 Discuss strategies to increase knowledge diffusion and utilization from grounded theory

3 Outline the challenges of competitive research funding for grounded theorists

4 Identify the contribution that essential grounded theory methods can make to contemporary paradigms of interpretive research

Introduction

We conclude this text by considering the contemporary face of grounded theory research and where it fits in the current research environment. Grounded theory has significantly influenced the research landscape of many disciplines in the last half century. Grounded theory methods have themselves evolved through the work of generations of researchers who believe in its continuing potential. Debates about how evidence is defined, how research is funded and the role of grounded theory within evolving paradigms of research are of interest in this discussion, as are potential new frontiers for grounded theory in the future.

The changing face of grounded theory research

The world today is a far different place than it was in 1967. We now communicate in ways that were unimaginable in this not so distant past. The internet and email connect us to the global community in such a way that we live in a 'woven world of distant encounters and instant connections' (Yergin & Stanislaw, 1998: 9). Such changes have implications for the type of research conducted. In years gone by, a researcher would often need to travel large distances to access published material and unpublished theses in support of their study. Undertaking a grounded theory study using concurrent data collection and analysis techniques meant that it was often necessary to return to the field to access data sources that were available only in hard copy. In the early days the field was, in fact, the field. Today the field may be a virtual environment, which, coupled with the accessibility of literature via online databases, reduces the need to travel or to search manually and access materials and individuals to support a research study.

 Activity 10.1

Research in the twenty-first century

What implications does the availability of technology have for research in the contemporary environment? Given that the process of undertaking a study is now aided by technology, what does this suggest for the end product of research? Should the researcher be expected to produce research outcomes in less time with less associated cost? Or should funding bodies and academic institutions expect a higher standard of research than was produced in the past?

Living within a global context has also impacted on the nature of studies that we undertake. Globalization has resulted in our changing the way we frame research questions. No longer do we only consider the local as a possible area of substantive enquiry, rather we think nationally and internationally when designing our grounded theory studies. At the same time that our global reach is expanding, qualitative researchers are living in a time of uncertainty, brought about by a conservative move towards redefining the production of evidence as solely the province of positivistic science (Denzin, 2009). It is therefore necessary to clarify how evidence can be defined in order to understand the implications that this situation has for the contemporary grounded theorist.

The question of evidence

At different points in this book, we have reflected on the genesis of grounded theory in an environment that was concerned with the accuracy of facts and the testing of theory in order to verify a 'truth'. Glaser and Strauss (1967) challenged researchers to move beyond 'too great an adherence to verification as the chief mandate for excellent research' (p. 2), and instead prioritize generating theory grounded in data. Since that time, grounded theorists have rigorously incorporated essential grounded theory methods into research designs based on their philosophical and methodological position, leading to innovation in the application of these methods in the generation of theory.

Over the past 43 years, grounded theorists have produced a large amount of evidence that contributes to bodies of knowledge about a range of substantive areas of enquiry. However, in many ways we have turned full circle to find ourselves facing many of the issues that Glaser and Strauss confronted in the late 1960s. The question of what constitutes evidence has never gone away, the paradigm wars of the 1980s stand testament to that; however, it appears that as we enter the second decade of the new millennium, our focus once more needs to shift to ways of successfully competing with researchers who position themselves as positivistic scientists.

For many policy makers, funders of research, faculty deans and researchers, the question of what counts as evidence is easy to answer – findings from a randomized control trial, or better still a systematic review of randomized control trials. Philosophically, such a position is positivistic in the way it conceives of a singular truth that can be deducted through the careful testing of various hypotheses. Now this is fine, if you want to know about things such as the outcome of using acyclovir for treating varicella in otherwise healthy children and adolescents, or the effect of hospital-at-home services on reducing admissions to hospital. However, life is often much messier than systematic reviews of randomized controlled trials might lead us to believe, and it is this need for solutions to messy situations that has generated a debate in the literature about how we legitimize and value research evidence (Forbes, 2003; Gerrish, 2003; Mantzoukas, 2007; Rolfe, Segrott, & Jordan, 2008; Walker, 2003).

The perceived value of these forms of evidence is reinforced through levels of evidence tables. At the top of this hierarchical pyramid sits the revered systematic review of randomized control trials, while research without experimental study, such as grounded theory, are positioned beneath this 'gold standard'. The problem with arranging categories of evidence in this way is that it overtly devalues interpretive findings as poor evidence for practice, regardless of the quality of the study that produced them.

In recent times, open warfare has been raging about the value of levels of evidence and this is particularly so in health care, where the term 'evidence-based practice' is now mainstream. On one side of this intellectual debate we have scholars such as Mantzoukas (2007) who argue that because 'daily practice is much closer to the interpretive or postmodern paradigms … the validity and value of evidence ought to be considered by the criteria of these paradigms' (p. 219), while there is a strong counterargument for the use of the traditional positivistic scientific method as opposed to alternative methods of enquiry to develop a competitive evidence base (Watson, 2003). Reading the work of many authors who are engaging in this debate, it becomes clear that the question of what constitutes science, and as a result evidence, is for all researchers tied to the philosophical and methodological position that they assume (Pearson, 2004).

Knowledge diffusion and utilization

Throughout the text, methods to ensure the quality of a grounded theory study have been emphasized. There are three elements that must be accounted for in a quality grounded theory study: researcher expertise, methodological congruence and procedural precision (see Chapter 3). As discussed previously, each of these elements is important; however, in particular the rigorous application of essential grounded theory methods, or in other words procedural precision, will result in high-quality evidence for use in the substantive area of enquiry and beyond. How then is it possible to increase the effectiveness of what is referred to as knowledge diffusion and utilization? This becomes a question that grounded theorists need to consider in order to increase the value of their research findings. Some suggested strategies for increasing a researcher's capacity to promote knowledge diffusion and utilization from their grounded theory are (Vingilis et al., 2003):

- Viewing research as a means and not as an end.

- Embracing a transdisciplinary research team.

- Bringing the university and researcher to the community.

- Identifying research translators in the substantive area of enquiry.

Considering the format of your findings, and the audience that will read them, will also increase their potential for knowledge diffusion and utilization. The use of research evidence for practice is a growing trend in policy work; however, Jewell and Bero's (2008) investigation of the facilitators and hindrances to evidence-informed health policy making found that the context of government was not always conducive to accessing and systematically analysing research findings. Furthermore, features of the political process affect how research findings are incorporated into policy and often the 'power of anecdotes' (Jewell & Bero, 2008: 190) and media campaigns carry more weight as sources of evidence than a carefully constructed research report.

Institutional characteristics such as different levels of government, fragmented service provision and access to resources are also very important influences on how policy makers conceptualize evidence as a source of knowledge for their work. Issues that make it hard for managers and policy makers to use research evidence when making decisions are: that there is too much evidence, not enough good evidence, evidence does not quite apply, people are trying to mislead you, and that, really, stories are more persuasive anyway (Pfeffer & Sutton, 2006).

A grounded theory possesses both persuasive explanatory power and the potential for application. These characteristics provide the researcher with a theory that has the potential to grab (Glaser & Strauss, 1967) a manager's or policy maker's attention, thereby increasing the chance of knowledge diffusion and utilization. Careful consideration of strategies to bring the university and researcher to the community and identifying a research translator or champion in a particular environment can also promote the adoption of a grounded theory as rigorous evidence that can have a positive impact on practice. Nowadays it is not enough to undertake a grounded theory study and rely on the dissemination of findings through peer review journals. Rather, our current funding milieu creates an impetus for the active application of findings that will result in a measurable impact. Meeting this challenge is one that all researchers find difficult, but a careful assessment of the disciplinary environment coupled with a multi-pronged approach to the dissemination of findings in a variety of formats will help (see Chapter 8) to get your message across.

Competitive research funding

For those of you at the beginning of your research career, it is hard to envisage a time when you might be a postdoctoral or even career researcher. Successfully completing doctoral studies trains you to be a competent researcher able to manage future funded research studies. So when it comes to competing with others for competitive research grants and tenders, what does it mean to be a grounded theorist?

Grounded theorists predominantly classify themselves as qualitative researchers, although by now your growing familiarity with essential grounded theory methods has no doubt led to the realization that this is not always the case. A general perception of grounded theory being an interpretive method with positivistic undertones also contributes to an image of what Denzin (2009) calls a model of 'good science' (p. 103). Being recognized as good science means grounded theory possesses a level of credibility that other more ethereal approaches to research do not. In the world of competitive research funding, however, this is often not enough. Those who review research funding applications may have only a superficial knowledge of grounded theory research designs, which results in their becoming confused about a lack of specificity of either research questions or hypotheses, and sample size. Other reviewers who do have a deeper understanding often equate grounded theory with lengthy periods of data generation or collection and analysis, thus making it unsuitable to fund for short-term studies. Even though this seems a rather depressing scenario, there is a place for grounded theory in competitive research. It is very much a case, however, of coming to grips with the realization that 'the type of funding sought affects the type of research that can be done' (Cheek, 2005: 390).

In the case of large competitive research grants funded for a minimum of three years, a grounded theory study can fit into a larger programme of research addressing the substantive area of enquiry. This is a particularly useful strategy for funding PhD candidates, or creating employment for postdoctoral fellows. Findings are reported both as a stand-alone study and in relation to findings from other concurrent studies being implemented as part of the wider project. It is usual for chief investigators on such grant applications to supervise or mentor the novice researcher in these roles. For the chief investigator, including a grounded theory study implemented by a PhD candidate or postdoctoral fellow in a larger programme of research is a cost-effective way of undertaking research that might otherwise not be funded.

 Activity 10.2

Competitive funding for grounded theory research

Search the internet, or obtain from your own academic or professional organization, information about potential funding sources for research. What criteria are established for the funding of studies from these sources? To what extent do the identified funding requirements reflect the discussion above? Reflect on the study you are undertaking or are considering undertaking in the future. Is it likely that your study would qualify for funding from any of these sources?

Now try searching for currently or recently funded research grants that include a grounded theory study. Different countries have national research bodies that publish funded studies that you may find helpful. Consider how successful researchers frame their grounded theory study to be successful in receiving competitive grants.

Grounded theory and mixed methods research

Given the discussion above, it is clear that grounded theorists face a number of challenges within the changing context of research. Mixed methods research designs have become much more palatable in this political environment, with the 'incompatibility thesis' (Denzin, 2009: 17) being destabilized by the blessing of methodological blurring between quantitative and qualitative methods of data generation and collection.

In Chapter 2 we discussed the selective use of essential grounded theory methods in diverse research designs, with a particular focus on mixed methods studies. Morse and Niehaus (2009) define this type of research design as 'the use of two (or more) research methods in a single study, when one (or more) of the methods is not complete in itself' (p. 9). Although this definition is a contested one (Johnson, Onwuegbuzie, & Turner, 2007), it fits well with the idea of using selected essential grounded theory methods in a mixed methods research design. While the idea of mixing methods of data collection has been a recurring theme in the research literature over time (Teddlie & Tashakkori, 2003) it has experienced a recent increase in popularity. Morse and Niehaus (2009) attribute this increase in attractiveness to it being easier to get quantitative research funded as opposed to qualitative research. Therefore, for those planning to investigate a substantive area of enquiry using a qualitative approach, considering a combination of quantitative and qualitative methods, with a dominant quantitative core, may be a practical way to increase the chance of being funded. This reflects our earlier discussion about how research evidence produced from different methodological paradigms is valued in the wider community.

There are many examples of mixed methods studies that have drawn upon essential grounded theory methods in the research design (for example, Cotterill, Norton, Avery, Abrams, & Donovan, 2008; Scott & Sutton, 2009; Scott et al., 2007; Sosulski & Lawrence, 2008). Of these methods, the most widely adopted appear to be concurrent data generation or collection and analysis, and theoretical sampling. In one study of the long-term benefits of pain management, the reason for not using grounded theory as the overall research design was the researchers' perception of grounded theory being a 'pure inductive process' (Kennett, O'Hagan, & Cezer, 2008: 322), which, you will be aware from your reading of Chapter 7, is clearly not the case.

Does a grounded theory research design not have the potential to be a mixed methods study in and of itself, being as it is that 'all is data' (Glaser, 1978)? Morse and Niehaus (2009) argue for a typology of mixed methods research designs where data can be generated or collected simultaneously or sequentially with either a core qualitative or quantitative theoretical thrust. They also discuss a form of contingency planning that meets the need for supplemental data in a research design, should it be that 'during the course of the inquiry, interesting or unexpected phenomena are revealed' (p. 41). This is termed an emergent mixed methods study, possessing strong echoes of Morse's history as a grounded theorist (Morse et al., 2009).

Clearly, however, the flexibility of grounded theory and the fact that it is not a methodology, but rather a *whole package of methods* anchored by the researcher's philosophical and methodological position, means that the only role for grounded theory in this zeitgeist research movement is in a multiple methods project, which is 'a series of inter-related studies conducted to address one programmatic aim' (Morse & Niehaus, 2009: 147). Sandelowski clarifies why it is that the mixed qualitative and quantitative methods of data generation and collection do not by themselves constitute a mixed methods study when she states that 'it is the distinctive execution and representation of these methods that signal key differences in inquiry' (2003: 324). The quality of your grounded theory study design is based on its methodological congruence (as we discussed in Chapter 3). Ensuring accordance between your personal philosophical position, the stated aims of your research and the methodological approach you employ to achieve these aims will account for the employment of data generation and/or collection techniques. These may include qualitative and quantitative sources, or they may not; either way grounded theory subsumes the notion of mixed methods through the simple elegance of its design where each of the essential methods locks together as one and all is data.

Contemporary paradigms of interpretive research

Reaching the end of the first decade of the twenty-first century brings us to a point in time where the paradigm wars that dominated interpretive research are no longer so fraught. Rather than being at war, we are entering a time of dialogue between paradigms (Denzin, 2009) that has an overriding concern for how research-ers 'can help change the world in positive ways' (Denzin & Lincoln, 2005: x). Grounded theorists are extremely well positioned to march to the beat of this drum should they choose to address substantive areas of enquiry concerned with issues of difference. Clarke (2005) voices the thoughts of many when she states that the workings of difference include but are not limited to injustice in the areas of 'gender, race, class, age, sexuality, transgender, ethnicity, nationality/ism, colonialism, imperialism' (p. 74).

In light of contemporary paradigms of interpretive research, the possibilities for grounded theory research are endless. Two areas of growing significance to the grounded theory researcher are research designs based on social justice and indigenous methodologies. Denzin and Lincoln's (2008) statement that 'it is time to chart a new decade, the Decade of Critical, Indigenous Inquiry' (p. ix) and the recent publication of the *Handbook of critical and Indigenous methodologies* has brought this arena in particular to the forefront of thinking about interpretive research. The flexibility of essential grounded theory methods creates the opportunity for contributing to this new movement.

Social justice

This text's reoccurring motif of positioning yourself philosophically and method-ologically is closely tied to enacting a grounded theory driven by a social justice agenda. Conceptually, social justice is not 'susceptible to a single simple definition' (Anderson et al., 2009: 287), rather it is an ethical and moral principle of justice embodied in human rights (Office of the High Commissioner for Human Rights, 2009). A grounded theory study begins with a substantive area of enquiry and within this is an identified unit of analysis or a research aim and associated questions that focus the researcher's attention. Making choices about the substantive area of enquiry is motivated by a range of factors that include the researcher's level of interest, the purpose of the research, the place of the research in relation to other concomitant studies if part of a larger programme of research, potential funding sources, and developing trends. Locating a substantive area of enquiry that is troubled by social justice concerns is as easily incorporated into a grounded theory research design as any other.

Edwards and Jones's (2009) study of college men's gender identity development is an outstanding example of a grounded theory study overtly framed by a social justice perspective. The aim of the study was to gain an understanding of the processes men enrolled at university use to manage internalized patriarchy. Using essential grounded theory methods, researchers identified a core category, 'performing masculinity', which included three fully realized and integrated categories: 'putting on a mask', why men perform masculinity; 'wearing a mask', how men perform masculinity; and the 'consequences of wearing a mask' that includes a sub-category of 'struggling to begin to take off the mask'. One of the important outcomes of this study was participants finding the interview process to be a critical event for how they acted as men. The findings were presented using a strong and meaningful metaphor, 'the mask of society's expectation of them as men' (p. 221), which became a powerful tool for renewed change in these participants' lives, resulting in affirmative action by some to shift away from living out a traditional hegemonic image of masculinity. As Charmaz (2005) states, and Edwards and Jones (2009) demonstrate, 'a social justice researcher can use grounded theory to anchor agendas for future action, practice, and policies in the *analysis* by making explicit connections between the theorized antecedents, current conditions, and consequences of major processes' (p. 512).

Clarke's work (2005) on bringing the situation of a grounded theory study to the forefront of analysis has created important tools for analysis that researchers concerned with explicating action and process concerned with social justice issues need to consider, including in their design. Critical social justice makes explicit the 'mutually constitutive social processes that shape individual experience' (Anderson et al., 2009: 287), a concern shared and addressed by Clarke (2005) through the use of situational, social worlds/arenas and positional mapping in a grounded theory study.

Indigenous research methodologies

Indigenous research methodologies are 'research by and for Indigenous peoples, using techniques and methods drawn from the traditions of those peoples' (Evans, Hole, Berg, Hutchinson, & Sookraj, 2009: 894). That research methods used within an indigenous methodology are cognisant of context is therefore integral to the study and the final research product needs to reflect this thinking. Grounded theory studies underpinned by an indigenous methodology are rare, with methods that have an explicit critical intent such as participatory action research being more commonly used (Evans et al., 2009). This state of affairs is possibly because of grounded theory's historical link to post-positivism (Mantzoukas, 2004) and the still currently stated intent of some (Glaser, 2002) to generate theory so highly abstract that it becomes totally decontextualized. As we have explored in each of the preceding chapters, the way that you choose to use essential grounded theory methods shapes the final product and unless you are conducting a formal grounded theory study, this product needs always to be grounded in the substantive area of enquiry. As novice indigenous researchers struggle to find their academic voice (Potgieter & Smit, 2009), the absence of an indigenous role model who is a grounded theorist is more likely a barrier to choosing grounded theory than the methods themselves.

In studies of substantive areas of enquiry related to indigenous people, essential grounded theory methods have been either successfully used as a whole package, or incorporated into broader qualitative research designs. Dylan, Regehr and Alaggia's (2008) study of Aboriginal victims of sexual violence living in Canada used unstructured interviews, theoretical sampling, concurrent data generation and analysis, and axial coding in the production of a series of interlinked themes. These researchers argue that each of these was pivotal to researching with indigenous people in a way that reflected their oral tradition of storytelling. In a study of the retention of indigenous Australian students during their first year at university, Day and Nolde (2009) also incorporated essential grounded theory methods in their overall research design. These researchers worked with an indigenous research assistant who facilitated the data collection phase of the study, and with whom the non-indigenous researchers credit the successful retention rate of participants over the 12-month period of data generation and analysis. In Chapter 7 Mary Whiteside, also a non-indigenous researcher, provided an example of a grounded theory study of empowerment in the context of indigenous Australia, in which she used secondary data for analysis. This strategy is supported by Glaser's (2008) comment that 'data overload is epidemic in the descriptive research world … secondary analysis is not only useful … but has an image of great potential for the … conceptual analysis of … many social problems' (p. 40). However, we reinforce the point made earlier: that participants must have provided informed consent for the use of this secondary data for the research to be considered ethically sound. The previous examples, while not underpinned by an Indigenous methodology, do demonstrate the potential fit between grounded theory methods and research with indigenous people.

To illustrate the potential of combining grounded theory methods with a critical indigenous methodology, Bainbridge (2009), an Aboriginal Australian researcher, tells of her experience undertaking a grounded theory study with Aboriginal Australian participants (Box 10.1).

 BOX 10.1 WINDOW INTO GROUNDED THEORY

Roxanne Bainbridge on grounded theory within a critical indigenous framework

As noted by the authors, much social science research conducted in indigenous contexts involves the use participatory action research that can be applied as an appropriate and culturally safe and respectful methodology. However, in the

(Continued)

(Continued)

instance of my recent research, the participants whose life-history narratives I brought together would not have ongoing collaboration to explore or define issues, implement action or accomplish other tasks. As such, participatory action research would not achieve the intentions of the research: to develop a substantive theory that identified and explained the processes of performing agency in the everyday for urban-dwelling Aboriginal women in contemporary Australian society.

I entered the research endeavour as both a 'knower' and the 'known', meaning I was what many would describe as an 'insider/outsider' researcher; in this particular instance, I was both a participant in the study and the researcher. I subsequently held concerns about imposing a prior frame of reference upon the participants' realities. I required a method that avoided the imposition of theory on the data and evaded the separation of knowledge and ways of producing it. I required of this methodology a certain amount of flexibility and freedom from which to work within my own boundaries, to explicate details of a particular situation, understand the local context in which that phenomenon occurs and the practices and actors who interact in that context. Critically, the methodology had to be authentic to the contexts and practices of the women with whom I collaborated to develop a theory of agency.

In my experience as an Aboriginal Australian researcher seeking to develop a theory of Aboriginal women's agency, I found that a constructivist grounded theory was consonant with my ontological, epistemological and methodological premises. However, coming to the decision to use grounded theory did not reflect an easy or seamless research journey. For Aboriginal people, there is no way of escaping the reality that formal 'research' is itself an instrument and product of the colonisers. I asked myself how one moves from Western research scholarship to anti-colonial practice in the search for knowledge. I pondered how my methodology would differ from conventional research methodologies; after all, I intended to use current Western research practices. I did not wish to replace the errors of colonial practice with the errors of another. I took solace in Linda Tuhiwai Smith's (1999) proposal of prioritising the research process and, like many Aboriginal researchers before me, I approached this process with a consciousness informed by an Aboriginal woman's standpoint. I intuitively worked to assert my own unique ontology and epistemology in the construction of knowledge and made use of Tuhiwai Smith's (1999) notion of decolonising methodologies. Thus, in the study I focused on 'centering our [Aboriginal] concerns and world views and then coming to know and understand theory and research from our own perspectives and for our own purposes' (p. 39) while using methods that were readily available in current research texts.

The decolonisation of research methodologies, however, requires more than a simple shift in conceptualisation of the process. Indeed, we also need to build knowledge that has relevance, practical application and vision for Aboriginal people. In a constructivist grounded theory I found opportunities to move beyond theory to inform the ethics of practice and the practice of ethics that problematises both colonial relations and practice and creates a critical link between theories and practice. In this way, Aboriginal ways of knowing, being and doing guided the research process and practice of grounded theory; an integration of Aboriginal and Western knowledge to facilitate a culturally safe and respectful and scientifically rigorous development of social science theory.

 Activity 10.3

Grounded theory research today

As a means of rounding off your reading of this text, discuss with your supervisor and colleagues their perspectives on grounded theory today, the ways in which it has evolved and the significance of its evolution to its position in the contemporary scholarly environment.

Conclusion

Throughout this text we have emphasized the flexibility of grounded theory as an approach to research suited to broad topic areas arising from a vast array of disciplines. This flexibility has seen it retain its relevance over the last half century as it has evolved to accommodate the changes on a global scale unprecedented for generations. The story does not end here, however, as grounded theory will continue to be a useful mechanism for investigating issues of importance for researchers from diverse backgrounds and with varying levels of experience and expertise. We trust that you too will recognize the continuing potential of grounded theory to contribute to, and make a difference in, your own world.

 CRITICAL THINKING QUESTIONS

1 What issues do you think are emerging as significant to grounded theorists? Have these arisen as a result of the changing methodological context and/or are they the result of societal, cultural, political, economic or global change?

(Continued)

(Continued)

2 What do you see as the impetus for the growing emphasis on social justice issues? Can you identify researchable problems in your own personal or professional environment that could be addressed using a social justice lens?

3 In addition to the contribution that grounded theory can make to the paradigms of interpretive research discussed in this chapter, consider other ways in which grounded theory might play a role in contemporary research.

 WORKING GROUNDED THEORY

Review the 'Working grounded theory' example presented in Appendix A. Note:

- The comments made by this researcher in respect of grounded theory and its relationship to other research designs.

- The potential contribution that essential grounded theory methods can make within contemporary paradigms of research.

- Suggestions made to promote the methodological significance of grounded theory as the complexity of the social world increases.

Glossary

Abduction: a form of reasoning that begins with an examination of the data and the formation of a number of hypotheses that are then proved or disproved during the process of analysis, thus aiding inductive conceptualization.

Advanced coding: techniques used to facilitate integration of the final grounded theory.

Analytical paralysis: feeling totally overwhelmed by the data to the point where analysis seems impossible.

Audit trail: a record of decisions made in relation to the conduct of research.

Basic social process: a process apparent in the categories and sub-categories constructed and the relationships between these.

Bracketing: using reflexivity to maintain a position of objectivity as a researcher.

Category: a higher level concept that represents a group of codes.

Code: a form of shorthand that researchers repeatedly use to identify conceptual reoccurrences and similarities in the patterns of participants' experiences.

Concept: an idea or notion that encapsulates a descriptive explanation of a phenomenon or characteristic of a phenomenon.

Conditional matrix: an analytical framework that accounts for context in the process of analysis.

Core category: a concept that encapsulates a phenomenon apparent in the categories and sub-categories constructed and the relationships between these.

Data: raw material generated or collected through sources such as interview, observation, literature, documents and artefacts for use in grounded theory research.

Data collection: a process of gathering data in which the researcher has limited influence on the data source, as occurs when data is extracted from static materials such as documents and the literature.

Data generation: the process by which a researcher directly engages with a data source to produce materials for analysis, such as occurs during in-depth interviewing.

Diagram: a visual representation that can assist in the process of data analysis.

Dimensions: variations of a property.

Epistemology: the nature of justifiable knowledge.

Extant theory: an existing theory outside of the current investigation.

Fieldnotes: contemporaneous records made during fieldwork to record events, activities and the researcher's responses to them.

Fieldwork: a broad range of data-gathering activities that include observation, informal conversation and accessing documents, in addition to formal interviews.

Formal grounded theory: theory developed to a higher level of conceptual abstraction thereby encompassing concepts spanning a number of substantive areas.

Gerund: verbs used as nouns that always finish with 'ing'.

Incident: an umbrella term for recurring actions, characteristics, experiences, phrases, explanations, images and/or sounds. Incidents are analysed for underlying concepts that can be coded.

Induction: a form of reasoning that begins with a large number of concepts that are then collapsed and integrated into an explanatory theory.

Initial coding: the process of fracturing the data in order to compare incident with incident, name apparent phenomena or beginning patterns, and begin the process of comparison between the codes applied. Also referred to as open coding.

Intermediate coding: the identification of properties, dimensions, patterns and relationships during the process of category development.

Interpretive research: studies based on a researcher's interpretation of non-quantifiable data.

In vivo **code:** participant's words used to encapsulate a broader concept in the data.

Memoing: a fundamental analytical process in grounded theory research that involves the recording of processes, thoughts, feelings, analytical insights, decisions and ideas in relation to a research project.

Metaphor: a figure of speech that can be used as a theoretical code where there is a sufficient fit between a metaphor and the grounded theory.

Methodological congruence: accordance between the researcher's personal philosophical position, the stated aims of the research and the methodological approach employed to achieve these aims.

Methodology: a set of principles and ideas that inform the design of a research study.

Methods: practical procedures used to generate and analyse data.

Model: an abstract representation of reality that is not real. Provides a summative visual representation of the findings.

Ontology: the study of the nature of reality.

Philosophical position: an assumed stance whereby a researcher draws upon a philosophical school of thought to inform their thinking and actions.

Process: dynamic activities occurring in all aspects of life, not necessarily limited to conceptions of time, phases or stages.

Properties: characteristics of a category.

Qualitative data analysis: analytical processes that seek to describe and explore, rather than to explain, data.

Reflexivity: an active, systematic process used by the researcher in order to gain insight into their work that will guide future actions and interpretations.

Relational statements: historically expressed as hypotheses or propositions during the process of intermediate coding. Used to explain action or process as it becomes apparent in a burgeoning grounded theory. Can also be used to link or integrate categories.

Rendering: to translate or make understandable to the reader the researcher's analysis of what is happening in a substantive area of enquiry.

Research design: a plan that accounts for the philosophical, methodological aspects of, and methods to be used in, a research study.

Rigour: control of the processes employed in a grounded theory study in order to accommodate or explain all factors that can impact on, and thereby potentially erode, the value of research outcomes.

Secondary data: data previously collected by another researcher for another research study.

Storyline: a strategy for facilitating integration, construction, formulation and presentation of research findings through the production of a coherent grounded theory.

Substantive codes: taken from the language of the data. Usually assume the form of gerunds or *in vivo* codes.

Substantive grounded theory: theory that aims to address a studied phenomenon in a specific situation.

Theoretical coding: the use of advanced abstractions to provide a framework for enhancing the explanatory power of a grounded theory.

Theoretical integration: the pulling together of the abstract theoretical scheme into a final grounded theory.

Theoretical sampling: the process of identifying and pursuing clues that arise during analysis in a grounded theory study.

Theoretical saturation: occurs when no new codes are identified pertaining to a particular category. Categories are clearly articulated with sharply defined and dimensionalized properties.

Theoretical sensitivity: the ability to recognize and extract from the data elements that have relevance for the emerging theory.

Theory: an explanatory scheme comprising a set of concepts related to each other through logical patterns of connectivity.

Thesis: a sustained argument. Term can be used interchangeably with dissertation.

In the following example, Melanie Birks (2007) describes her experience in undertaking grounded theory research. Along with the 'Working grounded theory' points for consideration at the end of each chapter, this example provides a practical illustration to enhance your understanding of the grounded theory process.

Discovering the essentials of grounded theory

I was first exposed to grounded theory when a colleague of mine employed it in her research design as an honours student many years ago. I had some prior experience in research, mainly through the use of statistical methods. Grounded theory seemed inherently complex. The language that my colleague used when talking about her research, the history of the approach and the uniqueness of the methods made me feel a degree of discomfort. Why, I wondered at the time, would anyone bother with such a difficult approach to research?

I am a black-and-white thinker. If I were at all mathematically inclined I would have stuck with statistical research. My professional world is a social one, however, and my inherent need to find meaning in situations would always bring me back to an interpretive paradigm. This need conflicts with my tendency to look for concrete explanations and so my view of the world is difficult to pigeonhole. In exploring methodological options for my doctoral research topic I struggled with this conflict. I needed an explanation for the focus of my study; I needed a structured approach to research that would suit my desire for certainty in process; and I needed enough freedom and flexibility to let the research phenomenon speak for itself. Grounded theory checked all the boxes.

It was not an easy road from that point, however. I bought a book on grounded theory and read it. I was ready to go! I started to write my chapter on methodology. I realized I wasn't going anywhere. On the advice of a recent doctoral graduate, I commenced reading all the seminal work in order of publication. It may suit some researchers but I found that it did not work for me. I read the work of others who had summarized the history, debates and evolutionary path of grounded theory.

Certain texts sat comfortably with me and now lay dog-eared on my desk along with chapters from broader works and articles written by others who had trodden the path before me. I like the frank nature of Glaser's work, the supportive undertones of Strauss and Corbin and the warmth and practicality of Charmaz. You will see the influences of them all in my work and I make no apologies for taking this non-partisan approach.

Getting to this stage of comfort required an important step. I was asked by my research supervisor 'how do you see the world?' I didn't know. I hadn't ever really thought about it. I started to think about it. I turned to writings on philosophy. Again I struggled with the shades of grey that characterize philosophical thinking. I started to keep a journal of my doctoral research experience. Like me, it was very black and white – objective and clinical. Over time this would change. The experience of writing made me see patterns in my thinking. Eventually the journal gave way to memos. With hindsight I can see this was a turning point, a signpost indicating that I had become comfortable with articulating my philosophical position. More importantly, bringing this process into my research through memoing meant that I would continue to grow with my study. Someone warned me before I commenced my doctoral studies that I may change how I see myself as a result of the experience. I was to discover that black and white is a façade that, when peeled back, gives way to dark grey and light grey, and ultimately a colourful spectrum of conceptual thinking.

Planning my grounded theory study

People often talk about the need to 'find' a topic for their doctoral research that speaks to their passion. I had contemplated undertaking research at this level for many years yet could not identify any topic that might hold the power to maintain my interest and burning passion. In the end, the topic for my research found me. I had been coordinating an off-campus Baccalaureate programme for Registered Nurses that used an outreach model to provide advanced educational opportunities to nurses in Malaysian Borneo. During one of the residential classes, a student commented in passing about how undertaking study had changed their lives. This comment stayed with me. I wondered what this really meant. What aspects of their lives had been changed? How had this occurred? What significance did it have for us as education providers? I toyed with the idea of pursuing the answer to these questions using research but had doubts about whether I had the elusive 'passion' for the topic. It was ultimately a doctoral research supervisor who insisted this topic had the potential to produce findings that would make a difference.

The nature of my research was clearly interpretivist and I leaned towards ethnography given the cultural aspects of the research situation. These were superficial considerations, however, and the substance of this research would ultimately transcend such issues. At the suggestion of my research supervisor I nervously approached grounded theory. As discussed above, I had reservations about this that would see me fight its use in my graduate work until I realized that there was something going on in my participants' world that needed to be explained. In the end I realized that using grounded theory would lead me to this explanation.

I was advised very early in my study to acknowledge my current assumptions about my substantive area of enquiry. My first official memo was written to this end. I listed all of the things I expected to be highlighted during my research. This was a useful exercise because it made me realize that I did harbour a number of assumptions that needed to be made transparent. I felt I understood, for example, the social and cultural factors that influenced the experience for these nurses. I even had preconceptions about who I felt would have the most interesting 'stories' to tell (as it turned out, I was wrong). I believe that you can't meaningfully prevent the imposition of your history on your work and would question whether you would wish to do so. You can, however, be honest and transparent with yourself and, if necessary, those who may benefit from your research.

Another piece of advice in the early stages of planning my study was to develop an embryonic table of contents for my thesis. Again, this was a difficult task but was an important step in planning because it made me identify all the practical issues that I would need to consider before embarking on my research. A standard thesis or dissertation contains chapters that mirror the research process. I was forced to start thinking at this early stage about what needed to be done and how it would be addressed in the research design. Having my study outlined in this way also enabled me to consider timelines. In the process of writing this book, some of the feedback we have received from experienced grounded theory supervisors is that students struggle with timelines when planning a study. It was suggested that less than 18 months is the absolute minimum time required for completion of a grounded theory study and that recruitment and data collection often take twice as long as expected. My experience reflected these words of wisdom. For example, my original proposed time for data collection and generation was only a few months. Fortunately, the exercise of writing a draft table of contents helped guide me to a more realistic timeframe during the early stages of my research.

As my understanding of grounded theory research methods grew, I realized that there would be elements of my research that may be challenged by those used to research employing quantitative methodologies. How could I meet institutional requirements without a clearly defined research question and aims? What about the literature review? How can I identify how many participants I will include when I don't yet know? I would ultimately negotiate these hurdles, albeit fuelled by a little stress (and a good deal of catastrophizing, my supervisors will tell you!). I stated my research question and aims in broad terms – how (in what way and by what means) has tertiary education changed the lives of nurses in Malaysian Borneo? In my final thesis the question and aims were reported as having evolved in response to the process. As I had always intended to use an interpretivist model, I steered clear of the literature specific to my topic and read around it in broad terms. My research was investigating an area about which little was known so this was not too difficult a task at this early stage. In my ethics application I specified a ball-park figure for my participant numbers and returned to this board on more than one occasion to seek clearance for necessary variations of my original research design.

With hindsight these issues were not as problematic as I had expected. Overall my research design was simple: individual interviews using a broad, unstructured approach. Data collection and analysis would be concurrent. Data would be analysed using a constant comparative approach. Codes would be identified. Categories would be developed. Whatever was going on in the data would become clear to me and my research question would be answered! Obviously it was not this straightforward but my simplistic research design was a starting point. I didn't know where the evolving processes would take me, but sometimes ignorance is bliss! My sense of security was enhanced when the bodies that were to review my proposal did not appear to have problems with the evolving nature of a grounded theory research design. These included the university, the ethics committee and the committee that awarded my scholarship. I was fortunate to have research mentors who were familiar with the system and knew what constituted a convincing proposal. To this end I ensured that any written proposal for my research was informed, broad and flexible and, where appropriate, open to future amendment.

Ensuring quality processes in my research

The issue of 'doing it right' was always at the forefront of my mind when undertaking my doctoral research. I was an experienced academic with skills in project management, writing and accessing resources. Nonetheless I still had some insecurities about my ability to undertake studies at doctoral level. I was keen from the outset to ensure that I applied a systematic approach to mitigate the limitations of a lack of familiarity with my chosen approach. My subsequent affinity with grounded theory no doubt stems from the fact that it provided greater structure than traditional interpretive methodologies. Before I even started I set up files in my office and on my computer to house the products of my labour. I learned early how to operate a bibliographic software program to manage the volumes of literature I would accumulate. I looked into data management software programs to aid my analysis. I took the attitude that this was a project to be run like any other major venture and I believed this preparation helped me both to manage the sheer size of the undertaking and to maintain the necessary standards in the process.

As I have stated, I was to become more comfortable with memoing. This level of comfort was to grow to the point where I became heavily reliant on memoing in support of my research (in fact, one of my supervisors was to refer to me as a 'rabid' memoer!). I used 'operational memos' to record *what* I did, *how* I did it and *why* I chose that course of action. I relied on 'coding memos' to explain *what* a code or category contained and *why* it belonged there. Eventually, as the analysis progressed, I would rely on 'analytical memos' to retain insights that explained the process of abstraction that would occur in the transformation of data into theory. Two points are now inescapable to me: operational activities, coding and analysis are so intertwined that overlap needs to be accepted if you choose to demarcate these processes; and anyone who says they are doing grounded theory without memoing cannot be doing grounded theory. Memoing is what makes theory *grounded*.

Positioning myself in my study

I would like to think that I had established my theoretical position as I moved into data collection and analysis, but the reality is that the very process of undertaking the study continued to shape me in this regard – as should be the case with doctoral studies, particularly in the interpretive paradigm. Becoming more comfortable with my role in the study took some time. I had an existing relationship with my participants and I thought I understood the process of interviewing for research. After my initial interviews in Borneo I emailed my supervisors late one night and lamented that the participants weren't telling me what I wanted to hear. *Who do you think you are?* Came the response. *This is not about* you!

I realized that my approach to that point had been to attempt to cut my participants open with a metaphorical scalpel and try to extract the data I wanted, or expected, to find. I understood the philosophical foundations of a constructivist approach but it took me some time to internalize these principles truly. Even later in my research I was still asking my supervisors 'how do I know if I've got it *right*?'. I would eventually come to realize that there is no 'right' outcome. The only truth that matters is that constructed through the correct application of grounded theory methods by the researcher in concert with their participants.

The existing relationship that I had with my participants, while aiding the process of establishing rapport, did cause me some concern. I had to work hard to diffuse potential power imbalances in our relationships and get them to tell me about *their* reality, not what they thought I wanted to hear. Developing insight into my preconceptions about potential outcomes from the interview process worked in tandem with my desire to become truly reflexive in the process of undertaking my research. The personal and professional growth that I was to experience as a result of my doctoral studies was borne from this insight. My participants would later tell me that they too had grown as a result of being able to discuss and reflect on how they had changed as a result of their university studies.

The more comfortable I was to become with the process of undertaking my research, the more theoretically sensitive I became to what was becoming evident in the data as it was generated and analysed. I'm sure I really didn't know what theoretical sensitivity was until relatively late in my research. I could define it, discuss it and even debate it, but it wasn't until I was deep inside the process that I discovered this subconscious ability to see parts of the data that would contribute to the whole. This is the skill of living out theoretical sensitivity. You have little idea what the final picture will look like but you know with a degree of certainty that this piece of data, this code, this category or this relationship, has relevance. I guess it's similar to how an artist sees those elements of a view that outsiders do not discern, but which ultimately bring to life their creation.

Generating and collecting my data

I was quite relaxed about commencing data collection for my study. I understood the concept of theoretical sampling and had experience in interviewing people in a professional capacity. I really wasn't prepared, however, for how different the research interview would be. Fortunately one of my research supervisors recommended that I 'practise' interviewing for my study with nurses in Australia who would not be included in the study but who had followed a similar academic and career path. This exercise proved invaluable. I was able to identify potential problems with my technique and discuss these with my supervisor, who acted as an observer.

In spite of my knowledge of this cultural group, I did not account for the cultural variations that would impact on my study. I found that I had to spend greater time ensuring that participants understood the unique nature of the research relationship and how it differed from the professional relationship that we already shared. I was careful to explain fully the nature of my research and commenced each interview with some broader questions about participants' motivation for and experience of study. These questions were only ever intended to 'warm up' the interview process, yet, as is the nature of grounded theory, I was later to find that they produced information of great value to my developing theory.

Another factor that I had to deal with was the enthusiasm with which news of my research was greeted. As I had to travel some distance, I purposefully sampled a small number of nurses, allowing sufficient time in between to commence analysis and direct future data collection. In my first location, five participants arrived to tell their stories. I learned a great deal about theoretical sampling from that experience. The reality is that analysis commences with the posing of your first question. I treasured the small amount of time available to me in between each of these initial interviews to review the data that had been generated and to make fieldnotes that would capture my rationale for any changes in direction in subsequent interviews. Of course I would later conduct a more detailed analysis of these interviews, yet did not find that my analysis suffered as a result of the baptism of fire that characterized my introduction to concurrent data collection and analysis.

After each interview I would listen to the recording and make preliminary notes, both on the content of the discussion and on my performance in an effort to improve my technique in future interviews. While those who know me will tell you that I have a tendency to talk too much, I was actually surprised at how much I had to say in these early interviews. There are of course times when it is important to clarify, paraphrase and respond to questions. And while we aim for a certain level of comfort it is important to maintain a focus on the purpose of the interview. I discovered that there is a lot to be gained from being constructively critical of your own performance in all aspects of your research in order to grow from the experience.

I relied heavily on interview recordings and the transcription of these. Listening to the recordings repeatedly imbeds the discourse in your brain, but I found my fieldnotes were equally important in helping to retain the contextual experience. Interview transcripts and fieldnotes together constituted the raw data of my study. The literature provided material for enhancing my theoretical sensitivity, understanding the context of the study and explaining the subsequent theory, but it was the participants' experience and my elicitation of it with them that formed the fodder for analysis.

Analysing my data

It was difficult to know where to start with data analysis once the initial data had been generated. I had read widely about coding and on the surface initial coding appeared simple: you become familiar with the data then extract codes from it as directed by your developing theoretical sensitivity. It became more complex, however, as subsequent data was generated and subjected to constant comparison. Did this data segment reflect this code? How was it different? How was it similar? Did this code need to be relabelled? Was this a new code that would be subsumed under a category that was yet to be developed? Axial coding did not sit comfortably with me and I eventually relied on a Glaserian approach informed by Charmaz. Like Charmaz (2006), my analysis would include an axial element in the identification of relationships but this was incidental to the process.

My initial attempts at analysis were manual, mostly for practical reasons, as I had not yet become proficient in the use of data analysis software. Having the opportunity to be so hands-on with my data proved extremely valuable. When I eventually moved my data into the software, the insights developed during the manual analysis phase were reinforced and refined as I continued the process of constant comparative analysis within the program. I nonetheless struggled with some basic concepts – what was the difference between a code, a category, a sub-category, a pattern, a theme? I stood fast in my use of essential grounded theory methods and all was to become clear as the theoretical picture evolved.

I don't think that anyone who has not engaged in analysis of qualitative data can truly understand how the process engulfs you. I heard people speak of being 'immersed' in the data and 'drowning' in data. I think it is somewhere between these two extremes. In reality you wallow in various depths of analysis. You don't see it coming with grounded theory. Analysis starts with the initial data collected and before you know it you are surrounded by it – physically, mentally and emotionally. Memoing was once again my saviour. Memoing helps you come up to the surface from your state of immersion and take an analytical breath.

I wrote memos in the early stages about the codes as they were identified, and later about the categories that were to develop. I invented what I called 'definitional statements' to guide my analytical decision-making (these were different in both structure and intent to 'relational statements' referred to by Strauss and Corbin, 1998). For the category 'being heard' for example, the definitional statement would be 'As a result of completing my studies, I now feel that I am being heard by others around me.' These statements reflected and summarized the content of each category and facilitated constant comparison for incoming data. Similarities and differences could be identified through this process as properties and dimensions were expressed. Definitional statements and the breadth and depth of each category were subsequent expanded as necessary. The evolutionary nature of constant comparative analysis saw the categories reform (divide or expand) in response to new data. Assigned labels and the definitional statements were refined to reflect such changes. As the analysis evolved, so too did my memos as I wrote about the analytical insights surrounding relationships and patterns that were becoming evident in the data.

My confidence in the process of analysis grew with my body of data and the production of memos. I realized that it was difficult to misread data or follow irrelevant leads; the reality is that grounded theory methods are self-correcting – if you are precise in their use. Any concept that is relevant will persist, and any that is not will eventually self-extinguish.

Integrating my theory

Applied correctly, the use of grounded theory methods results in the conceptual abstraction of data. The actual production of theory, however, requires a final analytical leap. This was certainly the case for me. I spent some time attempting to explicate my developing theory through the use of diagramming. As I approached the stage of theoretical integration, diagramming and memoing were my two best friends. Eventually I was to produce a schematic representation of what I thought was going on in the data. I returned to the field, this time using focus groups. With the embryonic theory as a foundation for discussion, I used these focus groups to generate more data. The different dynamic in the focus groups provided alternative perspectives that were reflected in the analysis.

Still there were elements in the evolving theory that I knew had relevance but struggled to clarify the relationships between these. I returned to my participants, again using focus groups. I produced cards labelled with the sub-categories I had identified and asked participants to sort them into the broader scheme of categories. It was clear that what I presented resonated with these participants, which was enormously gratifying for me. The categories and their relationships began to coalesce for me through these strategies, yet the final theory was yet to really come together. I was still to explicate the basic social process that I knew was there.

At this point I understood the concept of 'process' as it applies to grounded theory. I knew that it needn't be linear nor temporal. I also knew that people did not experience the world in a static way. It was serendipitous that Jane Mills found me staring at my computer screen through piles of notes in my office one morning as I tried to integrate my theory. We spent the better part of three hours with a whiteboard, moving through the final stages of analysis. A basic social process began to crystallize yet integration was not complete. It was only by writing my storyline that the theory would finally develop. Data collection and analysis is a recursive process, however, and I would need to return to my existing data set and generate additional data with my participants before I was happy that I had achieved complete integration and saturation of my grounded theory.

Producing my grounded theory as a storyline worked well for me. Not only did it aid integration, but also it enabled me to present my theory in a manner that captured the essence of the experience of my participants. The theory explained the phenomenon experienced by my participants through three phases: from *seeking knowledge*, *discovering learning*, these nurses went through a stage of *becoming different*, before ultimately *becoming professional*. Meanwhile I had discovered Roberts' (2000) theory of professional identity development and this resonated with my own findings. Although my participants had experienced this process in a unique cultural context, Roberts' work functioned as a theoretical code that explained the concepts, relationships and variations in my theory.

Presenting my grounded theory

The department in which I had enrolled for my doctoral studies had begun to encourage candidates to consider thesis by publication. This approach differs from what is sometimes referred to as a 'rubber-band thesis', where a collection of existing publications are bundled together and submitted for examination. Completing thesis by publication follows the usual path of doctoral research, with the exception that chapters, or sections of chapters, are submitted for publication across the period of candidature. Like many of my colleagues, I was initially a little reluctant to follow this route. I found, however, that this approach was eventually to become a natural progression of my study and it was to have many benefits both during and following my candidature. My final thesis comprised all my published work, woven together by introductory and summarizing sections and contained within opening and concluding chapters.

I relied heavily on narrative in presenting my theory. I produced a simple diagrammatic model of my theory but put my trust in storyline as the principal mechanism to communicate my findings. My theory explained a process that consisted of three phases; these phases were expounded in three separate published articles and the theory in its totality was expressed in a further published piece. The final thesis was constructed from these articles, along with eight others exploring the background to the study and methodological concepts.

Along the way I also presented at various conferences and research seminars during my candidature. Initially these presentations were terrifying for me, particularly during my ground-theory-phobic phase. As it happened, the opportunity to present my research enabled me to gain valuable feedback on my study as it evolved and increased my confidence in the process.

Evaluation and application of my grounded theory

While I was conscious of the importance of maintaining quality throughout the process of producing my grounded theory, I nevertheless also knew the importance of ensuring that the final product ticked all the boxes. More importantly, I felt I needed to demonstrate to my examiners and those who would read my thesis that it was indeed a 'real' grounded theory. To this end I included in my thesis my own evaluation of the grounded theory I had produced. By using criteria drawn from various sources in the literature (in particular Charmaz, 2006; and Chiovitti & Piran, 2003), I was able to discuss how my own work could be defined as grounded theory research. Most significantly I had produced a theory that was grounded in the data and demonstrated explanatory power in respect of the phenomenon that was the focus of my study.

In publishing my work throughout my candidature I felt that I was making a contribution to the knowledge base of my discipline early. While my findings would naturally be published in the later stages, the work I did on contributing to an understanding of grounded theory methods and their application has attracted interest from around the globe. While this was not my primary intent, it is gratifying to know that others may benefit from my own experience in undertaking grounded theory research. Naturally my professional work has been enhanced both substantively and in respect of my work with students of research.

Reflecting on grounded theory in the context of current debate

In the postdoctoral stage of my career I have found that, in spite of the rhetoric, interpretive research still struggles to achieve the same status as other studies employing highly controlled clinical trials. I think that the onus remains on the researcher to be clear about the potential contribution that their study will make to the knowledge base of their discipline. Publishing about the experience of undertaking research, in addition to dissemination of findings, increases the reach of grounded theory.

I remain concerned about the use of grounded theory as a 'catch-all' name for studies where research students (and often their supervisors) adopt selected methods for use when their research questions might be better addressed using another approach. The adaptability of the essential methods often see the name 'grounded theory' exploited in studies that are neither suited to this approach nor have the potential to generate theory that is grounded in the data. This is not to say that the powerful strategies developed since the discovery of grounded theory should not be used selectively within other research designs – provided, of course, that their use is acknowledged as such and that the research does not make claims about the outcomes of the research that are not kept.

As the social world becomes more complex, researchers have much to gain from the use of grounded theory methods, comprehensively and selectively. They have both stood the test of time and evolved with the changing, increasing complex nature of society. I for one celebrate the continuing contribution that grounded theory makes to those who employ its methods and those who will benefit from the evidence that is ultimately generated.

Appendix B   Windows into grounded theory – Contributor biographies

Merilyn Annells

Professor of Community Nursing. Division of Nursing & Midwifery, Faculty of Health Sciences, La Trobe University, Bundoora Campus, Melbourne 3086 Victoria. Tel. +61 3 9479 5956. Email: m.annells@latrobe.edu.au

Merilyn Annells RN PhD is Professor of Community Nursing at La Trobe University, Melbourne. Previously she had a wide range of nursing experience and has extensively taught nurses at undergraduate and postgraduate levels, including supervision of research students, many of whom have been PhD candidates. Over the past 20 years, she has regularly conducted and led nursing research studies but she is also a qualitative research methodologist with international publications concerning application of the grounded theory method. She commenced using the grounded theory method in 1991.

Roxanne Bainbridge

Senior Research Fellow. The Cairns Institute (School of Education), James Cook University, PO Box 6811, Cairns, QLD 4870, Australia Tel: +61 07 4042 1710. Email: roxanne.bainbridge@jcu.edu.au

Roxanne Bainbridge has family ties to the Gungarri and Kunja nations from the country around Charleville in South West Queensland. She currently works as a Senior Research Fellow in the Empowerment Research Programme located in The Cairns Institute (School of Education) at James Cook University. The Programme operationalizes Aboriginal-developed empowerment-based initiatives at the personal, organizational and structural levels with the aim of exploring the capacity and limitations such programmes hold in contributing towards improving the social determinants of health and well-being for Aboriginal people. Her research interests lie in expanding empowerment education across the developmental pathways of Aboriginal children. She holds a PhD in the field of Aboriginal women's agency.

Ann Bonner

Associate Professor. School of Nursing, Midwifery & Indigenous Health, Wagga Wagga Campus, Charles Sturt University, Locked Bag 588, Wagga Wagga NSW 2678. Australia

Ann Bonner, RN, PhD used grounded theory methods in her doctoral studies in which she examined the process of expertise acquisition in renal nursing. Currently she is the Postgraduate Courses Manager and she also supervises several doctoral candidates who are using grounded theory methods. Ann's research interests are clinical practice and chronic illness with a particular focus on renal health care, and she is recognized internationally as an expert renal nurse. She is also an Assistant Editor and Editorial Board Member for the *Renal Society of Australasia Journal* and reviewer for several national and international journals.

Gaile Cannella

Professor. Department of Teacher Education and Administration, College of Education, 1155 Union circle #310740. University of North Texas, Matthews Hall 206E, Denton, TX 76203-5017, USA. Tel. +001 940-565-4901. Email: Gaile. Cannella@unt.edu

Gaile Sloan Cannella is a Professor in the Department of Teacher Education and Administration and the Velma E. Schmidt Endowed Chair of Early Childhood Studies at the University of North Texas in the United States. Dr Cannella previously served as a Research Professor at Tulane University in New Orleans, Louisiana, where she explored the impact of disaster and neoliberalism on public schooling offered to young children. She is the author and editor of multiple publications, including *Deconstructing early childhood education: Social justice and revolution* (1997) and *Childhoods: a handbook* (In Press).

Vicki Drury

Associate Professor of Nursing. Alice Lee Centre for Nursing Studies, Yong Loo Lin School of Medicine, National University of Singapore, Block E3A, Level 3, 7 Engineering Drive 1, Singapore 117574. DID:+65 6516 3107. E-mail: nurvbd@ nus.edu.sg

Dr Vicki Drury is a Registered Nurse and a Registered Mental Health Nurse with additional qualifications in ophthalmic nursing and men's health. Over the past 15 years, she has worked at a number of universities in Australia as a Lecturer and Research Officer. Her main areas of interest and expertise are ophthalmology, mental health, resilience and self-efficacy. Currently an Assistant Professor in the Alice Lee Centre for Nursing Studies at the National University of Singapore, she continues to undertake research in chronic disease self-management, mental health and ophthalmology.

Yvonne Eaves

Assistant Professor. School of Nursing, University of Alabama at Birmingham, NB 446, 1530 3rd Avenue South, Birmingham, AL 35294–1210, USA. Tel +001 205–9346224. Email: yeaves@uab.edu
   Yvonne D. Eaves, PhD, RN is Assistant Professor of Nursing at The University of Alabama at Birmingham (UAB). She holds a PhD in nursing from the University of Michigan. Dr Eaves is an Associate Scientist at the UAB Minority Health and Research Center, and a Scientist in the UAB Center for Aging. She reviews manuscripts for several scientific journals. Dr Eaves' research foci are caregiving transitions, stroke, and long-term care decision-making in rural African Americans. A noted publication from 2006 is Caregiving in rural African American families for older adult stroke survivors. *Journal of Neuroscience Nursing, 38*(4), 270–81.

Caroline Eyles

Research Fellow. Complementary and Integrated Medicine Research Unit, Primary Medical Care, Aldermoor Health Centre, Aldermoor Close, Southampton SO16 5ST, UK. Tel. +44 (0)23 80 241072. Email: C.G.Eyles@soton.ac.uk
   Caroline Eyles, an experienced homeopathic practitioner and teacher of homeopathy, completed her Masters in 2000, which fired her enthusiasm for qualitative research leading to a PhD at the University of Southampton. The PhD explored the homeopathic consultation from the practitioner's perspective and inspired an interesting journey of exploration of grounded theory methodology and the challenges of practitioners researching practitioners. This finally led to a constructivist grounded theory approach being taken in her PhD. Since her PhD she has been working as a qualitative researcher on a study exploring patients' experiences of alcohol liver disease and a study exploring the effects of mindfulness meditation on women with metastatic breast cancer.

Foster Fei

Research Fellow. Diversity & Education Management Research Group (DeMRG), The Business School. University of Huddersfield, Huddersfield HD1 3DH, UK. Tel: +44 (0)1484 473 578. Email: x.fei@hud.ac.uk
   Dr Foster Fei is a Research Associate at the Cardiff Business School. He earned his PhD in management (organizational behaviour) from the School of Management, University of Bath. His doctoral thesis is entitled: 'Resourcing change: a grounded theory explaining the process by which managers address challenges in their

initiation of change as learning at work' (Fei, 2007). Over the past few years, he has been contributing significantly to the learning and teaching of grounded theory methodology in China. His research interests include: learning in organizations, management learning, education and development; internationalization of higher education; higher education law; grounded theory methodology.

Barry Gibson

Senior Lecturer in Medical Sociology. Unit of Dental Public Health, School of Clinical Dentistry, Claremont Crescent, University of Sheffield, Sheffield S10 2TA, United Kingdom.Tel. +44 (0)114 271 7889. Email: b.j.gibson@sheffield.ac.uk

Barry Gibson completed his PhD at The Queen's University of Belfast in 1997 titled 'Dangerous dentaling: a grounded theory of HIV and dentistry'. Since then he has been working in the field of the sociology of health and illness. His main interest in grounded theory is in the epistemology of classical tradition. Notable publications include a chapter 'Accommodating critical theory' in the *Sage handbook of grounded theory* and an article in the *Qualitative Sociology Review* on the epistemological similarities between Luhmann's social systems theory and classical grounded theory. He has acted as an external examiner for several grounded theory studies and continues to teach grounded theory at Masters and PhD levels.

Laurie Goldsmith

Assistant Professor. Faculty of Health Sciences, Simon Fraser University, Blusson Hall 10506, 8888 University Drive, Burnaby, BC, Canada V5A 1S6. Tel. +001 778-782-8145. Email: laurie_goldsmith@sfu.ca

Dr Laurie J. Goldsmith is an Assistant Professor in the Faculty of Health Sciences at Simon Fraser University in British Columbia, Canada. Her research interests include: access to health care, medical underservice, rural health, comparative health care systems, the politics of health care delivery and the use of qualitative methods in health research. She has conducted health services and health policy research in Canada and the United States working with health system decision makers at the federal, provincial, state and local levels. She has a PhD in health policy from the University of North Carolina and an MSc in health research methodology from McMaster University.

Andrea Gorra

Lecturer. Business School, Leeds Metropolitan University, Rose Bowl RB 562, Portland Crescent, Leeds LS1 3HB, UK. Tel. +44 (0)113 812 3862 Email: a.gorra@ leedsmet.ac.uk

Andrea Gorra completed her PhD at Leeds Metropolitan University (UK) in 2007 titled 'An analysis of the relationship between individuals' perceptions of privacy and mobile phone location data: a grounded theory study'. Her supervisors were Antony Bryant and Edward Halpin. She has worked as a researcher in the area of learning technologies and recently started teaching at the Business School at Leeds Metropolitan University. Andrea supervises PhD students using the grounded theory methodology and currently writes articles in English and German about the use of grounded theory.

Michelle Perez

Assistant Professor. Department of Curriculum and Instruction, College of Education, Southern Illinois University Carbondale, 1102 W Walkup Ave, Carbondale, IL 62901, USA. Tel. +001 504-432-7500. Email: michelle.s.perez@gmail.com

Michelle Salazar Perez recently graduated with a PhD in curriculum and instruction, early childhood education, from Arizona State University. She conducted her dissertation research in New Orleans, Louisiana, which examines discourses of power surrounding young children, charter schools and the privatization of public education post-Katrina. Dr Perez is currently an Assistant Professor in the Department of Curriculum and Instruction at Southern Illinois University in Carbondale.

Stella Walsh

Senior Lecturer, Hospitality and Retailing. Room: Bronte 204, Leeds Metropolitan University, Civic Quarter, Leeds LS1 3HE, Tel. +44 (0)113 812 3491. Email: S.M.Walsh@leedsmet.ac.uk

Stella Walsh currently teaches retailing and marketing at Leeds Metropolitan University. She has a long-standing interest in the subjects of food and food retailing. The research focus of her PhD was 'Food choices and consumption patterns among older working class women', in Leeds, UK. This included budgeting, retail choice, brands and shopping. She has extensive experience of teaching and research in higher education, has published refereed articles for academic and professional journals and book chapters, and has presented papers at international conferences on food, retailing and consumer issues.

Mary Whiteside

Lecturer. School of Social Work & Social Policy, Division of Allied Health, Faculty of Health Sciences, La Trobe University, Bundoora, Vic. 3068, Australia. Tel. +61 3-9479 2562. Email: Mary.Whiteside@latrobe.edu.au

Dr Mary Whiteside is currently a lecturer in the School of Social Work and Social Policy, La Trobe University. She has a long history of involvement in research and practice in the context of Indigenous Australia, supporting the development of local social and emotional well-being and health interventions. From 2000 she played a central role in the development of the James Cook University, School of Indigenous Australian Studies, Empowerment Research Programme which has sought to build the evidence base for indigenous social and emotional well-being interventions and explore the role of empowerment in addressing social and health inequalities.

References

Anderson, J. M., Rodney, P., Reimer-Kirkham, S., Browne, A. J., Khan, K. B., & Lynam, M. J. (2009). Inequities in health and healthcare viewed through the ethical lens of critical social justice contextual knowledge for the global priorities ahead. *Advances in Nursing Science, 32*(4), 282–94.

Annells, M. (1996). Grounded theory method: Philosophical perspectives, paradigm of inquiry, and postmodernism. *Qualitative Health Research, 6*, 379–93.

Annells, M. (2006). Triangulation of qualitative approaches: Hermeneutical phenomenology and grounded theory. *Journal of Advanced Nursing, 56*(1), 55–61.

Bahora, M., Sterk, C. E., & Elifson, K. W. (2009). Understanding recreational ecstasy use in the United States: A qualitative inquiry. *International Journal of Drug Policy, 20*(1), 62–9.

Bailey, D., & Jackson, J. (2003). Qualitative data analysis: Challenges and dilemmas related to theory and method. *American Journal of Occupational Therapy, 57*(1), 57–65.

Bainbridge, R. (2009). *Cast all imaginations: Umbi speak.* Doctoral thesis, James Cook University.

Bernstein, R. (1983). *Beyond objectivism and relativism: Science, hermeneutics, and praxis.* Philadelphia: University of Pennsylvania Press.

Birks, M. (2007). *Becoming professional by degree: A grounded theory study of nurses in Malaysian Borneo.* PhD thesis, Monash University.

Birks, M., Chapman, Y., & Francis, K. (2006). Moving grounded theory into the 21st century: Part 2 – Mapping the footprints. *Singapore Nursing Journal, 33*(4), 12–17.

Birks, M., Chapman, Y., & Francis, K. (2008). Memoing in qualitative research: Probing data and processes. *Journal of Research in Nursing, 13*(1), 68–75.

Birks, M., Chapman, Y., & Francis, K. (2009). Becoming different: Perspective transformation through post-registration baccalaureate nursing studies. In R. V. Nata (Ed.), *Progress in education* (Vol. 17, pp. 61–78). New York: Nova.

Birks, M., Mills, J., Francis, K., & Chapman, Y. (2009). A thousand words paint a picture: The use of storyline in grounded theory research. *Journal of Research in Nursing, 14*(5), 405–17.

Blumer, H. (1969). *Symbolic interactionism: Perspective and method.* Englewood Cliffs, NJ: Prentice Hall.

Bong, S. A. (2002). Debunking myths in CAQDAS use and coding in qualitative data analysis. *Forum Qualitative Sozialforschung/Forum Qualitative Social Research, 3*(2), 258–75.

Bonner, A., & Greenwood, J. (2005). Producing the magnum opus: A metaphor for nephrology nursing expertise acquisition. *Journal of Advanced Nursing, 51*(1), 64–72.

Bonner, A., & Greenwood, J. (2006). Acquisition and exercise of nephrology nursing expertise: A grounded theory study. *Journal of Clinical Nursing, 15*, 480–9.

Boslaugh, S. (2007). *Secondary data sources for public health: A practical guide.* New York: Cambridge University Press.

Bowen, G. A. (2008). Naturalistic inquiry and the saturation concept: A research note. *Qualitative Research, 8*(1), 137–52.

Bowers, B., & Schatzman, L. (2009). Dimensional analysis. In J. M. Morse, P. Noerager Stern, J. Corbin, B. Bowers, K. Charmaz & A. E. Clarke (Eds.), *Developing grounded theory: The second generation* (pp. 86–127). Walnut Creek, CA: Left Coast Press.

Boychuk-Duchscher, J. E., & Morgan, D. (2004). Grounded theory: Reflections on the emergence vs forcing debate. *Journal of Advanced Nursing, 48*(6), 605–12.

Bradbury-Jones, C. (2007). Enhancing rigour in qualitative health research: Exploring subjectivity through Peshkin's I's. *Journal of Advanced Nursing, 59*(3), 290–8.

Briley, M. E., Roberts-Gray, C., & Simpson, D. (1994). Identification of factors that influence the menu at child care centers: A grounded theory approach. *Journal of the American Dietetic Association, 94*(3), 276–81.

Bryant, A. (2003). A constructive/ist response to Glaser. *Forum Qualitative Sozialforschung/ Forum: Qualitative Social Research, 4*(1). Retrieved 30 March 2006 from www.qualitative-research.net/fqs-texte/1–03/1–03bryant-e.htm

Bryant, A. (2009). Grounded theory and pragmatism: The curious case of Anselm Strauss. *Forum Qualitative Sozialforschung/Forum: Qualitative Social Research, 10*(3). Retrieved 6 January 2010 from http://nbn-resolving.de/urn:nbn:de:0114-fqs090325

Bryant, A., & Charmaz, K. (2007). *The Sage handbook of grounded theory.* London: Sage.

Burns, N. (1989). Standards for qualitative research. *Nursing Science Quarterly, 2*(1), 44–52.

Cagle, C., & Wells, J. (2008). Journey to a mixed methods approach for understanding Mexican American female cancer caregiving. *Journal of Theory Construction & Testing, 12*(2), 50–7.

Carpenter, J. (2008). Metaphors in qualitative research: Shedding light or casting shadows? *Research in Nursing & Health, 31*(3), 274–82.

CEBM. (2009). Levels of evidence. *Centre for Evidence Based Medicine.* Retrieved 15 December 2009 from www.cebm.net/index.aspx?o=1025

Charmaz, K. (1991). Turning points and fictional identities. In D. Maines (Ed.), *Social organization and social process: Essays in honor of Anselm Strauss* (pp. 71–86). New York: Aldine De Gruyter.

Charmaz, K. (1995). Grounded theory. In J. Smith, R. Harre & L. Langenhove (Eds.), *Rethinking methods in psychology* (pp. 27–65). London: Sage.

Charmaz, K. (2000). Grounded theory: Objectivist and constructivist methods. In N. K. Denzin & Y. S. Lincoln (Eds.), *The handbook of qualitative research* (2nd ed., pp. 509–35). Thousand Oaks, CA: Sage.

Charmaz, K. (2001). Qualitative interviewing and grounded theory analysis. In J. F. Gubrium & J. A. Holstein (Eds.), *Handbook of interview research: Context and method* (pp. 675–94). Thousand Oaks, CA: Sage.

Charmaz, K. (2005). Grounded theory in the 21st century. In N. K. Denzin & Y. S. Lincoln (Eds.), *The Sage handbook of qualitative research* (3rd ed., pp. 507–35). Thousand Oaks, CA: Sage.

Charmaz, K. (2006). *Constructing grounded theory: A practical guide through qualitative analysis.* London and Thousand Oaks, CA: Sage.

Charmaz, K., & Mitchell, R. (1996). The myth of silent authorship: Self, substance and style in ethnographic writing. *Symbolic Interaction, 19*, 285–302.

Charmaz, K., & Mitchell, R. G. (2001). Grounded theory in ethnography. In P. Atkinson (Ed.), *Handbook of ethnography* (pp. 161–74). London: Sage.

Charon, J. M. (2001). *Symbolic interactionism: An introduction, an interpretation, an integration* (7th ed.). Upper Saddle River, NJ: Prentice Hall.

Cheek, J. (2002). Advancing what? Qualitative research, scholarship, and the research imperative. *Qualitative Health Research, 12*(8), 1130–40.

Cheek, J. (2005). The practice and politics of funded qualitative research. In N. Denzin & Y. Lincoln (Eds.), *The Sage handbook of qualitative research* (3rd ed., pp. 387–409). Thousand Oaks, CA: Sage.

Cheek, J., Garnham, B., & Quan, J. (2006). What's in a number? Issues in providing evidence of impact and quality of research(ers). *Qualitative Health Research, 16*(3), 423–35.

Chiovitti, R. F., & Piran, N. (2003). Rigour and grounded theory research. *Journal of Advanced Nursing, 44*(4), 427–35.

Christianson, C. L., & Everall, R. D. (2009). Breaking the silence: School counsellors' experiences of client suicide. *British Journal of Guidance & Counselling, 37*(2), 157–68.

Clare, J. (2003). Writing a PhD thesis. In J. Clare & H. Hamilton (Eds.), *Writing research: Transforming data into text* (pp. 19–32). Edinburgh: Churchill Livingstone.

Clark, P. (2009). Resiliency in the practicing marriage and family therapist. *Journal of Marital and Family Therapy, 35*(2), 231–47.

Clarke, A. (2005). *Situational analysis: Grounded theory after the postmodern turn*. Thousand Oaks, CA: Sage.

Collins, P. (1998). Negotiating selves: Reflections on 'unstructured' interviewing. *Sociological Research Online*. Retrieved 13 March 2005 from www.socresonline.org.uk/3/3/2.html.

Corbin, J. M. (1991). Anselm Strauss: An intellectual biography. In D. Maines (Ed.), *Social organization and social process: Essays in honor of Anselm Strauss* (pp. 17–42). New York: Aldine De Gruyter.

Corbin, J. M., & Strauss, A. L. (2008). *Basics of qualitative research: Techniques and procedures for developing grounded theory* (3rd ed.). Los Angeles: Sage.

Corti, L., Witzel, A., & Bishop, L. (2005). On the potentials and problems of secondary analysis. An introduction to the FQS special issue on secondary analysis of qualitative data. *Forum: Qualitative Social Research, 6*(1). Retrieved 23 December 2009 from www. qualitative-research.net/index.php/fqs/article/view/498

Cotterill, N., Norton, C., Avery, K., Abrams, P., & Donovan, J. (2008). A patient-centered approach to developing a comprehensive symptom and quality of life assessment of anal incontinence. *Diseases of the Colon & Rectum, 51*(1), 82–87.

Covan, E. (2007). The discovery of grounded theory in practice: The legacy of multiple mentors. In A. Bryant & K. Charmaz (Eds.), *The Sage handbook of grounded theory* (pp. 58–74). London: Sage.

Cutcliffe, J. R. (2000). Methodological issues in grounded theory. *Journal of Advanced Nursing, 31*(6), 1476–84.

Cutcliffe, J. R. (2003). Reconsidering reflexivity: Introducing the case for intellectual entre-preneurship. *Qualitative Health Research, 13*(1), 136–48.

Cutcliffe, J. R., & McKenna, H. P. (2004). Expert qualitative researchers and the use of audit trails. *Journal of Advanced Nursing, 45*(2), 126–33.

Day, D., & Nolde, R. (2009). Arresting the decline in Australian Indigenous representation at university. *Equal Opportunities International, 28*(2), 135–61.

Dent-Brown, K., & Wang, M. (2006). The mechanism of storymaking: A grounded theory study of the 6-part story method. *Arts in Psychotherapy, 33*(4), 316–30.

Denzin, N. (2009). *Qualitative inquiry under fire: Toward a new paradigm dialogue.* Walnut Creek, CA: Left Coast Press.

Denzin, N., & Lincoln, Y. (2005). *The Sage handbook of qualitative research* (3rd ed.). Thousand Oaks, CA: Sage.

Denzin, N., & Lincoln, Y. (2008). *The handbook of critical and Indigenous methodologies.* Thousand Oaks, CA: Sage.

Devers, E., & Robinson, K. M. (2002). The making of a grounded theory: After death communication. *Death Studies, 26*(3), 241–53.

Dey, I. (2007). Grounding categories. In A. Bryant & K. Charmaz (Eds.), *The Sage handbook of grounded theory* (pp. 167–90). London: Sage.

Dick, B. (2005). Grounded theory: A thumbnail sketch. *Resource papers in action research.* Retrieved 26 June 2005 from www.scu.edu.au/schools/gcm/ar/arp/grounded.html

Dowling, M. (2006). Approaches to reflexivity in qualitative research. *Nurse Researcher, 13*(3), 7–21.

Draucker, C. B., Martsolf, D. S., Ross, R., & Rusk, T. B. (2007). Theoretical sampling and category development in grounded theory. *Qualitative Health Research, 17*(8), 1137–48.

Drury, V., Francis, K., & Chapman, Y. (2008a). Letting go and moving on: A grounded theory analysis of disengaging from university and becoming a registered nurse. *Nurse Education Today, 28*(7), 783–9.

Drury, V., Francis, K., & Chapman, Y. (2008b). Mature learners becoming registered nurses: A grounded theory model. *Australian Journal of Advanced Nursing, 26*(2), 39–45.

Duffy, K., Ferguson, C., & Watson, H. (2004). Data collecting in grounded theory: Some practical issues. *Nurse Researcher, 11*(4), 67–78.

Dylan, A., Regehr, C., & Alaggia, R. (2008). And justice for all? Aboriginal victims of sexual violence. *Violence against Women, 14*(6), 678–96.

Edwards, K., & Jones, S. (2009). Putting my man face on: A grounded theory of college men's gender identity development. *Journal of College Student Development, 50*(2), 210–28.

Evans, M., Hole, R., Berg, L. D., Hutchinson, P., & Sookraj, D. (2009). Common insights, differing methodologies: Toward a fusion of Indigenous methodologies, participatory action research, and white studies in an urban Aboriginal research agenda. *Qualitative Inquiry, 15*(5), 893–910.

Eyles, C., Walker, J., & Brien, S. (2009). Homeopathic practitioner's experiences of the homeopathic consultation: A protocol of a grounded theory study. *Journal of Alternative and Complementary Medicine, 15*(4), 347–52.

Fei, F. (2007). *Resourcing change: A grounded theory explaining the process by which managers address challenges in their initiation of change as learning at work.* Doctoral thesis, University of Bath.

Fielding, N. (2005). The resurgence, legitimation and institutionalization of qualiative methods. *Forum Qualitative Sozialforschung/Forum: Qualitative Social Research, 6*(2). Retrieved 15 December 2009 from http://nbn-resolving.de/urn:nbn:de:0114-fqs0502324

Forbes, A. (2003). Response to Kim Walker: Why evidence-based practice now? A polemic. *Nursing Inquiry, 10*(3), 156–8.

Francis, K., Mills, J., Chapman, Y., & Birks, M. (2009). Doctoral dissertations by publication: Building scholarly capacity whilst advancing new knowledge in the discipline of nursing. *International Journal of Doctoral Studies, 4*, 97–106.

Gerrish, K. (2003). Evidence-based practice: Unravelling the rhetoric and making it real. *Practice Development in Health Care, 2*(2), 99–113.

Glaser, B. G. (1978). *Theoretical sensitivity: Advances in the methodology of grounded theory*. Mill Valley, CA: Sociology Press.

Glaser, B. G. (1992). *Basics of grounded theory analysis*. Mill Valley, CA: Sociology Press.

Glaser, B. G. (1998). *Doing grounded theory: Issues and discussions*. Mill Valley, CA: Sociology Press.

Glaser, B. G. (2001). *The grounded theory perspective: Conceptualization contrasted with description*. Mill Valley, CA: Sociology Press.

Glaser, B. G. (2002). Constructivist grounded theory? *Forum: Qualitative Sozialforschung/ Forum: Qualitative Social Research, 3*(3). Retrieved 15 September 2005 from www.qualitative-research.net/fqs-texte/3-02/3-02glaser-e.htm

Glaser, B. G. (2004). Remodeling grounded theory. *Forum: Qualitative Sozialforschung/Forum: Qualitative Social Research, 5*(2). Retrieved 21 January 2008 from www.qualitative-research.net/fqs-texte/2-04/2-04glaser-e.pdf

Glaser, B. G. (2005). *The grounded theory perspective III: Theoretical coding*. Mill Valley, CA: Sociology Press.

Glaser, B. G. (2007). *Doing formal grounded theory: A proposal*. Mill Valley, CA: Sociology Press.

Glaser, B. G. (2008). *Doing quantitative grounded theory*. Mill Valley, CA: Sociology Press.

Glaser, B. G., & Strauss, A. L. (1965). *Awareness of dying*. New York: Aldine.

Glaser, B. G., & Strauss, A. L. (1967). *The discovery of grounded theory: Strategies for qualitative research*. New York: Aldine.

Goldsmith, L. J. (2007). *Access to health care for disadvantaged individuals: A qualitative inquiry*. Doctoral dissertation, University of North Carolina at Chapel Hill.

Goulding, C. (2002). *Grounded theory: A practical guide for management, business and market researchers*. Thousand Oaks, CA: Sage.

Guba, E., & Lincoln, Y. (2004). Competing paradigms in qualitative research. In S. N. Hesse-Biber & P. Leavy (Eds.), *Approaches to qualitative research: A reader on theory and practice* (pp. 17–38). New York: Oxford University Press.

Gubrium, J. F., & Holstein, J. A. (2001). From the individual interview to the interview society. In J. F. Gubrium & J. A. Holstein (Eds.), *Handbook of interview research: Context & methods* (pp. 3–32). Thousand Oaks, CA: Sage.

Hand, H. (2003). The mentor's tale: A reflexive account of semi-structured interviews. *Nurse Researcher, 10*, 15–27.

Heath, H., & Cowley, S. (2004). Developing a grounded theory approach: A comparison of Glaser and Strauss. *International Journal of Nursing Studies, 41*(2), 141–50.

Hesse-Biber, S. N. (2007). Teaching grounded theory. In A. Bryant & K. Charmaz (Eds.), *The Sage handbook of grounded theory* (pp. 311–38). London: Sage.

Hill, D. M., Hanton, S., Fleming, S., & Matthews, N. (2009). A re-examination of choking in sport. *European Journal of Sport Science, 9*(4), 203–12.

Hohl, M. (2009). Designing the art experience: Using grounded theory to develop a model of participants' perception of an immersive telematic artwork. *Digital Creativity, 20*(3), 187–96.

Holloway, I. (2008). *A–Z of qualitative research in healthcare* (2nd ed.). Oxford: Blackwell.

Holloway, I., & Fulbrook, P. (2001). Revisiting qualitative inquiry: Interviewing in nursing and midwifery research. *NT Research, 6,* 539–50.

Holton, J. (2007). Coding process and its challenges. In A. Bryant & C. Charmaz (Eds.), *The Sage handbook of grounded theory* (pp. 265–89). London: Sage.

Hood, J. C. (2007). Orthodoxy vs. power: The defining traits of grounded theory. In A. Byrant & C. Charmaz (Eds.), *The Sage handbook of grounded theory* (pp. 151–64). London: Sage.

Huberty, J. L., Ransdell, L. B., Sidman, C., Flohr, J. A., Shultz, B., Grosshans, O., et al. (2008). Explaining long-term exercise adherence in women who complete a structured exercise program. *Research Quarterly for Exercise and Sport, 79*(3), 374–84.

Jacobson, N., Oliver, V., & Koch, A. (2009). An urban geography of dignity. *Health & Place, 15*(3), 725–31.

Janasik, N., Honkela, T., & Bruun, H. (2009). Text mining in qualitative research: Application of an unsupervised learning method. *Organizational Research Methods, 12*(3), 436–60.

Jewell, C., & Bero, L. (2008). 'Developing good taste in evidence': Facilitators of and hindrances to evidence-informed health policymaking in state government. *Millbank Quarterly, 86*(2), 177–208.

Joanna Briggs Institute. (2008). *JBI levels of evidence.* Retrieved 15 December 2009 from www.joannabriggs.edu.au/pubs/approach.php

Johnson, R. B., Onwuegbuzie, A. J., & Turner, L. A. (2007). Toward a definition of mixed methods research. *Journal of Mixed Methods Research, 1*(2), 112–33.

Kearney, M. (2007). From the sublime to the meticulous: The continuing evolution of grounded formal theory. In A. Bryant & K. Charmaz (Eds.), *The Sage handbook of grounded theory* (pp. 127–50). London: Sage.

Kelle, U. (2007). The development of categories: Different approaches in grounded theory. In A. Byant & K. Charmaz (Eds.), *The Sage handbook of grounded theory* (pp. 191–213). London: Sage.

Kennett, D. J., O'Hagan, F. T., & Cezer, D. (2008). Learned resourcefulness and the long-term benefits of a chronic pain management program. *Journal of Mixed Methods Research, 2*(4), 317–39.

Knoblauch, H., Baer, A., Laurier, E., Petschke, S., & Schnettler, B. (2008). Visual analysis. New developments in the interpretive analysis of video and photography. *Forum Qualitative Sozialforschung/Forum: Qualitative Social Research, 9*(3), Art. 14.

Kotabe, M., Parente, R., & Murray, J. Y. (2007). Antecedents and outcomes of modular production in the Brazilian automobile industry: A grounded theory approach. *Journal of International Business Studies, 38*(1), 84–106.

Kubler-Ross, E. (1973). *On death and dying.* London: Tavistock.

Lambert, S. D., & Loiselle, C. G. (2008). Combining individual interviews and focus groups to enhance data richness. *Journal of Advanced Nursing, 62*(2), 228–37.

Lamott, A. (1994). *Bird by bird: Some instructions on writing and life.* New York: Pantheon.

LaRossa, R. (2005). Grounded theory methods and qualitative family research. *Journal of Marriage and Family, 67*(4), 837–57.

Lather, P. (2004). This is your father's paradigm: Government intrusion and the case of qualitative research in education. *Qualitative Inquiry, 10*(1), 15–34.

Lee, L. (2009). 'Boys like smart girls more than pretty girls': Young Korean immigrant girls' understanding of romantic love in American popular culture. *Journal of Instructional Psychology, 36*(1), 87–94.

Lempert, L. B. (2007). Asking questions of the data: Memo writing in the grounded theory tradition. In A. Bryant & K. Charmaz (Eds.), *The Sage handbook of grounded theory* (pp. 245–64). London: Sage.

Lincoln, Y. S., & Guba, E. G. (1985). *Naturalistic inquiry*. Beverly Hills, CA: Sage.

Lofland, J., & Lofland, L. (1995). *Analyzing social settings: A guide to qualitative observation and analysis* (3rd ed.). Belmont, CA: Wadsworth.

Lösch, A. (2006). Combining quantitative methods and grounded theory for researching e-reverse auctions. *Libri, 56*(3), 133–44.

Mantzoukas, S. (2004). Issues of representation within qualitative inquiry. *Qualitative Health Research, 14*(7), 994–1007.

Mantzoukas, S. (2007). A review of evidence-based practice, nursing research and reflection: Levelling the hierarchy. *Journal of Clinical Nursing, 17*, 214–23.

McGhee, G., Marland, G., & Atkinson, J. (2007). Grounded theory research: Literature reviewing and reflexivity. *Journal of Advanced Nursing, 60*(3), 334–42.

Meadus, R. J. (2007). Adolescents coping with mood disorder: A grounded theory study. *Journal of Psychiatric & Mental Health Nursing, 14*(2), 209–17.

Melendez, M. C. (2008). Black football players on a predominantly White college campus: Psychosocial and emotional realities of the Black college athlete experience. *Journal of Black Psychology, 34*(4), 423–51.

Meyer, D. Z., & Avery, L. M. (2009). Excel as a qualitative data analysis tool. *Field Methods, 21*(1), 91–112.

Mills, J., Bonner, A., & Francis, K. (2006). Adopting a constructivist approach to grounded theory: Implications for research design. *International Journal of Nursing Practice, 12*(1), 8–13.

Mills, J., Chapman, Y., Bonner, A., & Francis, K. (2007). Grounded theory: A methodological spiral from positivism to postmodernism. *Journal of Advanced Nursing, 58*(1), 72–9.

Mills, J., Francis, K., & Bonner, A. (2008). Getting to know a stranger – rural nurses' experiences of mentoring: A grounded theory. *International Journal of Nursing Studies, 45*(4), 599–607.

Mishler, E. (1991). *Research interviewing: Context and narrative*. Harvard, MA: Harvard University Press.

Mitchell, R. G., & Charmaz, K. (1996). Telling tales, writing stories. *Journal of Contemporary Ethnography, 25*(1), 144–66.

Montgomery, P., & Bailey, P. H. (2007). Field notes and theoretical memos in grounded theory. *Western Journal of Nursing Research, 29*(1), 65–79.

Morse, J. (2006). The politics of evidence. *Qualitative Health Research, 16*(3), 395–404.

Morse, J., & Niehaus, L. (2009). *Mixed method design: Principles and procedures*. Walnut Creek, CA: Left Coast Press.

Morse, J., Stern, P., Corbin, J., Bowers, B., Charmaz, K., & Clarke, A. (2009). *Developing grounded theory: The second generation*. Walnut Creek, CA: Left Coast Press.

Morse, J. M. (1995). The significance of saturation. *Qualitative Health Research, 5*(2), 147–9.

Morse, J. M. (2007). Sampling in grounded theory. In A. Bryant & K. Charmaz (Eds.), *The Sage handbook of grounded theory* (pp. 229–44). London: Sage.

Mullen, P. D. (2006). Generating grounded theory: Two case studies. *International Quarterly of Community Health Education, 25*(1–2), 79–114.

Nagy, S., Mills, J., Waters, D., & Birks, M. (2010). *Using research in healthcare practice*. Sydney: Lippincott, Wilkins & Williams.

Neill, S. J. (2006). Grounded theory sampling: The contribution of reflexivity. *Journal of Research in Nursing, 11*(3), 253–60.

Neill, S. J. (2007). Focus. Grounded theory sampling: 'Whole' family research … including commentary by H. Heath. *Journal of Research in Nursing, 12*(5), 435.

Nelson, A. M. (2008). Addressing the threat of evidence-based practice to qualitative inquiry through increasing attention to quality: A discussion paper. *International Journal of Nursing Studies, 45*(2), 316–22.

NHMRC (2009). *NHMRC Additional levels of evidence and grades for recommendations for developers of guidelines*. Retrieved 15 December 2009 from www.nhmrc.gov.au/guidelines/developers.htm

Nilsson, F. (2006). Logistics management in practice: Towards theories of complex logistics. *International Journal of Logistics Management, 17*(1), 38–54.

Nordvik, E., & Broman, N. O. (2009). Looking at computer-visualized interior wood: A qualitative assessment using focus groups. *Journal of Wood Science, 55*(2), 113–20.

Oakley, A. (1981). Interviewing women: A contradiction in terms. In H. Roberts (Ed.), *Doing feminist research* (pp. 30–74). London: Routledge & Kegan Paul.

O'Connor, D. (2001). Journeying the quagmire: Exploring the discourses that shape the qualitative research process. *AFFILA, 16*, 138–58.

Office of the High Commissioner for Human Rights. (2009). *What are human rights?* Retrieved 15 December 2009 from www.ohchr.org/EN/Issues/Pages/WhatareHumanRights.aspx

Olson, L. N., Daggs, J. L., Ellevold, B. L., & Rogers, T. K. K. (2007). Entrapping the innocent: Toward a theory of child sexual predators' luring communication. *Communication Theory, 17*(3), 231–51.

Pearson, A. (2004). Balancing the evidence: Incorporating the synthesis of qualitative data into systematic reviews. *JBI Reports, 2*, 45–64.

Pearson, A., Baughan, B., & Fitzgerald, M. (2005). *Nursing models for practice* (3rd ed.). London: Butterworth–Heinneman.

Perez, M. S., & Cannella, G. S. (In Press). The neoliberal construction of early childhood education/care policy: Examining childhood and disaster capitalism in post-Katrina New Orleans. In G.S. Cannella, & L.D. Soto (Eds.), *Childhoods: A handbook, critical histories and contemporary issues, rethinking childhood series*. New York: Peter Lang.

Peshkin, A. (1988). In search of subjectivity – one's own. *Educational Researcher, 17*(7), 17–21.

Pfeffer, J., & Sutton, R. (2006). Evidence-based management. *Harvard Business Review, January*, 63–74.

Plummer, K. (2009). *On pragmatism and poetics*. Retrieved 10 January 2010 from www.dur.ac.uk/writingacrossboundaries/writingonwriting/kenplummer/

Potgieter, F., & Smit, B. (2009). Finding academic voice: A critical narrative of knowledge-making and discovery. *Qualitative Inquiry, 15*(1), 214–28.

Reichertz, J. (2007). Abduction: The logic of discovery of grounded theory. In A. Bryant & K. Charmaz (Eds.), *The Sage handbook of grounded theory* (pp. 214–28). London: Sage.

Reinharz, S. (1992). *Feminist Interview Research*. New York: Oxford University Press.

Richards, L. (2005). *Handling qualitative data: A practical guide*. London: Sage.

Richardson, L., & Adams St Pierre, E. (2005). Writing: A method of inquiry. In N. Denzin & Y. Lincoln (Eds.), *The Sage handbook of qualitative research* (3rd ed., pp. 959–78). Thousand Oaks, CA: Sage.

Roberts, S. J. (2000). Development of a positive professional identity: Liberating oneself from the oppressor within. *Advances in Nursing Science, 22*(4), 71–82.

Rolfe, G. (2006a). Judgements without rules: Towards a postmodern ironist concept of research validity. *Nursing Inquiry, 13*(1), 7–15.

Rolfe, G. (2006b). Validity, trustworthiness and rigour: Quality and the idea of qualitative research. *Journal of Advanced Nursing, 53*(3), 304–10.

Rolfe, G., Segrott, J., & Jordan, S. (2008). Tensions and contradictions in nurses' perspectives of evidence-based practice. *Journal of Nursing Management, 16*(4), 440–51.

Ruppar, T. M., & Russell, C. L. (2009). Medication adherence in successful kidney transplant recipients. *Progress in Transplantation, 19*(2), 167–72.

Russell, S. (2006). An Overview of Adult-Learning Processes. *Urologic Nursing, 26*(5), 349–70.

Ryan-Nicholls, K. D., & Will, C. I. (2009). Rigour in qualitative research: Mechanisms for control. *Nurse Researcher, 16*(3), 70–85.

Sandelowski, M. (1993). Rigor or rigor mortis: The problem of rigor in qualitative research revisited. *Advances in Nursing Science, 16*(2), 1–8.

Sandelowski, M. (2002). Keynote address: Second Annual Advances in Qualitative Methods Conference. Reembodying qualitative inquiry. *Qualitative Health Research, 12*(1), 104–15.

Sandelowski, M. (2003). Tables or tableaux? The challenges of writing and reading mixed methods studies. In A. Tashakkori & C. Teddlie (Eds.), *Handbook of mixed methods in social & behavioral research* (pp. 321–50). Thousand Oaks, CA: Sage.

Sandelowski, M. (2004). Using qualitative research. *Qualitative Health Research, 14*(10), 1366–86.

Sandelowski, M. (2007). Words that should be seen but not written. *Research in Nursing & Health, 30*(2), 129–30.

Sandelowski, M. J. (2008). Justifying qualitative research. *Research in Nursing & Health, 31*(3), 193–95.

Scott, C., & Sutton, R. E. (2009). Emotions and change during professional development for teachers: A mixed methods study. *Journal of Mixed Methods Research, 3*(2), 151–71.

Scott, S. B., Bergeman, C. S., Verney, A., Longenbaker, S., Markey, M. A., & Bisconti, T. L. (2007). Social support in widowhood: A mixed methods study. *Journal of Mixed Methods Research, 1*(3), 242–66.

Shibutani, T. (1962). Reference groups and social control. In A. Rose (Ed.), *Human behavior and social processes: An interactionist approach*. London: Routledge & Kegan Paul.

Skeat, J., & Perry, A. (2008). Grounded theory as a method for research in speech and language therapy. *International Journal of Language & Communication Disorders, 43*(2), 95–109.

Smolander, K., & Rossi, M. (2008). Conflicts, compromises and political decisions: Methodological challenges of enterprise-wide e-business architecture creation. *Journal of Database Management, 19*(1), 19–40.

Sosulski, M. R., & Lawrence, C. (2008). Mixing methods for full-strength results: Two welfare studies. *Journal of Mixed Methods Research, 2*(2), 121–48.

Stanley, L. (2008). It's a craft and a job and requires practice. *Writing on Writing*. Retrieved 10 January 2010 from www.dur.ac.uk/writingacrossboundaries/writingonwriting/lizstanley/

Stern, P. (2009). In the beginning Glaser and Strauss created grounded theory. In J. Morse, P. Stern, J. Corbin, B. Bowers, K. Charmaz & A. Clarke (Eds.), *Developing grounded theory: The second generation* (pp. 24–9). Walnut Creek, CA: Left Coast Press.

Stern, P. N. (2007). On solid ground: Essential properties for growing grounded theory. In A. Bryant & K. Charmaz (Eds.), *The Sage handbook of grounded theory* (pp. 114–26). London: Sage.

Strauss, A. L. (1987). *Qualitative analysis for social scientists*. New York: Cambridge University Press.

Strauss, A. L. (1993). *Continual permutations of action*. New York: Aldine De Gruyter.

Strauss, A. L., & Corbin, J. M. (1990). *Basics of qualitative research: Grounded theory procedures and techniques*. Newbury Park, CA: Sage.

Strauss, A. L., & Corbin, J. M. (1994). Grounded theory methodology: An overview. In N. K. Denzin & Y. S. Lincoln (Eds.), *Handbook of qualitative research* (pp. 273–85). Thousand Oaks, CA: Sage.

Strauss, A. L., & Corbin, J. M. (1998). *Basics of qualitative research: Techniques and procedures for developing grounded theory* (2nd ed.). Thousand Oaks, CA: Sage.

Strubing, J. (2007). Research as pragmatic problem-solving: The pragmatist roots of empirically-grounded theorizing. In A. Bryant & K. Charmaz (Eds.), *The Sage handbook of grounded theory* (pp. 580–601). London: Sage.

Sullivan, P. (2009). *Writing with your head in your hands*. Retrieved 10 January 2010 from www.dur.ac.uk/writingacrossboundaries/writingonwriting/patricksullivan/

Teddlie, C., & Tashakkori, A. (2003). Major issues and controversies in the use of mixed methods in the social and behavioral sciences. In A. Tashakkori & C. Teddlie (Eds.), *Handbook of mixed methods in social & behavioral research* (pp. 3–51). Thousand Oaks, CA: Sage.

Tuhiwai Smith, L. (1999) *Decolonizing Methodologies: Research and Indigenous Peoples*. London: Zed Books Ltd.

UCSF (2007). *1906–2006 Centennial Celebration – UCSF School of Nursing – University of California, San Francisco*. Retrieved 25 January 2010 from http://nurseweb.ucsf.edu/centennl.html

University of Essex/University of Manchester (2006). About ESDS Qualidata. Retrieved 23 December 2009 from www.esds.ac.uk/qualidata/

Urquhart, C. (2007). The evolving nature of grounded theory method: The case of the information systems discipline. In A. Bryant & C. Charmaz (Eds.), *The Sage handbook of grounded theory* (pp. 339–59). London: Sage.

Vågan, A. (2009). Medical students' perceptions of identity in communication skills training: A qualitative study. *Medical Education, 43*(3), 254–9.

Vingilis, E., Hartford, K., Schrecker, T., Mitchell, B., Lent, B., & Bishop, J. (2003). Integrating knowledge generation with knowledge diffusion and utilization: A case study analysis of the consortium for applied research and evaluation in mental health. *Canadian Journal of Public Health, 94*(6), 468–71.

Wales, R. C., Shalin, V. L., & Bass, D. S. (2007). Requesting distant robotic action: An ontology for naming and action identification for planning on the Mars exploration rover mission. *Journal of the Association for Information Systems, 8*(2), 75–104.

Walker, K. (2003). Why evidence-based practice now? A polemic. *Nursing Inquiry, 10*(3), 145–55.

Walton, J. (2007). Prayer warriors: A grounded theory study of American Indians receiving hemodialysis. *Nephrology Nursing Journal, 34*(4), 377–86.

Wasserman, J. A., Clair, J. M., & Wilson, K. L. (2009). Problematics of grounded theory: Innovations for developing an increasingly rigorous qualitative method. *Qualitative Research, 9*(3), 355–81.

Watson, R. (2003). Scientific methods are the only credible way forward for nursing research. *Journal of Advanced Nursing, 43*(3), 219–20.

Weed, M. (2009). Research quality considerations for grounded theory research in sport & exercise psychology. *Psychology of Sport and Exercise, 10*(5), 502–10.

Whiteside, M. (2010). *A grounded theory of empowerment in the context of Indigenous Australia.* PhD Thesis, James Cook University.

Wiener, C. (2007). Making teams work in conducting grounded theory. In A. Bryant & K. Charmaz (Eds.), *The Sage handbook of grounded theory* (pp. 293–310). London: Sage.

Williams, S., & Reid, M. (2007). A grounded theory approach to the phenomenon of pro-anorexia. *Addiction Research & Theory, 15*(2), 141–52.

Wilson, H. S., Hutchinson, S. A., & Holzemer, W. L. (2002). Reconciling incompatibilities: A grounded theory of HIV medication adherence and symptom management. *Qualitative Health Research, 12*(10), 1309–22.

Wishart, P. (2006). Letting go of preconceptions: A novel approach to creating memorial services. *Health Care for Women International, 27*(6), 513–29.

Wolcott, H. (1990). *Writing up qualitative research.* Newbury Park, CA: Sage.

Yergin, D., & Stanislaw, J. (1998). *The commanding heights: The battle between government and the marketplace that is remaking the modern world.* New York: Simon & Schuster.

Index

Research Methods
Books from SAGE

Read sample chapters online now!

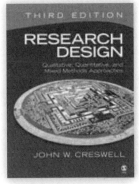

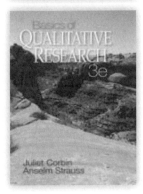

www.sagepub.co.uk

Research Methods Books from SAGE

Read sample chapters online now!

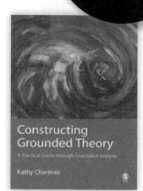

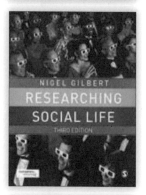

www.sagepub.co.uk

⑤SAGE